APPROACHING PRIMARY SCIENCE

A Reader edited by

Barbara Hodgson and Eileen Scanlon
at the Open University

Harper & Row, Publishers
London

Cambridge		San Francisco
Hagerstown		Mexico City
Philadelphia		São Paulo
New York		Sydney

Harper & Row, Publishers
in association with
The Open University

Selection and editorial material
copyright © The Open University 1985

First published 1985

Harper & Row Ltd
28 Tavistock Street
London WC2E 7PN

British Library Cataloguing in Publication Data

Approaching primary science.
  1. Science—Study and teaching (Elementary)
  I. Hodgson, Barbara   II. Scanlon, Eileen
  372.3'5   LB1585

ISBN 0-06-318319-6

Typeset by Burns & Smith, Derby
Printed and bound by St Edmundsbury Press,
Bury St Edmunds, Suffolk.

Course Team

Ann Diack (BBC)
Barbara Hodgson (Joint Chair)
George Loveday
Roger Lowry (Editor)
Eileen Scanlon (Joint Chair)
Jane Sheppard (Designer)
Adrian Thomas
Glenna White (Course Manager)

Consultants
Wynne Harlen
Brenda Prestt

CONTENTS

GENERAL INTRODUCTION

This collection of papers has been prepared as a Reader to accompany Open University pack EP 531 *Primary Science: Why and How,* which is designed to encourage primary teachers to include some science in their curriculum.

There is a tremendous amount of teacher and pupil material available in primary science. Much of this material is excellent but very little used. Many primary school teachers have little or no background in science and consequently lack the confidence to introduce science teaching in their classroom. Many primary schools lack any school-wide policy regarding science teaching. A need for a wider appreciation of the contribution that can be made by science to the primary curriculum is therefore apparent.

Over the past 25 years much has been written and said about science in the primary school – why it should be included in the primary curriculum, how to teach it, what to teach, why it is not taught, whether or not what is done is useful. The 1978 HMI survey of primary education indicated that only some 10 percent of schools incorporated science into their curricula, and there is nothing to indicate any major change since then. Recent reports by the Assessment of Performance Unit indicate that the uptake of primary science activities into the school curriculum is very limited except in isolated cases. This collection of papers plus the other components of the pack should provide an adequate grounding in the debate.

The pack itself contains four main texts: *The Study Book, The Science Book, The Planning Book* and *The Resource Book.*

The Study Book considers whether science should be introduced into the primary curriculum and discusses curriculum projects which have attempted to produce suitable material. This component of the pack draws on readings from Parts 1 and 2 of this Reader.

The Science Book provides the science background to the topic of force and energy, which is the theme chosen for the pack. It also discusses the appropriateness of various topics and activities for certain stages of the primary curriculum, with particular regard to the work of Piaget. This component of the pack draws on readings from Part 3 of this Reader, which deals with Piagetian influences on science education, and Part 4, which describes research into the difficulties children experience with the concepts of force and energy.

The Planning Book and *The Resource Book* provide guidelines for the construction and evaluation of science lessons and describe resources available to be drawn on by the teacher. This component of the pack is supported by Part 5 of this Reader, which consists of case studies describing the responses of individual teachers to the challenge of carrying out 'good' science lessons with their children.

The selection of material for this Reader reflects the variety of audiences we hope the pack will serve. Teachers who do not currently teach science will be attracted by Parts 1, 2 and 5, while Parts 3 and 4 should be useful to teachers with some experience of teaching science and who wish to consider the psychological basis of their teaching and perhaps undertake research in the area. Teachers in the latter category should note that the pack will also form a module of the Open University's *Advanced Diploma in Curriculum and Teaching*.

PART ONE

Aims and Policy

Introduction

If we take as a yardstick the number of curriculum projects and schemes of work currently available on the subject, we might reasonably conclude that primary science is flourishing. Cursory examination of this wealth of resources suggests that there is reasonable agreement on the broad aims of science education for children aged 5–13 though not necessarily on the means of achieving them. These aims include the development of skills and attitudes necessary for scientific inquiry and problem solving and an introduction to a range of basic concepts.

How realistic are these aims and to what extent are they being achieved? Is primary science indeed flourishing? Do teachers need more, or different, resources and support in order to implement a policy for primary science in their schools and classrooms? What does science contribute to the primary curriculum and to children's intellectual development? These are the themes which run through the papers in this Reader, starting in this first part with views on science and its importance in the primary curriculum.

In 1978 HMI surveyed primary education in England and reported that few primary schools visited had effective programmes for the teaching of science. The state of affairs they describe, in the first paper in this part, obviously falls far short of their expectations and implicit aims for primary science. They conclude that despite some 15 years of considerable stimulus and support, there was little sign of progress in the teaching of science at primary level. The ideas and materials produced by curriculum development projects did not appear to have had any major impact.

Another concern of the Inspectorate was that only a minority of head-teachers recognized the important contribution that science can make to children's intellectual development. The second paper in this part explores what science is and the distinctive contribution that the study of science can make to the primary curriculum. It includes definitions and descriptions of the processes of science.

To what extent can the teaching and learning of science in primary schools match the aims and aspirations of curriculum developers or the Department of Education and Science? Kerr and Engel, in comparing the aims and policies of curriculum innovations with the present situation in schools, suggest a need for the 'tempering of theoretical "ideals" ... to take realistic account of practical constraints'. These constraints include the poor science background of many teachers, little recognition of the potential contribution of science to the curriculum and inadequate provision of resources. They also argue that to improve primary science we need a deeper knowledge of how children acquire both scientific skills and attitudes and their understanding of essential concepts.

In working towards a policy for science for children aged 5–16, the DES produced a discussion paper on science in primary schools. The first part of this paper, reprinted here as 'Science and the curriculum', explores a view of the processes and content of science appropriate for children of primary school age, and considers effective teaching and learning in science and the relationship of science to the rest of the curriculum.

In the context of an individual school, the headteacher has a vital part to play in developing and promoting a policy for science teaching. The final paper in this part not only looks at the place of science in a balanced curriculum but also suggests ways in which headteachers might encourage and support their staff in science teaching.

1.1

SCIENCE IN PRIMARY EDUCATION

Her Majesty's Inspectorate

Few primary schools visited in the course of this survey had effective programmes for the teaching of science. There was a lack of appropriate equipment; insufficient attention was given to ensuring proper coverage of key scientific notions; the teaching of processes and skills such as observing, the formulating of hypotheses, experimenting and recording was often superficial. The work in observational and experimental science was less well matched to children's capabilities than work in any other area of the curriculum.

Heads' statements showed that the degree to which programmes of work in science had been thought out varied considerably from school to school. A number of heads referred to the importance of developing children's powers of observation, and to the responsibility of schools to encourage enquiry and curiosity. One wrote that his intention was 'to encourage in the children an attitude of wonder and enquiry so that these may become a lasting part of their life and outlook and to assist children's desire to communicate and construct; and help them to gain an insight into the happenings of everyday life'.

Some heads also mentioned the scientific subject matter they considered children should study; for example, 'practical work in nature study, plant and animal life, and an introduction to a study of the environment'. Another head wrote: 'The children should be able to perceive relationships and pose hypotheses to be tested through experiments, to be discarded if found untenable; they should become acquainted with the evolution and

Source: Her Majesty's Inspectorate (1978) *Primary Education in England*, London, HMSO, pp. 58–63

metamorphosis of animals; learn the simple properties of air and water; and understand how simple machines work'.

Science is a way of understanding the physical and biological world. However, the general impression given by heads' statements was that only a small minority recognized the important contribution which science could make to children's intellectual development. Although some science was attempted in a majority of classes, the work was developed seriously in only just over one class in ten, either as a study in its own right, or in relation to other topics being studied. The attention given to science did not vary greatly with the age of the children.

In science it is essential that children should develop observational skills and begin to recognize similarities and differences. The study of living and non-living things can stimulate children to ask the sort of questions which can lead, with careful guidance, to the formulation of hypotheses and the devising of experiments to test them.

In about two-thirds of all the classes a nature table or 'interest' table was kept, where objects such as pieces of wood, sea shells, building materials, old clocks or radios were collected and displayed. In a similar number of classes plants were either grown in school or brought in for study. About half the classes kept small mammals such as hamsters or gerbils and a similar proportion undertook some work arising from outdoor activities such as a nature walk, a visit to a local park or a study of a local habitat such as a canal or pond.

Unfortunately, although children in a fair proportion of the classes were introduced to plants, animals and objects intended to stimulate scientific enquiry, in very few classes were opportunities taken to teach children how to make careful observations or to plan and carry out investigations of a scientific nature. For example, collections of autumn leaves were commonly used for decorative purposes or to stimulate work with pattern and colour; they were seldom used to help children to recognize similarities and differences in formation, such as the different forms of multiple leaf in ash and horse-chestnut trees, or notions or stability and change in living things.

In about two-fifths of the classes some use was made of television broadcasts for the teaching of science, but radio was used in less than one class in ten. In some classes a particular television or radio broadcast was selected to fit in with a topic the class was studying, and in others part of a term's work was planned around a series of programmes. Used in these ways, television and radio broadcasting made a valuable contribution to the work in science and it is surprising that, in a subject where many teachers lacked confidence in their own abilities, more use was not made of this resource to support the work in science.

Textbooks or assignment cards were used to initiate work in science in only about a fifth of all the classes, although their use increased with the age of the children. At the 11-year-old level about a quarter of the classes made use of assignment cards and a similar proportion worked with textbooks. The discriminating use of carefully chosen textbooks or assignment cards can help to sustain work in science if their use is carefully planned to supplement a programme of work; more use of this resource to support a particular line of scientific enquiry could have been made. Considerable use was made of reference books in nearly two-thirds of the 7-year-old classes and four out of five of the 11-year-old classes. However, in only about a fifth of the classes were reference books well used to support first hand observation or experimental work or to develop sustained work on a particular topic.

Children's interests arising from their life at home, outside school or on holiday sometimes provide starting points for work in science. There was some evidence in about two-fifths of the classes that work had arisen in this way, although the potential of such work was seldom exploited. Children may collect shells, pebbles or fir cones; may wonder why aeroplanes stay in the air or how a canal lock works; may become interested in the behaviour and characteristics of animals or immersed in the details of the latest space exploration reported on television. There is a wealth of experience for teachers to draw on, and most children are willing to bring things to school and discuss their enthusiasm in class.

Although four-fifths of all classes had access to some resources for their work in science, the provision was generally inadequate. Simple equipment for measuring, observing and discriminating, for example, thermometers, hand lenses, tuning forks, and materials such as batteries, bulbs and wire for work with electricity, can be assembled easily but were rarely seen to be available in the classroom. Older children were only marginally better catered for than the younger children in this respect.

Content

In interpreting the findings relating to the content and quality of children's work in science it has to be kept in mind that there was no evidence of such work in nearly a fifth of all the classes. In those classes where work in science was undertaken, about half had touched on topics which contributed to children's understanding of the characteristics of living things and to notions of stability and change in living organisms. Fewer classes gave attention to reproduction, growth and development in plants and animals. Sources of energy were considered in about half of the 11-year-old classes but rarely by the younger children.

In only half the 11-year-old classes and about a third of the 7-and 9-year-old classes were children prompted to look for and identify significant patterns, for example, the way leaves are arranged on a twig, patterns of bird migration, the way materials react to heat or light, or the arrangement of colours in a rainbow, and the way light behaves when it is reflected, casts shadows or is dispersed into its component parts. Such topics can be developed without specialized facilities, using simple materials such as twigs, water, salt or mirrors or simply carrying out observations in a natural habitat. In only a very small minority of classes were activities requiring careful observation and accurate recording developed beyond a superficial level and in less than one class in thirty was there evidence of investigations which had been initiated as a result of questions asked by the children.

In those classes where efforts were made to introduce children to science as both a body of organized knowledge and an experimental process the emphasis tended to be placed on work relating to plants and animals. This probably reflects the fact that rather more teachers were knowledgeable in the field of biology than in the physical sciences, although some were able to extend the work to take account of physical as well as biological aspects. For example, in one 9-year-old class the teacher had arranged a visit to a bird sanctuary. The preparatory work involved drawing children's attention to the characteristics of different species of birds which would assist in their identification, examining the construction of birds' nests and relating the materials used and the method of construction to the size of the bird and the shape of the beak. At a later stage the children constructed a bird table and went on to collect bird droppings; they placed them in sterilized seed compost and witnessed the germination of seeds which had been carried by the birds. In an 11-year-old class where germination was being studied, the children were growing plants under different conditions and recording their findings in a systematic way. They were being encouraged to make predictions and generalize from their findings; the teacher was also able to introduce the notion of the need for a control sample.

Another school had its own small area of woodland in part of a nearby Forestry Commission plantation. The children in the 11-year-old class had planted seedlings and were carrying out systematic observations of their growth. They also made careful comparisons of other plants and animals found on open ground, on the fringes, and in the centre of the woodland. This included the observation and identification of living things found under stones and logs and on the trees. In the course of these activities the children designed and constructed clinometers and other instruments to enable them to measure dimensions such as the height and girth of the trees and the spread of the branches. The children had learned to distinguish hard and soft timber and had employed a rigorous technique for comparing the hardness of woods by dropping a weight from a standard height on to a nail in the wood. The children were knowledgeable about the kinds of wood appropriate to different forms of manufacturing, for example, paper and matchsticks, and the types used in the construction of different household articles.

Studies relating specifically to man-made artefacts or mechanical actions were comparatively rare, although one 9-year-old class had paid a visit to a working water mill. During the visit the children made notes and drawings and, on their return to school, were able to construct a working model to illustrate the action they had observed at the mill. Subsequently the children looked at other applications of the mechanics of a chain of cogwheels including the gears of a bicycle, the action of an alarm clock and a rotary food whisk. The study of mechanical artefacts supported by constructional activities is an aspect of the work in science which is seldom exploited and which could usefully be developed at the primary stage.

Comment

During the past few years considerable efforts have been made to stimulate and support science teaching in primary schools. There have been curriculum development projects at national level and in some areas local authority advisers and teachers' centres have been very active. Guidance about the kind of science which is suitable for young children, its place in the curriculum and teaching methods is readily available in the publications of the Schools Council, the Nuffield Foundation, the Department of Education and Science and elsewhere. Yet the progress of science teaching in primary schools has been disappointing; the ideas and materials produced by curriculum development projects have had little impact in the majority of schools.

The most severe obstacle to the improvement of science in the primary school is that many existing teachers lack a working knowledge of elementary science appropriate to children of this age. This results in some teachers being so short of confidence in their own abilities that they make no attempt to include science in the curriculum. In other cases, teachers make this attempt but the work which results is superficial since the teachers themselves may be unsure about where a particular investigation or topic in science could lead.

Making good the lack of science expertise among existing teachers is a complex matter but the careful deployment of those teachers who do have a background of study in science is a straightforward step that should be taken. Such teachers should be encouraged to use their expertise to the full, as class and specialist teachers, to bring about an improvement in the standards children achieve in science. Teachers with a particular responsibility for science need to be supported fully by heads and advisers and where necessary receive further in-service training, particularly courses which are designed to help them to further their own knowledge of science. The planned acquistion and use of resources for science teaching would also contribute to a general improvement of the work in this area. In addition, more attention should be given to the ways in which initial training courses can best equip new teachers to undertake the teaching of science whether as a class teacher, as a science consultant, or as a specialist in the primary school.

1.2

WHAT IS SCIENCE?

United Nations Educational, Scientific and Cultural Organization

Lord Bullock, Master of St. Catherine's College, Oxford, and, himself, a historian has deemed science to be ['the greatest intellectual and cultural achievement of modern man] He perceives science to be [an open-ended process in which imagination, hypothesis, criticism and controversy – not to mention passion and error – play a role]. It is not, nor was it ever, 'the closed dogmatic system of immutable laws beloved of nineteenth-century positivists'. Bullock, then, sees science as a humane study, deeply concerned with man and society, providing scope for imagination and compassion as well as for observation and analysis (1976). [. . .]

Science, it has been said, is what scientists do. Nature is vast, complex and interesting. In the belief that nature is also comprehensible, scientists are inquisitive people who are for ever trying to solve her riddles. Like detectives hunting for clues and building theories from them, they seek to make sense of apparent complexity by trying to relate one observation to another. These relationships, they find, are related to other relationships. Then the interrelationships grow in structure and strength until scientists arrive at giant theories like special relativity and quantum mechanics. Once the code is cracked, it can be applied to solve a wide range of puzzles.

Mendel's work on genetics, for example, provided generalizations that led eventually to the establishment, by Crick and Watson, of the structure of the DNA molecule. With this, a lot of pieces in the puzzle fell into place, and genetic engineering is now possible. Even the educated layman can now understand something of the way in which parents pass on certain characteristics to their offspring.

Source: United Nations Educational, Scientific and Cultural Organization (1980) *Unesco Handbook for Science Teachers*, Paris, Unesco/London, Heinemann, pp. 17–33. Reproduced by permission of Unesco

Quote Bullock.

In school we ought to take children as far along this search for sense as we can, for, as the Dean of Clare College, Cambridge, a cleric, addressing the Association for Science Education, has said: (Peacocke, 1976)

> 'It is really only within the last 150 years, the second half of the last 300 years of the scientific revolution and indeed, more specifically, only within the last twenty years, that the full grandeur and scope of what has been going on in the universe has yielded to the human adventure we call science, still the finest and most distinctive flower (saving, perhaps, music) of our Western civilization.'

The questions that a scientist asks of nature are *what* and *how* questions; a scientist describes. He cannot answer *why* questions, which are matters for religion and metaphysics. *Why* questions are important, but science cannot answer them. There is no conflict here, as a Hindu science teacher has observed, since he can be concerned with *what* and *how* while he is being a scientist, and with *why* while he is being a Hindu.

Thus a science teacher may ask, 'What does this reaction tell us about the substances we mixed in the test-tube?', but *not* 'Why is a gas given off when we put vinegar on a sea shell?' He may ask, 'How do red blood corpuscles keep mammals alive?' but *not*, 'Why do mammals have red blood corpuscles?' Who knows why? When children observe mosses growing on one side of a tree but not the other, the scientist (teacher or child) may ask, 'What are the conditions on that side rather than the other that make it a suitable place for mosses?' Finding answers to *what* and *how* questions is the job of the 'pure' scientist. Making use of his discoveries is the job of the applied scientist and the technologist. The teacher of science must take account of the findings of all three.

Although the distinction between pure science and applied science or technology is not always clear, the scientist is in general a questioner of nature, while the technologist manipulates nature. The manipulation is intended to be for the well-being of man, which is undoubtedly the effect of a doctor's technology. The weather technologists are aware that they are dealing with dangerous forces. So are the engineers who design roads, bridges, factories, and hydroelectric plants. They know that, unless care is taken, the construction of a deep-water harbour may turn the sea into a desert. They are conscious of the fact that a bauxite smelter fuelled by reserves of petroleum will bring riches at the cost of consuming materials that took millions of years to form and which could have been converted to agricultural chemicals. Cutting away a mountain for road materials can destroy man's heritage of beauty and wildlife, and upset the water balance. Alert, sensitive and educated masters and public are needed to preserve our heritage, because we cannot manufacture it again. With the technology explosion there has arisen an urgent need for a good preparation of tomorrow's decision-makers and citizens. Mankind is at risk, and science teachers must recognize that they have a responsibility to future generations. They should examine 'not just the *how* of technology but also the *why* and the *should* '.

In science teaching, as in science, values, too, are important. Scientists are aware of ignorant critics who describe science as flying in the face of God, interfering with nature, materialistic, unconcerned with aesthetics, taking the rainbow to pieces (Bronowski) instead of putting it together, turning the beauty of a flower into a cold and intellectual mathematical formula. On the contrary, the marvellous engineering of a flower or a beehive can best be appreciated by those who have studied and described them minutely. Weisskopf, addressing the International Union of Pure and Applied Physics, argued that science is a very important way of establishing a relation between mankind and its natural and social environment (1976). Einstein has described how his science helped him to believe in God. Bronowski was another scientist for whom science is a humanity in which judgements of value, goodness, beauty, right conduct and especially freedom of human ideas are absolutely essential concerns (1973, 1960).

Older science teaching failed to reflect these aspects of science and, among others, Baez and Alles (1973) and Goldsmith (1974) have insisted that integrated science for social responsibility is required. The recent curriculum developments like SCISP [Schools Council Integrated Science Project] and ASEP [Australian Science Education Project] see society as a subject for scientific analysis, and discuss the impact of science on society.

Science evolves

As we have seen, scientists are slowly unravelling the secrets of nature. The unravelling technique, however, is one that man had to *invent*. In inventing science, man invented a way of thought. To satisfy his curiosity, he had to work out a way of thinking that would be sure to give him reliable answers. This way of thinking, resulting from man's search for reliability, is called scientific thinking. It has been going on for at least 2000 years. The growth of scientific thought is an exciting story. To appreciate it, we must imagine ourselves to be back 2000 years, stripping ourselves of the heritage of the educated. We would be perhaps like a tribe which is cut off from the twentieth-century brotherhood of men, a tribe which has had to work out its own ways of thought without written communication from the past or any communication from other thoughtful tribes. That was approximately the position of the Greek philosophers of the fourth century B.C.

At first it was generally believed that events in the world were governed by the unpredictable will of the gods. Then Aristotle in the fourth-century B.C. and his successor Ptolemy in A.D. 140 claimed that the celestial system was created by a God who acted according to understandable philosophical and mathematical principles. The earth, planets and stars were spheres within spheres, all moving with uniform velocity; this must be so, they said, since the most perfect of all bodies is a sphere and the most perfect motion is uniform motion. If they could arrive at the principles of the universe by theoretical thinking, observation was unnecessary, the philosophers believed.

There was difficulty when some observations, such as the motion of the planets, conflicted with theory. At first the theory was extended, but when observations and theory could no longer fit, the philosophers claimed that the observations must be wrong. (We find echoes of this in some teaching laboratories to this day!)

It may be remarkable to us that these ideas were accepted until the sixteenth century. But the Middle Ages were the dark ages in European civilization (although the Arabs were further advanced in science and medicine) and the sort of question that needed to be asked had simply not occurred to the scholars.

The Scientific Revolution was the triumph of observations as truth. The sixteenth-century Polish astronomer Copernicus set up a milestone in the invention of science. His view of the universe (that the sun, not the earth, is the centre of the system) was significant not so much in its content as in its simplicity and ability to absorb the observations that came later from Tycho Brahe and others. A beautiful theory is one which is simple and able to accommodate earlier observations and new ones. We could theorize that the activity in a pot of boiling water is due to demons, but we should have to go on inventing new properties for these demons as more observations were collected (Science Teacher Education Project, 1974). The particle theory is simpler and has so far agreed with all observations. The theory of Copernicus, after it had been tidied up by Kepler, was of that kind.

Another major step forward in man's thinking came from Galileo in the seventeenth century. Although it was not appreciated at the time, and indeed upset the Church and universities profoundly, Galileo gave mankind the principle of experiment, the idea of actively confronting nature with his questions. Galileo may not have actually dropped balls from the Leaning

Tower of Pisa, but we certainly owe to him the idea of planned observation, reproducibility and objectivity, instead of philosophical theory and subjectivity. At about the same time van Helmont in Holland carried out his famous experiment to test Aristotle's theory that trees eat soil. The Scientific Revolution (1500–1700) was under way and its culmination was the work of Newton, who has been called the greatest scientist of all time. The laws of Kepler and Newton were able to incorporate observations from as far back as the Babylonian, Greek and Moorish astronomers. Man had learnt to think differently, and this development was critical in the creation of modern civilization. Only 40 years after Galileo was forced by the Church to recant his opinions, Newton, faced with a scientist who believed that with a new telescope he had destroyed entirely the Newtonian system, simply replied, 'It may be so. There is no arguing against facts and experiments'. And Newton also said: 'If I have seen a little further, it is by standing on the shoulders of Giants' (Weber, 1973).

The following centuries brought great advances in man's understanding of his world. The lessons learnt from the study of astronomy gave rise to the science of chemistry, the study of heat, and eventually to the science of biology (which did not enter American schools until the twentieth century). It was in the nineteenth century that the one science, natural philosophy, became separated into the branches physics, chemistry and biology. The nineteenth century, probably coincidentally, was also characterized by the certainty of scientists. When it was proposed to establish laboratories at Cambridge, the mathematician Todhunter in 1873 (200 years after the great Newton's humble statement just quoted) objected that it was unnecessary for students to see experiments performed, since the results could be vouched for by their tutors, probably clergymen of mature knowledge, recognized ability and blameless character! Lawrence Bragg, who was to go on to his great work in X-ray crystallography, has said that when he was an undergraduate at Cambridge at the beginning of the twentieth century, classical physics appeared to be complete. There was really little else to find out and it only remained to determine physical constants to a further place of decimals (1970).

The twentieth century brought a revolution that in its own way was as big an earthquake as the seventeenth-century one. At the turn of the century, Thomson discovered the electron. Einstein showed Newton's laws to be inadequate (which Newton would have approved) and scientists are still testing Einstein's theories by trying to disprove them (which Einstein would approve). Theories about the structure of the atom have constantly been fashioned, discarded, and refashioned. A profoundly important dimension to science – perhaps the most important one of all – has become apparent: science is uncertain and its knowledge is constantly changing. If science is knowledge, it is dynamic knowledge. 'Prove' is a word that may be appropriate to mathematics or logic, but it is now usually out of place in science. When a scientist fails to find life on Mars, he has not proved that no life exists there.

The twentieth-century scientist should be certain of only one thing: that in the end everything he knows may turn out to be wrong. However, the 1970 Nobel Physics Prize winner, Hannes Alfvén, has warned that if scientists are not continually on their guard they may believe in mythical theories just as firmly as did Ptolemy and Artistotle. The difference between science and myth, he says, is the difference between critical thinking and the belief in prophets (1976). There is a danger that the theories accepted at present will not be examined critically enough, but will be regarded as the wisdom of prophets, not to be questioned.

There is a lesson here for schools. Nearly all pre-1960 science teaching contained the positivism of the nineteenth century. 'Modern physics' was anything that happened after 1900. It was dealt with at the end of an advanced course. In many schools the situation has not changed significantly. Schoolchildren can still be found 'proving' Boyle's law or copying diagrams of perfectly symmetrical leaves. But if children are to learn science, they must be given the view of science of the late twentieth century. We must give them respect for observations rather than for the pronouncements of the textbook and teacher prophets. Otherwise we shall leave them with pre-Copernican thinking and a willingness to accept Aristotelian pronouncements. If we want to take them as far as Galileo, we must see to it that children understand experimentation as a means of compelling nature to answer their questions. And if we are to bring them into the present century, they must be made to appreciate the uncertainty of science, and to know that theories are speculations or guesses that must be discarded or modified as soon as they fail to fit the observations. Children must know that *no one really knows*. If we can give children these insights, they will have learnt science, no matter what content they have covered. If we tell them, as hard fact, the theories of Newton, Darwin, Boyle, etc., we shall be teaching the kind of thinking of the Middle Ages and earlier. The children will not be learning science. They will have been denied what might be man's greatest achievement. We shall have left them unprotected against the myths of the politicians, advertisers and other dangerous prophets.

The distinctiveness of science -- *Characteristics*

Continuing with the question 'What is science?' we now consider whether science has special characteristics not found in other disciplines. We have seen that science asks *what* and *how* questions, but not *why* questions; and we have seen that in science evidence is very important. Is it possible, however, to be sure that a given scholarly actvity is science (or is not science)? Is social science a science? Is there a difference between social science and social studies? What is the relationship between mathematics and science? Can learning be classified into branches?

Science and other disciplines

It is agreed that the various disciplines have their own central concepts (gravity, photosynthesis and elements, for example, in science); that the concepts of a discipline form a network of relationships within the discipline; that each discipline has its own language, symbols and means of communication; and that the disciplines have their own techniques and skills (Hirst, 1972). Science depends crucially on experiment and observation. Social studies and history may use these techniques (indeed, an archaeologist is a scientific historian), but they are not crucial to the discipline, and if evidence is absent, it is still history. Phenix puts the social sciences together with psychology, physical sciences and life sciences into the 'realm of meaning' that he calls empirics. Since the social scientist is dealing with people and human populations, the variables are many and not easy to manipulate; but if evidence, experiment and observation are crucial to social science, it is easy to accept it as a science. Hirst, on the other hand, separates the human sciences from physical science, putting the former with history.

Both philosophers agree that mathematics is not empirical and is not classified with any form of science. Hirst puts mathematics with logic, while Phenix puts it with language. There is no doubt that mathematics is a language, one that is much used by scientists since it allows them to say beautifully in half a line what might take a whole book of words in the mother tongue. Mathematics is also logic, a deductive way of working beginning with certain general assumed truths, or axioms, and moving through theorems to individual cases. In mathematics one 'proves' things.

When science is taught in this way, as it very often is in schools which see scientists and mathematicians as interchangeable, the science is destroyed. Deductive teaching of science takes children backwards through man's experience, assuming first the particle theory (for example) and then applying it to the structure of crystals, the gas laws, and all the other specifics of particle behaviour. Children are being taught about science in a way that is contrary to scientific thinking. The modern science curricula work the other way, approaching problems inductively. Children observe that crystals have a regular geometric structure, that Brownian motion occurs in a smoke cell, that air exerts pressure, that liquids and gases diffuse. From these phenomena, they are led to appreciate that, in order to relate these observations together, it is reasonable to assume that matter is particulate, grainy, discrete, not continuous. The working is from individual observations to a general principle, conveying the nature of a great scientific theory.

If the curricula of the sixties approached science inductively, this may not be exactly how the scientist in the field works. Medawar is one who argues that induction in science is a myth. Opponents of the inductive view assert that meaningful observations simply cannot be made without some sort of guess (hypothesis) to start with. Popper sees hypothesis and observation as a chicken-and-egg situation. Just as the chicken is preceded by an earlier kind of egg, so is the observation preceded by an earlier kind of hypothesis. There are signs that science teaching is becoming dissatisfied with the extreme inductive approach, but it is unlikely that there will be a swing back to the deductive teaching of the past. Meanwhile, science teachers should be on their guard against the teaching of science as mathematics or logic, because science is certainly not that. Science must always be 'I wonder if ...'.

Both Hirst and Phenix believe that their divisions of 'forms of knowledge' or 'realms of meaning' arise logically, that the very nature of the disciplines distinguishes them. There is another school of thought that believes that each discipline simply emerged and proceeded to define and develop its realm. A discipline is seen as a community of human beings with a heritage striving to bring their field to a continually higher or more fruitful stage of knowledge and meaning. This point of view is expressed by King and Brownell (1966), who believe that a field of knowledge is whatever the members of the community claim it to be. In other words, 'science is what scientists do'. If we reflect on the way in which science emerged, the latter view seems more acceptable than that of Hirst and Phenix.

The conclusion is that it is not possible to delimit science and other disciplines except by using the criteria outlined earlier, in the paragraph headed 'Science and other disciplines'. Science is also done by historians, artists, musicians, mathematicians and ordinary people, and it is no wonder that the boundaries are in a constant state of flux. It is equally difficult to delimit physics, chemistry and biology which, as Whitfield points out, began to distinguish themselves from one another about 1800 but whose boundaries began to break down about 1920 into studies like biochemistry and biophysics. Towards the end of the twentieth century we find that the distinctions persist only in the upper levels of schools and the lower levels of universities, a band that is rapidly narrowing.

The implications for teaching

It seems self-evident that schools should provide children with exposure to a broad spectrum of the forms of thought, however they are classified. Whatever labels are given to school subjects, children deserve the experience of empirics, aesthetics and all the other fields of human endeavour. A child whose learning is confined to physics, chemistry, biology, mathematics and his own language is just as deprived as the child whose learning consists only of history, geography, art, mathematics, literature and his language. The growth in the seventies of integrated science and social studies stems partly from a recognition of the need for a balanced curriculum for all children until as late a stage in their schooling as possible.

If science is what scientists do, what do scientists, in fact, do? This question has been partly answered already. Scientists confront nature, compelling her to reveal her secrets. In effect, science has two dimensions, the body of knowledge that has been accumulated by scientists, and the ways in which they acquire this knowledge. These two dimensions will now be looked at more closely in the context of school science.

The body of scientific knowledge

This body of knowledge may be seen as a collection of knots in a rather untidy net. The many little knots are the specifics of science (how to prepare oxygen, transpiration through the stomata of leaves, the structure of the mammalian heart, series and parallel circuits, for instance). Taken separately, these specifics do not tell us much about nature as it is, and schoolboys find them hard to remember. Isolated from one another, and without the network, they are little facts for the sake of little facts, providing few new insights. Unfortunately, school science very often ends at these little facts, which are no more science than a heap of bricks is a home.

When the little knots are tied into bigger knots, making generalizations, science begins to make sense. Psychologists like Ausubel and Bruner point out that a child needs hooks on which to hang new knowledge, that new learning needs to be related to the old. Thus teaching for generalization is not only consistent with what science is to scientists, it leads to better learning in children. Failure to make the generalizations explicit to children usually means that children miss the point.

In choosing his topics, the teacher has the opportunity to make the science relevant to the interests and needs of the community he serves. Different topics like 'Fish Farming', 'Traffic', 'Our Street' and 'Cooking' may be appropriate to different communities, but all of them offer the opportunity to teach children the body of knowledge accumulated by scientists.

As a child becomes more mature and acquires more and more of the concepts and generalizations, the big knots in the net of knowledge can be brought together into really giant knots. These will include the great principles, laws and theories which are the triumph of science. Not all children will learn science long enough or have the ability to think in the abstract, so that many will not reach this stage. A good many science teachers do not themselves have the scientific knowledge necessary to teach at this stage. However, if the main purpose of science teaching is to provide scientific knowledge, it will have maximum meaning if taken as far as possible towards this stage. Children in primary school can travel only a little distance along this road; thus the main purpose in teaching science to young children should not be the provision of knowledge. For one thing, such a purpose is unattainable. We have mentioned before that the teacher of young children does not need a great store of scientific knowledge himself. Even if he does not know much about atoms or anatomy, he has little to fear. Unfortunately, educators of teachers often fail to recognize this, and college courses tend to emphasize content more than may be wise.

The processes of science

The second dimension of science is the processes by which knowledge is acquired. Ritchie (1971) says, 'Scientific method basically involves confronting ideas with experience, that is, designing experiments to test ideas or hypotheses and predictions based on them.' This section looks at what is involved in designing experiments to test ideas or hypotheses and predictions.

While we have asserted that the body of scientific knowledge must be a secondary concern for the teacher of young children, scientific processes, although neglected in the older curricula, make a vital contribution to the education of students of any age. Some of these processes are part of other branches of learning and there seems to be general agreement that primary-school studies are best integrated. It follows that the primary-school teacher is not a teacher of science or art or language, but a teacher of children. Good teaching requires an awareness of, among other things, the skills that can be developed by working in a scientific way. Whether or not the child will continue his studies in science, the development of these skills provides an essential component for the achievement of the goals of general education.

In an attempt to define the processes of science, the American Association for the Advancement of Science (AAAS) asked scientists to say what they actually do. The following list of thirteen processes came from this inquiry, and we attach some explanatory notes.

1. Observation. (Using all the senses, of course.) One cannot be curious until one has observed, and the powers of observation can be learnt. Since the senses are bombarded with stimuli, consciousness is selective, so that many events escape notice. Some casual observations make us stop to think, others are dismissed. Observations are not in themselves so valuable as the questions that follow them ('That's odd! I wonder what made that happen?'). Children can be guided and trained to make observations-with-a-purpose, just as a detective hunts for clues in order to find the murder weapon, the motive for the crime and then the criminal. 'Let us collect as many clues as we can so that we can describe what is going on. No guesswork just yet, just say what you see, hear, smell, etc. Find facts.' Thus children learn to collect evidence discriminating between observation and inference.

2. Classification. To bring order to their inquiries about nature, scientists have developed systems of classification. Some of these classifications are plant/animal, vertebrate/invertebrate, solid/liquid/gas, the periodic system, sedimentary/metamorphic/igneous rocks, metal/non-metal. Other systems of classification (such as striped/plain and rough/smooth) are not wrong; it is just that scientists do not find them useful and do not use them. When children are beginning to learn what classification is all about, they may be allowed to develop any system they like. There is no need to hurry children into knowing the scientists' classifications.

There is no point in classification for its own sake, and many teachers worry unnecessarily that they do not know the scientific classification of common plants and animals. It might be just as useful, at a given time, if one classifies plants according to whether they grow in the shade or sun, or whether they are considered locally to be food or non-food. It is only when one goes deep into the study of science that the scientists' classifications are really needed.

3. Number relations. Information can be described and analysed economically and meaningfully in the language of mathematicians, so scientists count, measure, draw graphs, work out equations and so on. This process of science must not be overdone with young or slow children, because they may find it discouraging and boring. There is much opportunity here for integrating work in school.

4. Measurement. Measurement (with string, ruler, balance, thermometer, cup, for instance) gives us useful information in our explorations. Since they are not valuable for their own sake, measurement techniques are better taught as they are needed, rather than by the class spending a few weeks learning measurement in isolation. Very often, estimations or rough measurements are much more meaningful than precise measurements, and these techniques have to be taught. The child has to learn when it is better to estimate and when one ought to be precise. It is wrong and misleading, for instance, to say, 'Limes weight 8 grams and grapefruit weigh 314 grams'.

5. Space/time relations. This involves the investigation and use of shapes, distance, motion and speed. The process is related to studies of the shapes of animals or crystals, of balls rolling down slopes, or perhaps of crab-racing.

6. Communications. Communication is a skill surprisingly neglected in schools, although the art of communication can be learnt only through practice. Children tend to be inarticulate, especially if the language of school is not the one they use at home. When a child cannot express his or her thoughts in words, oral or written, he or she is reduced to gestures or silence. One of the most important tasks of the teacher is to give each child the opportunity to think and to put his or her thoughts into spoken and written words, drawings and pictures, graphs and equations. The surest way to inhibit the development of communication skills is for the teacher to do most of the talking, and to insist that children use the formal language of textbooks.

7. Prediction. Science being much more than description of observations, the intelligent guess, or prediction, is an essential part of the scientist's work. He plans a path of investigation by asking, 'What would happen if ...?', making his guess and then proceeding to test it. Children should know that their teacher is anxious for them to ask 'What would happen' questions, and then to make their own predictions; and that it does not matter if they guess wrong, since this is always happening to scientists. The teacher knows he is doing well when a child says to himself, 'I wonder what the wood louse will do if I poke it. I think it will run away. Funny, it just curled up into a ball! I wonder if ...'. True learning is characterized not so much by the answering of questions as by the asking of them. Bronowski has said, 'That is the essence of science: ask an impertinent question and you are on the way to the pertinent answer.'

8. Inference. This is another kind of guess, a subjective explanation for observations. A scientist observing a wick sticking out from each end of a candle may infer that there is a single wick going right through the candle. The inference could be more useful, leading somewhere, than the observation by itself. When it is clear that there has been an inference, another scientist might say, 'That might be the explanation; I think I shall try to test it.' And so science advances.

9. Making operational definitions. Definitions provide economy of communication since a single word or term may be used repeatedly in place of a lengthy description if the user first makes clear the meaning to be assigned to the word or term. Imagine the tortuous language that would be needed if our predecessors had not defined *force* as that which causes *acceleration*, acceleration as rate of change of *velocity* and velocity as rate of change of position. These words have operational definitions, because they are defined in terms of how they are measured or what they do.

10. Formulating hypotheses. This list of processes is a hierarchy. Each process represents a higher level of skill than the ones before it, and includes them. Hypothesis-formulation therefore is a relatively advanced skill, and one that should not be laboured with young children. A hypothesis is a guess. A causal hypothesis is one which suggests causes. A testable hypothesis is one which can be tested in order to find out whether it will be supported or disconfirmed. Here are some examples:

Fertilizer X is good for all growing things (might be easily disconfirmed, but can never be proved beyond doubt).
Fertilizer X is good for growing gungo peas (testable).
Fertilizer X is good for growing gungo peas because it contains a nitrate (causal, and testable with difficulty).

Even if a teacher is not consciously developing this skill in children, he should be on the alert for the occasions when they are unconsciously making tentative hypotheses. To a child who says, 'Birds will not eat chenille worms', the teacher might ask, 'What makes you think so, Anna?' And Anna might answer that she believes that birds will be afraid of the spikes. Anna and the teacher could then work out a way of finding out if birds really will not eat chenille worms. In a well-known activity from Nuffield Chemistry, children are asked where the black stuff comes from when a piece of copper is heated in a flame. Some think it comes from the flame, others think it comes from the air, and others think it comes from the copper, so this leads to a rewarding investigation.

11. Interpreting data. Data by themselves are of little interest. What is important is the new light shed by the data. What generalizations can we make? What is their meaning in terms of large questions? How much do they tell us and how little do they tell us? A graph of population growth or a cooling curve leads to a consideration of the story told by the picture and the implications for food supply or for our understanding of the energy in the system. Data collection and interpretation serve the search for the big answers.

12. Identifying and controlling variables. The ability to identify and to control the variables in an experiment comes with experience, and should be treated at progressive levels of complexity as the child matures. It is not until quite late in his or her development that the child will understand all the implications of the well-known bell-jar demonstration in which one jar, the control, has a flask of sodium hydroxide to absorb the carbon dioxide, and whose plant is shown not to photosynthesize. By the time children are ready to understand the science in this exercise, most of them have already found out from somewhere else that carbon dioxide is taken up in photosynthesis, and it would be pointless and unscientific to pretend that they have not. The demonstration could, however, be useful to 'show how scientists work' rather than to 'show that carbon dioxide ...'. Older children who are, for example, investigating the effect of dissolved salt on the lather obtained with different detergents should be able to recognize that there are a number of variables that can be manipulated, such as quantity of salt, brand of detergent, quantity of detergent, and temperature. The teacher's guidance may be needed to help them decide which of these variables they will, in fact, vary; and the teacher will see to it that they understand *why* they vary only one at a time.

13. Experimenting. This represents a high level of the scientist's art, and it will be remembered that science made little progress until Galileo invented the process in the seventeenth century. The experimenter makes a hypothesis from observations that have interested him, and then he devises a way to test his hypothesis. 'How can I find out?', says the scientist. 'How can you find out if your guess is right?', says the teacher, and then, 'Try it and see'.

In the belief that it is the processes of science that should be learnt by the primary-school child, AAAS developed *Science: a Process Approach*. An examination of most modern curricula, especially those for primary schools, should show that the developers of the curricula have put a heavy emphasis on the processes of science [. . .].

Conclusion

Should all children be taught science? We say yes, even if the science they learn is taught the way most of us learnt it in school.

If, however, we can provide children with opportunities to work as scientists, to think as scientists, to make mistakes, then we are providing them with opportunities for intellectual and personal growth that they will not get in any other way. Bronowski has said. 'Let us not be contemptuous of mistakes; they are the fulcrum on which the process of life moves.' If we invite our pupils to ponder on the theories of science, on their power, elegance and beauty, and above all on their uncertainty, we shall be reflecting the greatest intellectual and cultural achievement of which Bullock spoke. If we can do these things, then all children should learn science.

Teachers trying out new techniques usually sense any lowering in the quality of the teaching–learning situation. Similarly, a two-finger typist attempting to touch-type becomes frustrated by his new slowness and his errors. No new technique ever goes well at the first few attempts, but we may reflect that the mistakes of teachers can be as valuable as the mistakes of children. If the teacher is aware of this he continues to refine his techniques as his pupils come to understand the new ways of learning. Teaching and learning science will then be a dynamic and exciting process for all who share in the explorations.

References

Alfvén, H. (1976) Cosmology: myth or science? *The British Association for the Advancement of Science, supplement no. 1, 3 September,* to *The Times Higher Education Supplement.*

Baez, A.V. and Alles, J. (1973) Integrated science teaching as a part of general education – looking ahead, in Richmond, P. (ed.) *New Trends in Integrated Science Teaching.* Vol. II, ch. 9, Paris, Unesco.

Bragg, L. (1970) *Ideas and Discoveries in Physics.* London, Longman (Longman Physics Topics).

Bronowski, J. (1960) *The Common Sense of Science.* Harmondsworth, Penguin.

Bronowski, J. (1973) *The Ascent of Man.* London, BBC Publications.

Bullock, Lord (1976) Presidential address to the Association for Science Education, *School Science Review,* Vol. 57, No. 201, p.621.

Goldsmith, M. (1974) The social significance of the teaching of science and mathematics in the Commonwealth, in Richmond, P. (ed.) *New Trends in Integrated Science Teaching,* Vol. III, ch. 19, Paris, Unesco.

Hirst, P.H. (1972) Liberal education and the nature of knowledge, in Archambault, R.D. (ed.) *Philosophical Analysis and Education.* London, Routledge & Keegan Paul, p. 113–38.

King, A. and Brownell, J. (1966) *The Curriculum and Disciplines of Knowledge*. New York, Wiley.

Peacocke, A.R. (1976) Natural science and Christian meaning. *School Science Review*, Vol. 58, No. 202, p.153–6.

Ritchie, B. (1971) Physics, in Whitfield, R. (ed.) *Disciplines of the Curriculum*. Maidenhead, McGraw-Hill, p.127.

Science Teacher Education Project (1974) *Activities and Experience*. London, McGraw-Hill (SCI 4.).

Weber, R.L. (comp.) (1973) *A Random Walk in Science*. London, The Institute of Physics, p.187, p.192.

Weisskopf, V.F. (1976) Is physics human? *Physics Education*, Vol. 11, No. 2, p.75–9.

1.3

SHOULD SCIENCE BE TAUGHT IN PRIMARY SCHOOLS?

Jack Kerr and Elizabeth Engel

A positive answer to the question posed in the title of this article is conceded at the outset, but a detailed response must surely depend on the resolution of a number of problems. First, what precisely do we mean by primary science? Has the approach as represented by the Nuffield Junior Science and Science 5–13 Projects resulted in more scientific investigations in classrooms? Is the time appropriate to re-examine the current orthodoxy which lays so much more emphasis on ways of behaving scientifically than on science itself? At the 5–11-year stage, should the case for a more ordered and deliberate introduction of essential scientific concepts be given further thought? Do we know how children learn to behave in scientific ways? How adequate is the provision for the preparation of primary school teachers, at both initial and post-experience stages, to cope with scientific activities in their classrooms? Attention must be focused on these important questions if planned scientific experiences are to become accessible to young children [. . .].

Although we believe it is essential to provide opportunities for children of all ages to enjoy scientific experiences, translation of this conviction into practice is known to be far from simple. And the dichotomy (which has always been a dichotomy in theory only) between, at the one extreme, science as a means of acquiring skills and attitudes characteristic of the discipline and, at the other, science as learning information has not necessarily provided us with a useful framework for practice. Wynne Harlen, in a recent article (1978), has analysed the alternative approaches to primary science and attempts to find some guidelines for avoiding the errors of both extreme positions. The

Source: Kerr, J. and Engel, E. (1980) Should Science be Taught in Primary Schools?, Education 3–*13*, 3 (1), pp.4–8 Pb. Studies in Education Ltd, Driffield, N. Humberside

questions we have posed need to be re-examined, but perhaps a de-emphasis of the processes/content polarization and a conscious avoidance of extreme views of science may provide a more useful context for this re-examination.

Assessment of progress in primary science

Judged on the basis of published material alone the reader might conclude that the past 20-year period had been one of unusual progress and innovation. Apart from the mass of commercially-produced books, kits and resources of all kinds, since 1964 at least six project teams in Britain alone have been actively developing curricular materials for teachers to stimulate and support scientific activities and experiences with young children. Many reports have been published by the Association for Science Education, the Department of Education and Science, the British Association and other bodies. The Interim Report of the Schools Council's Impact and Take-Up Project (1978) suggests that in quantitative terms the outcome of all this activity has been disappointing. The Nuffield Junior Science Project materials were familiar (that is, 'read parts or know well') in only 18 percent of a random sample of 279 primary schools. According to the headteachers, 13 percent of schools in the sample were using the materials but only 7 percent of the teachers agreed that they were doing so. The Science 5-13 Project was known to 30 percent of the same sample, 36 percent of the headteachers claiming the books were used, as against 22 percent of their teachers. Science 5-13 books were actually seen by members of the project team in 50 percent of the schools visited. It is interesting that when about six hundred teachers were asked which national curriculum project was 'best known' Science 5-13 ranked very highly – fourth out of 107 projects listed. In Ashton's study (1975) based on data collected in 1969-72 — 1513 teachers rated 72 aims of primary education in order of importance. That the child should 'know some basic scientific procedures and concepts' was ranked 62nd; 'know basic facts of sex and reproduction' 63rd; and 'understand how the body works', 64th. Yet scientific activity in the classroom would be a powerful means of achieving other, more highly-ranked aims in Ashton's study. For example, 'to make reasoned judgements and choices' was 23rd in importance of the same 72 aims ; 'a questioning attitude to his environment' ranked 24th; 'inventiveness and creativity', 30th; and 'to observe carefully, accurately, and with sensitivity', 37th. This discrepancy, between the ranking of aims which specifically mention science and the ranking of more generally expressed aims which in fact describe important aspects of scientific (and of course other) activity, is interesting. It may be that many primary teachers simply do not recognize the particular contribution science could make to the achievement of aims which they themselves rank highly, or it may be that they would prefer to try to achieve these aims in non-scientific contexts in which they feel more comfortable. The most recent report on the state of science in primary education in England is based on a survey of 1127 classes in 542 schools by HM Inspectorate (1978). They found that the 'work in observational and experimental science was less well matched to children's capabilities than work in any other area of the curriculum' ... 'only a small minority recognized the important contribution which science could make to children's intellectual development' ... and ... 'the ideas and materials produced by curriculum development projects have had little impact in the majority of schools' (Chapter 5, iv, p.58).

In summary, the evidence suggests that many primary teachers are aware of the existence of important curricular developments in primary science, they rank highly objectives which science educators would recognize can be achieved through planned scientific activity, and yet there seems to be precious little scientific activity going on in our classrooms. Apart from inspired work by a minority of schools and teachers' centres, it is clear that our efforts to spread science teaching in primary schools over the past decade have been largely ineffective. Why is there so little visible progress? Is it simply that the pace of any educational change is always painfully slow? Are there any other reasons?

A reassessment of policy

Factors commonly thought to impede the improvement of science at the primary stage include (a) the poor science background of teachers, resulting in lack of confidence to attempt work in science; (b) failure of headteachers to recognize the potential contribution of science to the curriculum; and (c) inadequate provision of simple apparatus and materials. These obstacles to change will be looked at later, but there may be a more fundamental reason why progress has been so slow.

The writings on child development of Isaacs, Dewey, Piaget and others had a powerful influence on most of us in the 1960s. The case for more openness, more activity and more concern for the individual child won over the Plowden Committee, whose work was in progress at the same time as the Nuffield Junior Science Project. This project team followed suit, and recommended that children should be allowed to investigate the environment by working at self-appointed tasks to develop skills of observing, questioning, exploring, interpreting findings and communicating, across the curriculum. The team argued that at this stage starting to *do* science was more important than science itself. The so-called 'process approach' to primary science had arrived. Few noticed the much-less publicised Oxford Primary Science Project supported by the Ministry of Education which produced its report (Redman, Brerton and Boyers, 1969) in 1969, a little later than Nuffield Junior Science. The Oxford group argued that it was impossible to ignore the fact that 'children will bring science into the school' and it was vital to include the contribution of science in the interpretation of the environment. Children must be given an understanding of some of the essential ideas used by scientists. Four main concept areas – energy, structure, chance and life – were explored by methods which were not *in fact* dissimilar to those recommended by the Nuffield group. But to no avail. The all-embracing child-centred philosophy dominated discussion about the whole of the primary curriculum, and generally precluded consideration of materials such as the Oxford project which delineated content areas for scientific exploration.

The process-content debate, referred to earlier, has been with us since the start of science teaching. It figured in varying degrees in Henry Armstrong's campaign for discovery methods a hundred years ago, the general science movement of the 1950s and all the Nuffield Science Teaching Projects. But at no time did we try to lay so much emphasis on process and attitude objectives as in recommendations for primary science a decade ago. This sophisticated orthodoxy – for this is what the process approach has become for teachers – was so deep-rooted that, until recently, few people were prepared to appear so heretical as to question it. Could it be that progress in primary science has been limited because the *general* principles controlling primary policy have been applied unbendingly in the case of science? In Harlen's paper, referred to earlier, she lists examples of 'guidelines to content' to meet the process criteria (pp.622–4), but at the same time emphasizing that 'the content objectives must not be allowed to replace the process and attitude objectives'. The same shift to a more practical balance, albeit tentative, is detectable in the HMI's report and, more overtly [in an article by Norman Booth in 1980]. At present the content of primary science is left almost entirely to chance, a state of affairs which puts a considerable strain on conscientious teachers who lack sufficient background and experience of science. We conclude that if science *should* continue to be taught in primary schools, an adjustment of policy is desirable. Perhaps we should begin by forgetting all about the process-content dichotomy, and look more closely at how the child acquires scientific skills and attitudes as well as an understanding of essential concepts, and then at what the teacher is required to do about it.

Children's scientific ideas

The fact that learning depends on the learner successfully relating new experience to what is already known is crucial to all theories of cognitive development, and is an idea familiar to teachers. It follows that what a learner brings to a learning situation is of great importance. Irene Finch (1971) makes a very interesting distinction in this connection. She suggests that teachers of English show interest in children's own ideas and opinions, but by contrast, science teachers frequently give the impression that children's ideas are not worth much consideration beside those of great scientists. She goes on:

> 'But the English teacher is not, and cannot, be aiming at producing a class of Shakespeares, and we cannot be aiming at producing a class of scientists ... Somehow we must arrange for children to produce useful scientific ideas in our lessons, and to get credit and kudos for them'(p.407).

Many teachers would agree, and some science educators (e.g. Driver and Easley 1978, Deadman and Kelly 1978) have suggested that there is a need to look more fundamentally and in detail at pupils' own understandings and ways of thinking about scientific ideas, and to use this information in planning teaching strategies. Thus the traditional Curriculum/Pupil model would be reversed; pupil understanding would be investigated *first* and then gradually incorporated into teaching and curricular plannng. As with classical botany and zoology (on which the modern study of these subjects is founded), it may be that the first job is description and classification.

But is this any more than good teachers have always done? Good practice has always included listening carefully to individual children's ideas and then beginning from the vantage point of the learner's own experience. This is quite true, but we believe that research can provide valuable suppport for this approach.

There are indications from the small body of qualitative research into children's understandings that *common belief patterns* emerge. Frequently these patterns, which may be totally 'wrong' ideas, or may represent a partial understanding, persist despite instruction. This seems to be particularly true for scientific notions which defy 'common sense'. (For example, the fact that all matter is made up of molecules and atoms, or the fact that sideways pressure at a given depth in fluid is the same as downwards pressure.) Sometimes the alternative explanations offered by children are unanticipated, and even bizarre. Documentation of these common patterns of understanding in children of different ages (and, ideally, in the same children at different ages) should yield useful information on developmental trends and on individual pupil differences.

Two examples of investigations with young children may perhaps serve to illustrate the points made so far in this section. Nussbaum and Novak (1976) interviewed 52 7–8 year olds in an attempt to elucidate their ideas on the 'Earth' concept. The interviews, which included the use of models and drawings, began with a set of questions which included: How do *you* know that the Earth is round? Which way do we have to look in order to see the Earth? Why don't we see the Earth as a ball? etc. From analysis of the data, Nussbaum and Novak identified five common patterns of children's thinking about the Earth, ranging from primitive notions of a flat earth with no concept of space to a notion of a spherical planet, surrounded by space and with things falling to the centre. They concluded that the problem of developing a conception of cosmic space is central in learning the Earth concept, and yet this aspect is not emphasized by teachers or in textbooks. Similarly, they thought there was a need to explore ways of helping young children to understand that 'down' directions were towards the centre of the Earth. Many children who 'know' that 'a person on the other side of the Earth does not stand upside down, and does not fall off because gravity pulls him towards the Earth' still do not completely comprehend the meaning of this statement.

Using a similar approach, Albert (1978) identified eleven 'thought patterns' which underlie the concept of heat found in children from 4–9 years. Just one of her findings will suffice as illustration. The adult conception of heat implies that cold, warm and hot are a single dimension. Albert found that the 4,5 and 6 year olds in her sample did not consistently distinguish between 'hot' and 'warm', even though they used both terms. But at the age of 8 children began to distinguish clearly between 'hot' and 'warm', at the same time regarding them as different instances of the same dimension. They did this by reflecting on how *they* act on and react on objects at different temperatures. For example, Ron (age 9) pointed out: 'Like hot is sort of burn you, and warm is just feeling nice'. Teachers of older children will be aware that the idea of 'cold' as an entity, and a separate one from 'hot', is held quite frequently up to 15 years (and probably beyond!).

Many primary teachers would accept the need to take account of the learner's perspectives. If the approach outlined above could demonstrably identify difficult areas, isolate problems (perhaps ones which impede any further development of understanding) and suggest ways of overcoming them, teachers are likely to respond positively. Over-generalizations are no use – justice must be done to the rich variety of children's ideas.

To summarize, it has been suggested that descriptive studies of children's understandings could be accessible and very useful to teachers. If research can identify common belief patterns, some of the 'spade work' will have been done for teachers. These patterns would not be considered as 'norms' or 'stages', but would certainly alert teachers to the possible perspectives their pupils may bring to learning. A build-up of information from studies of this kind, one conceptual area at a time, is bound to be slow (but then most 'instant' educational solutions turn out to be ephemeral). The *application* of information gleaned from these studies must be investigated by classroom-based research, preferably by teachers themselves. One thing is quite clear. It is obvious that the requirement for primary teachers to be well-trained in science will become no less urgent if this approach is adopted.

Professional training of primary teachers in science.

How adequate is the preparation of primary teachers at both initial and post-experience stages to meet the demand for scientific activities in their classrooms? As far as initial training is concerned, attention given to science is *less* than it was 20 years ago. A survey of 36 of the 109 training colleges in England and Wales was carried out in 1960 for use at a British Association conference on 'The Place of Science in Primary Education', the proceedings of which were published in 1962 (Kerr). At that time, about three-quarters of the students 'were getting some science instruction', 40 percent of the colleges required all primary students to attend science courses, and 45 percent allocated 30 hours or less for primary science. Two provided over 100 hours. This was thought by the delegates to be a highly unsatisfactory picture. What would they have thought about our present provision?

Since the introduction of B.Ed. degree courses in colleges, the majority of students are given the most scanty professional training in science. Many are given none at all. The fact that the study of curricular areas, other than English and mathematics, usually operates on an options system is partly responsible for this deterioration. The preparation of primary teachers to cover all the areas of the curriculum has been a major problem for decades. Part of the intention of setting up separate Professional Studies Departments and Educational Studies Departments in the majority of training institutions was to enrich professional training and underline its importance. In fact, too often the consequence has been quite the opposite. Universities and the CNAA have imposed their views of what kind of knowledge is academically acceptable for the award of degrees, and the development of professionally-relevant courses (seen by the teaching profession to be necessary) has been neglected. McNamara and Desforges (1978) claim the time is ripe to abandon the disciplines of education at the initial training stage and develop 'the teaching of professional studies as an academically rigorous, practically useful, and scientifically productive activity' (p.17). Through a project funded by The Nuffield Foundation, they aim to work out a more clearly articulated rationale for professional studies, one which is informed by practical knowledge (which they call 'craft knowledge'). The project seeks to develop professional skills through the generation of classroom-based theories of instruction and teacher behaviour. The Science Teacher Education Project (Haysom and Sutton, 1974) was a move in this direction, that is towards building theory from professional practice. Given the present pattern of teacher education programmes, the professional preparation of teachers is unlikely to be improved until the aims of these projects are taken seriously.

Opportunities for the further professional training of primary teachers in science, especially at teachers' centres, have been generously provided until the recent financial cuts. These courses and workshops have been actively supported by teachers. School-based courses, using the staff as the 'unit' rather than individual teachers, seem to be the most promising method of bringing about change.

Looking to the future

It is clear that progress will depend on the tempering of theoretical 'ideals' (which are anyway rather subject to fashion) to take realistic account of practical constraints. Some of these constraints, such as the low level of scientific training of many primary teachers, may be very unpalatable. To ignore them is simply escapist. Sometimes the contrast between consultative reports from 'experts and teachers' opinions is striking. In a recent evaluation of a health education course in some Sheffield primary schools, it was found that the project appealed to teachers precisely because it was prescriptive, in terms of content especially, and because it offered the necessary in-service training and resource back-up.

The recent shift from the practice of producing only teachers' materials for primary science to preparing materials for use by pupils is another example of a realistic response to practical constraints. Local curriculum development groups and commercial publishers have been turning out children's science work cards and assignment sheets for some time. The HMI's report (p.59) acknowledges that 'the discriminating use of carefully-chosen' pupil material can 'help to sustain work in science'. The Director of the most recent Schools Council project, 'Learning Through Science', plans to produce pupil materials, although as a team they 'are wedded to the idea of getting children to show initiative and to devise some of their own methods of carrying out investigations'.

Seemingly, these advisers perceive the danger of worksheets becoming the syllabus. We would agree with this view. It would be an extreme and totally retrograde step to finish up with a prescribed science course for primary schools. Even so, if we expect primary teachers to plan scientific activities for children, more understanding of children's scientific ideas is needed, more rigorous and relevant professional training in science for all primary teachers must be introduced, headteachers must be persuaded of its importance, and the resources for the children to engage in these activities must be provided.

References

Albert, E. (1978) Development of the concept of heat in children, *Science Education*, 62, pp.389–99.

Ashton, P. et al. (1975) *The Aims of Primary Education: A Study of Teachers' Opinions*. Macmillan Schools Council Research Studies.

Booth, N. (1980) Science in the middle years, *Education 3–13*, 6, 2, pp.37–41.

Deadman, J.A. and Kelly, P.J. (1978) What do secondary school boys understand about evolution and heredity before they are taught the topics? *Journal of Biological Education*, 12 (1), pp.7–15.

Driver, R. and Easley, J. (1978) Pupils and paradigms: a review of literature related to concept development in adolescent science students, *Studies in Science Education*, 5, pp.61–84.

Finch, I.E. (1971) 'Selling science', *School Science Review*, 53, pp.405–10.

Harlen, W. (1978) Does content matter in primary schools? *School Science Review*, 59, pp.614–25.

Haysom, J.T. and Sutton, C.R. (eds) (1974) *Science Teacher Education Project* publications. McGraw-Hill.

HM Inspectorate (1978) *Primary Education in England: A Survey by HM Inspectors of Schools*, HMSO.

Kerr, J.F. (1962) Training for learning through investigations, in Perkins (ed.) *The Place of Science in Primary Schools*. The British Association, pp.33–44.

McNamara, D. and Desforges, C. (1978) The social sciences, teacher education and the objectification of craft knowledge, *British Journal of Teacher Education*, 4, 1, pp.17–36.

Nussbaum, J. and Novak, J.D. (1976) An assessment of children's concepts of the Earth utilizing structured interviews, *Science Education,* 60, pp.535–50.

Redman, S., Brerton, A. and Boyers, P. (1969) *An Approach to Primary Science* (The Oxford Primary Science Project). Macmillan.

Steadman, S.D. et al. (1978) *An Enquiry into the Impact and Take-Up of Schools Council Funded Activities.* Schools Council publications.

1.4

SCIENCE AND THE CURRICULUM

HMI Science Committee

The intellectual processes of science

Science with its emphasis on the study of the environment and concern for direct observation and practical investigation matches what we know of how children best learn. It can assist pupils to bring questioning minds to their experience of things around them. The teaching of science in primary schools should seek to develop the processes of scientific thinking such as:

observing	explaining	communicating
pattern seeking	experimenting	applying

Observing does not mean simply looking and recording. It means being alert to the many features that may be observable and not only to those that are most obvious. Children studying trees might include the sycamore. Certain features spring immediately to mind – the general shape of the tree, its size, the shape of its leaves, and its method of seed dispersal. The helicopter action of the seeds is fascinating in itself but alert children may also notice the distribution of seeds on the ground, the distance they travel from the tree and whether or not they seem to travel further in some directions than in others. They might be led on to speculate about the growth of sycamore seedlings and their distribution or to conduct experiments with the seeds, dropping them from various heights and in various conditions to observe their flight. They might try making a working model of a sycamore seed. They are then taking the first steps along the road to the formulation of a pattern in which their

Source: HMI Science Committee (1983) *Science in Primary Schools,* London, Department of Education and Science, pp.1–5

observations are related to one another so that those factors that are common, and those that are not common, can be seen and distinguished. In part of the Schools Council Science 5–13 Project, children make a model siege engine and, in playing with it, learn something about projectiles. They can discover the conditions that produce maximum range and go on to ask whether this is part of a larger pattern concerning the flight of projectiles or whether it is peculiar to this model. At a more sophisticated level they might be led to ask whether some features of the operation of the model are part of a common pattern while others are not.

Explaining an observed pattern of events is an important part of true scientific activity. There may be several possible explanations for a particular pattern and children may not always be able to determine the correct one immediately, although they may very well have ideas about which is most likely to be correct. Two 10-year-old boys attached a model soldier to a pulley and ran the pulley down an inclined string. They used different heights and lengths for the string to make the model go faster. They then hit on the idea of attaching another long string to pull the model back to the starting point. The model went more slowly and less far after being released. The boys could offer several possible explanations in this order: the string was an extra weight; pulling the string after it caused the model to slow down; the friction of the additional string on the ground impeded the model.

To arrive at a clearer idea of the most likely explanation they needed to carry out some experiments to test the various possibilities. They tried removing the extra string but attaching an equivalent weight to the model; they tried attaching a number of short strings of equivalent total length; and they tried holding the string up off the ground as the pulley descended. They decided that friction was the over-riding factor. To carry out these experiments successfully meant careful thought about their design and about which factors should be varied and which kept the same. Experimenting always involves careful design, a clear basis of observation, and knowledge. They could well have used their knowledge to design a pulley transport system with particular characteristics such as to carry a particular weight at a particular speed. This would have been an example of their growing awareness of technology and technological processes.

Scientific facts and principles are capable of expression in a variety of ways – in speech or writing, pictorially or graphically, or by the use of number or mathematical relationships. For example, pupils who have hamsters in the classroom can learn about them through handling them and talking about them but they will learn more if they can also draw or make a painting of them, measure their lengths, plot graphs of their growth, and tabulate their increase in weight against their intakes of food. Understanding is strengthened through having to make the effort required to produce a satisfactory description or statement.

Given sufficient opportunity to think scientifically, pupils are able to apply ideas and knowledge to problems new to them. A general knowledge of the needs of plants will enable them to suggest reasons why certain wild plants appear in some places and not in others. The boys who found difficulty with friction in one situation will be likely to recognize it in another and perhaps suggest ways of overcoming it or using it.

The content of science

It is impossible to develop a mode of thought without some basic content about which to think. Or, to put it another way, we cannot be certain we are thinking scientifically unless we have a substantial experience of thinking about matters that are recognizably scientific. There are certain fundamental facts and ideas that pupils must meet and grasp if they are to make any significant progress in their studies. The teacher must be very clear about which scientific concepts are to be used or developed in any particular piece of work so that it may be appropriate to the age and development of the pupils. There are, too, some scientific ideas that call for a carefully chosen sequence in what is done if concepts are to be thoroughly grasped and progress is to be made from year to year [. . .]. Aspects of science that children should meet in the primary school include:

The study of living things and their interaction with the environment

Materials and their characteristics

Energy and its interaction with materials

Forces and their effects.

The approach can be made through a variety of activities but it is important to understand which part of the activity contributes to the science and at what level. It will often be necessary to supplement a particular activity beforehand or afterwards (or possibly both) so that ideas can be thoroughly grasped. To move towards an understanding of forces, pupils first need a considerable amount of simple, everyday experience of forces and what they can do. Having gained some rough and ready ideas, both qualitative and quantitative (e.g. roughly twice the force produces roughly twice the effect), they are then ready to apply forces to materials in more systematic ways and to study examples of the application of forces.

Systematic enquiry

A generalized school activity can be extremely useful if it is well planned. Preparation is needed beforehand, the teacher and the children need to know what is to be studied during the activity, and sufficient follow-up is necessary to ensure learning. The point to be emphasized is that science is being done when the pupils are carrying out a systematic enquiry, but not all activities meet this requirement. For example a visit to the countryside or the seashore can offer many possibilities – geographical, historical, artistic, scientific and so on. The children may decide to study birds. They may draw and paint pictures of birds, make collections of feathers, bring to school collections of birds' eggs which they have been given (but, it is to be hoped, not made themselves). They may find information about birds and broaden their investigation to aeroplanes. Pupils often find this kind of work interesting and rewarding and it has a part to play in improving their skills in classifying, assembling information and in writing and speaking. However, it is very easy for pupils to do a great deal of work on birds with almost nothing that could be called scientific being included. To draw or paint birds, to make collections about them, to assemble pictures, even to read and write about them may not be at all scientific. A systematic enquiry might involve looking not only at the birds themselves but at their mode of living; investigating their food preferences and the way they are adapted to their habitat; it might include comparison between birds of different types, different habits and different distributions geographically and numerically. Explanations might be sought for the appearance of certain birds in certain places and for seasonal variation in the bird population. To take another example, this time from technology: the building of a model bridge is not in itself either scientific or technological. But scientific and technological development is taking place when a sustained investigation is being made of forces and structures, when pupils are asking questions and seeking answers through experiment or in books, and when what they have learned begins to influence their design of the model bridge.

Teaching and learning

For science to be taught effectively teachers must have an understanding of its requirements and a knowledge of its content, particularly of those facts and concepts that are of fundamental importance. They need to be able to strike the right balance between these factors and the time necessary to ensure that for each child there is some recognizable structure in his scientific thinking and in the scientific content presented to him so that he has at least a patchwork quilt and not just a rag-bag of material. Teachers also need to understand the importance to science of experimental investigation. Very few teachers in their own science education were given the experience of designing or carrying out their own experiments and this probably accounts for the difficulty that so many of them say they have with this aspect of the work. Nevertheless, experimenting is an essential component of science and experience has shown that, given advice and support, teachers find the obstacle surmountable. There is certainly a great deal of evidence to suggest that children do not have great difficulty with the process although it has to be recognized that, as with observation and pattern-seeking, there will be a steady progression with age and experience. For example, some 6-year-old children tested their ideas on lifting weights with a lever by changing the position of a block of wood under a plank until they could lift their teacher by pressing on the other end of the plank with one foot. Some 9 and 10 year olds examined the relationship much more systematically by hanging weights from a strip of peg board pivoted by placing a knitting needle horizontally through one of the holes and holding it in a clamp. In this way they determined the mathematical relationship involved.

The ideal in learning is achieved when children are led through a rich variety of experience while along the way the teacher is able to extract, exemplify, reinforce, clarify and relate ideas and knowledge so that the pupils are provided with education that forms a whole, although they still understand and gain from its separate parts. As far as science is concerned and possibly other subjects too, the more this ideal is pursued, the greater is the demand made upon the teacher's understanding and knowledge of the subject and its requirements, and also upon his or her professional skill and expertise. Teachers have to bring to the task the kind of professional skill, which, beginning with a thorough knowledge of the children and how they learn, leads to an understanding of the contribution that can be made to general education by a variety of experiences and by the ways in which those experiences can be both analysed and synthesized; they must also gain a knowledge of science, and an understanding of its nature and of its particular contribution to general education. It seems wholly unreasonable, not to say unrealistic, to expect all primary teachers, or even most, to be able to meet this kind of demand and any insistence on it is unlikely to result in good science. It is perfectly proper to make small beginnings, with teachers taking some of the science content they feel most confident about and, at the start, organizing the children's investigation and learning in a fairly formal way. Experience brings greater confidence, and encourages expansion into a wider field; links with other subjects and activities will soon begin to suggest themselves [. . .].

Links with other subjects

Important relationships exist between science and other areas of curriculum. Practical enquiry by children in groups or as a class involves debate and discussion, as well as reading and writing. Science gives opportunity for the development of language based on first hand experience. Children's language is extended through use in a variety of forms aimed at particular audiences, as well as for dealing with reference and general reading texts. Often there is a demand for the application of mathematical skills such as computation and the construction and interpretation of graphs. Science may start from or lead to the study of historical events or characters. Movement and physical education can include good examples of force or friction. Transport is a common topic in primary schools and a knowledge of science would help teachers to offer children a deeper understanding of its history, its development and its use. A study of canals in Britain may lead to an investigation into the shapes of boats that travel in restricted waterways, or into the operation of locks. The question 'How was the water maintained in the canals?' could give rise to some practical experiments as well as to some research in schools or local library.

The intellectual processes listed at the beginning of this chapter are not unique to science and this facilitates links across the curriculum such as those mentioned above. But there are also pitfalls. It is sometimes thought that all or most of the science experience children need can be included in or extracted from a whole range of activities which have other and different objectives. Unfortunately it is very seldom that such an approach leads to good science education. The reasons lie in fragmentation of the subject; the labelling of parts of the activity as science when they may not be scientific at all; and the use of unsuitable science topics because they seem to fit the general topic. Science can be taught and learned through more general studies and it can be splendidly done but it is far from easy and requires outstanding knowledge, expertise and insight from the teacher. Links are desirable but they should not become chains which restrict pupils' development in science.

1.5

THE HEADTEACHER AND PRIMARY SCIENCE

Primary School Sub-committee of the Association for Science Education

The role of the headteacher

In any consideration of the headteacher's role, it is necessary to remember that his or her concern must be with the school as a whole and the extent to which all parts of the curriculum meet the needs of its children. Today this school will be a dynamic place. Careful observation of children and the ways in which they learn has brought about many changes. Widespread interest in curriculum development, fostered by the Schools Council and local efforts, is preventing complacency and encouraging critical thought about all aspects of school life. As a result, teachers are constantly being introduced to additional teaching materials and innovations relating to organization. This is a development that can make their work exciting but it also provides problems because the length of the children's day remains unchanged. This fact makes selection of the experiences that children should meet inevitable. The headteacher will create opportunities for staff consultation and co-operation within the school, so that new ideas can be considered and all teachers can be fully involved in making the decisions which enable the children to use their time to the greatest advantage.

In the early days of elementary education, there were strong external pressures, such as payment by results, and later the 11+ selection tests, to convince teachers of the importance of the basic skills. This concern rightly

Source: Primary Schools Sub-committee of the Association for Science Education (1981, revised edition) *The Headteacher and Primary Science* (Science and Primary Education Paper No.2), Hatfield, Association for Science Education, pp.4–14, 19–21, 25–26. Details of this and other booklets of the ASE may be obtained from the ASE Bookselling Department, College Lane, Hatfield, Herts, AL10 9AA

persists, but if the children's curriculum is not to be over-dominated by a narrow approach to this work, teachers must recognize the value of other types of experience. Many teachers will need help in gaining deeper understanding of what they are trying to do and of the philosophy from which this liberal attitude springs.

In what follows we shall [. . .] concentrate on the vital part all headteachers of primary schools must play if all their children are to have opportunities of learning through science.

The justification for scientific experience

The desire and ability to interest members of a staff in any development must stem from personal conviction, so we must begin by stating some of the major arguments which may help to convince headteachers of the value of scientific experience.

Science is concerned with things in our surroundings that can be investigated with the aid of the senses. These are things of great interest to children, who readily ask questions about them. If they are encouraged to try to find answers by practical investigation, they will become actively involved in making observations and comparisons, testing their own ideas and considering evidence. Such experience of tackling problems can help them to develop the powers of judgment that members of a democracy are free to exercise and, at the same time, give them some of the understanding that will help them to come to terms with their surroundings. Today, also, demands on land and natural resources, brought about by population growth and rising standards of living, are making it necessary for all to co-operate in using the environment wisely and to work for its improvement. Some of the knowledge required for doing this can come through scientific experience [. . .].

We do not think we are being unrealistic in asking that a headteacher, ultimately responsible for all aspects of the curriculum and organization of a school, should try to gain some understanding of what is meant by science and its value, for blind enthusiasm can never be as effective as enthusiasm based on knowledge and thought.

The place of science in a balanced curriculum

Encouraging staff to provide wide-ranging programmes of experience for the children in their care and helping them to see science within this context, is a much more complex task for the headteacher than the development of personal conviction and enthusiasm.

Science in infant and first schools

At one time it was generally accepted practice for headteachers to control what was done in their schools each day by constructing timetables in which packets of time were allocated to all the subjects considered necessary. The infant children's programme was usually arranged in larger blocks of time but even then work in the basic skills usually occupied most of the mornings and aesthetic and environmental experiences were provided during the afternoons. It has become obvious that the conception of separate subjects in watertight compartments is artificial. Young children think of the world as a whole; only gradually do they come to appreciate the distinctions between the different areas of knowledge.

Also there is much more awareness among teachers of children's individuality, or variation. This causes children to perform the same actions and gain understanding of the same conceptual ideas at different rates. It follows that a flexible organization of the school day, giving all children the time they need to finish each job properly, is likely to keep them all working to capacity.

The response of many teachers to this knowledge has been to establish something analogous to a busy supermarket. The materials and equipment set out in working areas for the children's use represent the goods on the shelves. The children, as customers, are encouraged to make use of these things in whatever order seems sensible as they work through programmes of interesting occupations, devised with their teacher's help or suggested by the provision in various working areas.

Since the length of time children will spend on each activity and their order of working will vary, it will be possible for many of them to use the same pieces of equipment at different times. Consequently the money available for apparatus can be spent on a wide range of items in preference to large sets of the same things. This is another factor making for rich experience.

There will still be times when it will be appropriate for the whole class to come together each day for planning sessions, some direct instruction, and for discussions about what has been done.

In the situations created by a flexible type of organization it becomes easier for a teacher with no interest in science to avoid it. A greater danger is that some teachers may not recognize the many starting points for scientific experience that are created in a good primary school, and so fail to encourage the children to exploit these opportunities to the full.

This can be avoided if teachers form the habit of looking critically at the children's curriculum in order to check on the scientific experience it offers,

Infant related.
- the children think of
the world as a whole
So need to distinguish
as (outdoor)
? could be an issue?
- do they lack of confid
ch should know
such ex gain
within the
curric

'n be expected to achieve through such work.
cher to initiate.

'le which illustrates the type of useful
nsultation between the headteacher and
school:

Starting points for scientific experience

...an ...or	One thing related to another, for example, crockery to dresser, blanket to bed. Matching, sorting and arranging crockery and other utensils. Washing and drying dolls' clothes under different conditions, such as in moving and still air.
2. Cooking.	Experience of: liquids and solids, wet and dry things, hot and cold substances. Smelling and tasting. Mixing solids, liquids, and liquids and solids. Weighing and timing.
3. Role playing with the help of 'dressing up' clothes. Children can become local, adventurous, fairy tale or religious characters.	Mother's role of cooking, cleaning and attending to children. The activities of doctors and nurses. } Health Education
4. Construction with: kits (jigsaws, Lego, Bilofex), large blocks, scrap material.	Development of manipulative skill. Spatial experience – position and proportion of one thing in relation to another. Discrimination and arrangement of shapes. Symmetry.

Activities	Starting points for scientific experience
5. Work with the teacher on development of the skill of reading, for example: pre-reading activities; phonic teaching; practice in expression and fluency.	Collection, at second-hand, of factual information about scientific things. (**Note:** This is not science, but it is a way in which children can add to the first-hand information they gain by using their senses.)
6. Individual work in library corners with: picture books; supplementary readers; books of information.	Use of aids to recognition of things that may be found out of doors such as flowers, trees, small animals and common materials. Gaining knowledge of relationships between these objects and printed words.
7. Writing involving: formation of letters and words; adding captions to pictures; communication of observations, discoveries and imaginary ideas.	Development of the skills that make communication of scientific observations possible. Consolidation of scientific ideas through attemps to express them in words.
8. Work with mathematical equipment.	Contact with numerical and spatial ideas that are common to both mathematics and science, such as conservation of discrete and continuous quantities; length; mass; speed.
9. Work with water.	Experience of some of the physical properties of this liquid, for example, transparency, fluidity. Things that float and sink in water. Measurement of different volumes of water. Experience helping towards an understanding of conservation of volume. The effect of water on substances, wetting, dissolving.

Activities	Starting points for scientific experience
10. Work with sand.	Experience of a material composed of particles. Measuring masses and volumes. Again experience in leading towards understanding of conservation of volume. Comparison of ways in which sand can be used in its wet and dry states.
11. Work with other materials: using paints on different paper; modelling with plastic substances; carving rigid substances such as Sunlight soap, chalk, etc.; using fabrics for collages; sewing and puppetry; printing on papers and fabrics with paints and dyes; making things with wood, polystyrene and scrap materials; testing adhesives.	Effects of mixing and superimposing colours. Effects of adding different quantities of white or black to other colours. Experience of ways in which solids with different properties can be used. Experience of shapes, space, proportion. Opportunities for estimating and measuring. Investigation of alternation, repetition and symmetry.
12. Music making with different types of instruments (home made, Orff Schulwerke).	Opportunities for discriminating between differences in the pitch and rhythm of sounds. Discovery of distances different sounds can travel. Opportunities of testing other children's varying abilities to hear sounds. Discovery of more about travelling sounds.
13. Setting up beautiful and interesting displays of objects and words, possibly concerned with environmental topics such as wheels, bottles, toys.	Comparison of shapes, sizes, colours. Ways in which objects can be sorted and arranged. Vocabulary associated with natural and man-made objects.

Activities	Starting points for scientific experience
14. Problem tables.	Early investigation of things like prisms, mirrors, magnets, bulbs and batteries. Finding out how things work, such as mechanical toys, old clocks.
15. Outdoor activities: use of adventure equipment; care of pets; cultivation of garden plots; walks and visits in a gradually extended area.	Spatial experiences (high and low, sideways, underneath). Experience of animals' needs. ⎫ Observations of plant growth. ⎬ Health Education Growth of plants under different conditions. ⎭ Useful and harmful garden creatures. Comparison of collections from places where environmental conditions vary. Observations of weather conditions, puddles, shadows, etc.

When the children gather in larger groups, or whole classes, for literary and religious stories, poems and speech rhymes, they will often be offered factual information about living things and the physical world, which can reinforce what they have learnt from first-hand experience. Physical education and movement to music will give them opportunities of finding out more about ways in which they can use parts of their own bodies.

Teachers will find many useful suggestions for infants in the Science 5-13 books *Early Experiences* and *Early Explorations*.

Topic work for older children

As children in junior and middle schools become more experienced investigators they often like to concentrate their attention on topics they find particularly interesting and then to produce more extended studies.

In schools where this is recognized it is usual to find children spending time on what may be called topic or project work, centres of interest or environmental studies, this integrated approach replacing some of the separate subject teaching.

The curiosity and questioning attitude in children, from which the impetus to investigate comes, may be aroused by evocative materials and situations set up in school by the teacher, or from exploration of the outdoor surroundings. Many teachers also make good use of class discussions, broadcast programmes, films, visits and seasonal events to stimulate general interest in a particular theme and thus help the children to find good reasons for wishing to share the labour of exploiting it. In any case a variety of studies is likely to be selected from such starting points by individual children or small groups.

Children can gain a great deal of scientific experience through this 'topic work'. Headteachers, in attempting to ensure that this does happen, might encourage members of their staffs to make use of flow charts for estimating and checking on the type of experience the children meet.

A flow chart is a concise summary of the various studies that can develop, or flow, from a good starting point. It can be constructed for a number of purposes.

In the first place, it can be the teacher's record of his or her preliminary thought about the range of work a topic could offer. The chart on the following pages, for example, might be related to the capacity of older children in a junior or middle school interested in houses and homes.

A teacher who is fully aware of the lines of investigation a particular topic can offer will be well equipped for dealing with discussions through which children make their choices of the actual investigations they wish to tackle.

The children's choices can then be set out on a second, smaller type of flow chart and this can serve as an initial working plan for the class or group exploring the topic. It can also give the teacher useful guidance about the resources likely to be needed for the work. These can be assembled while the children undertake more detailed planning of the ways in which they might work individually.

Finally, the ground covered by different children as the topic work progresses can be recorded by the teacher on a third type of flow chart.

Such charts, whether forecasts or records, can serve as a basis for discussion when teachers come together to consider the extent to which the children's studies are providing them with opportunities for collecting information by observing and testing, and therefore with scientific experience.

While these consultations are in progress it is also important for teachers to be reminded that 'all is grist to the mill' and consequently that children, using secondary sources of information for studies that are not obviously scientific, will often be stimulated by such material to raise questions that can be answered through practical investigation. The teachers' background booklet

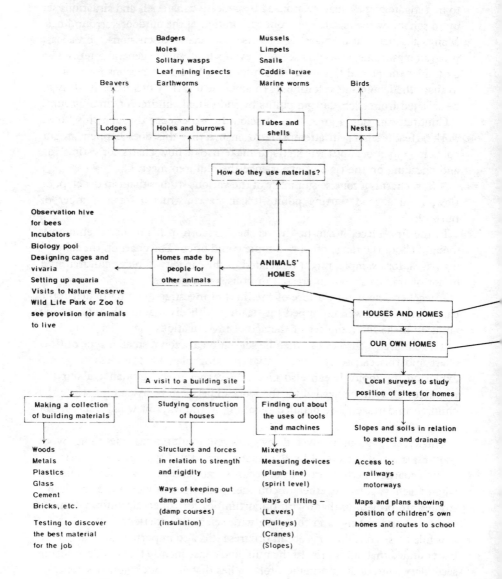

Beavers

Badgers
Moles
Solitary wasps
Leaf mining insects
Earthworms

Mussels
Limpets
Snails
Caddis larvae
Marine worms

Birds

Lodges | Holes and burrows | Tubes and shells | Nests

How do they use materials?

Observation hive
for bees
Incubators
Biology pool
Designing cages and
vivaria
Setting up aquaria
Visits to Nature Reserve
Wild Life Park or Zoo to
see provision for animals
to live

Homes made by people for other animals

ANIMALS' HOMES

HOUSES AND HOMES

OUR OWN HOMES

A visit to a building site

Making a collection of building materials

Studying construction of houses

Finding out about the uses of tools and machines

Local surveys to study position of sites for homes

Woods
Metals
Plastics
Glass
Cement
Bricks, etc.

Testing to discover
the best material
for the job

Structures and forces
in relation to strength
and rigidity

Ways of keeping out
damp and cold
(damp courses)
(insulation)

Mixers
Measuring devices
(plumb line)
(spirit level)

Ways of lifting —
(Levers)
(Pulleys)
(Cranes)
(Slopes)

Slopes and soils in relation
to aspect and drainage

Access to:
railways
motorways

Maps and plans showing
position of children's own
homes and routes to school

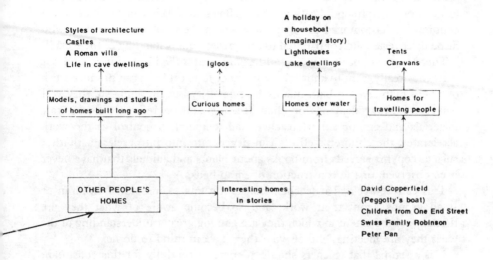

Styles of architecture
Castles
A Roman villa
Life in cave dwellings

Igloos

A holiday on
a houseboat
(imaginary story)
Lighthouses
Lake dwellings

Tents
Caravans

Models, drawings and studies
of homes built long ago

Curious homes

Homes over water

Homes for
travelling people

OTHER PEOPLE'S
HOMES

Interesting homes
in stories

David Copperfield
(Peggotty's boat)
Children from One End Street
Swiss Family Robinson
Peter Pan

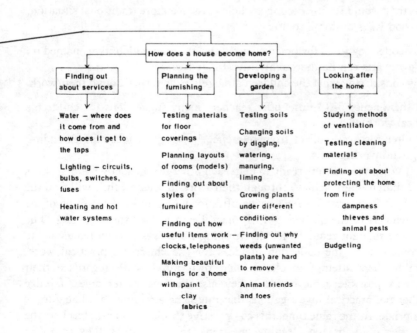

How does a house become home?

Finding out
about services

Planning the
furnishing

Developing a
garden

Looking after
the home

Water — where does
it come from and
how does it get to
the taps

Lighting — circuits,
bulbs, switches,
fuses

Heating and hot
water systems

Testing materials
for floor
coverings

Planning layouts
of rooms (models)

Finding out about
styles of
furniture

Finding out how
useful items work —
clocks, telephones

Making beautiful
things for a home
with paint
clay
fabrics

Testing soils

Changing soils
by digging,
watering,
manuring,
liming

Growing plants
under different
conditions

Finding out why
weeds (unwanted
plants) are hard
to remove

Animal friends
and foes

Studying methods
of ventilation

Testing cleaning
materials

Finding out about
protecting the home
from fire
dampness
thieves and
animal pests

Budgeting

Science and History (Collins, 1967) produced by the Nuffield Junior Science team is one helpful publication which shows how this can be done when children are 'encouraged to put themselves in the position of the men who made discoveries and contributed to our present understanding of the world'.

There is no doubt that lively children, fully absorbed in trying to find out what they really want to know about many different things, can produce work of a very high level in both quality and quantity but, in doing so, they will make very heavy demands on their teachers and on reference books, raw materials and equipment. If teachers fail to maintain control as the work accelerates, the children's efforts can degenerate into purposeless activities, such as copying screeds from books about plants and animals that have never been observed, or the construction of scrap books.

This can be avoided if teachers constantly talk to individual children or small groups about their work, and so become aware of what they are thinking, of the extent to which they are gaining greater understanding of the ideas they are meeting, and of what they have in mind to do next.

It is essential that teachers should prepare as carefully for this consultant role as they would for instructing a whole class in a more traditional situation. Two good ways of doing so are:

1. By collecting ideas for practical activities through which items named on the flow charts can be thoroughly investigated, and
2. By considering what the children are likely to achieve through their work.

All the Science 5–13 units offer teachers many suggestions for children's practical work.

Children also can collect from reference books good ideas for extending their own investigations.

[. . .] When teachers are ready to help each other to consider what objectives their children might achieve through their work in science, they will find the book *With Objectives in Mind* very helpful, for it contains a description of the way members of the Science 5–13 Project Team tackled the same task. The study and thought required for determining objectives is complementary to that required for the collection of ideas for the children's practical work. When teachers attempt to clarify their own minds with regard to their children's possible achievements, they also become better able to judge whether the practical investigations that might be attempted are likely to be appropriate. At the same time, this co-operative thinking can give teachers the ideas they need for good leading questions, through which they can offer children constructive help in taking their 'finding out' activities as far as possible, for example:

'I wonder what would happen if . . . . . . ?'

'Have you ever thought of trying . . . . . . ?'

'Was your test really fair ? How do you know that the blow that broke up the lump of cement was no harder than those given to the other materials ?'

Headteachers should try to make sure that teachers realize that work on a topic cannot be considered to be finished until the children have examined and discussed the displays which other children have produced. Only in this way can they all be helped to think of their own efforts in relation to the whole theme. Equally important, in trying to present their findings to those who have not been engaged in the same work, the children can consolidate their own understanding of what they have studied.

The headteacher will naturally be a very interested visitor to any class or group exhibition of topic work, and his appreciation will encourage children and their teachers to work even harder on the next occasion. Furthermore, an objective observer is often in a better position to note the improvements and developments that may still be possible than those who have been deeply involved in the work.

Planning for progression

The headteacher is in the best position for considering the curriculum planned by the staff in relation to the development of the children, and therefore to initiate staff discussion on the question of progression.

In comparing the activities of the older and younger children in the same school one would expect to find the majority of older children placing less emphasis on the mechanics of learning to read and write, and more on using these skills for gathering and comparing information and for communicating ideas and discoveries. Junior children should be much more adept than infants in using the techniques of estimation, measurement and ideas about proportion. Their drawings, models, charts and plans should give reasonably accurate information about what has happened or how things work, whereas the earlier efforts would only be likely to convey impressions.

One of the most important advances one could hope for when children try to work scientifically will be a growing readiness to explain 'How they know' something, or in other words, to support statements with evidence. As their ability to think abstractly increases, children can be expected to make much more use of their memories of previous experiences in predicting the possible outcome of something they think of doing. Their prediction will be followed by a test (an experiment) to try to discover whether their thinking is on the right track.

The curriculum of a primary or middle school should reveal plans for a continual broadening of the children's experience of places where environmental conditions vary, and for encouraging them to make use of an increasing range of materials and resources, including documents, museum specimens, aids to magnification and measurement and audio-visual equipment.

When teachers wish to consider signs of progression in their school in relation to the development of children, the headteacher might suggest that they refer to 'Objectives for children learning science' to be found at the end of every source book produced for the Science 5–13 Project. Although the title says 'science' the material in this summary is applicable to many aspects of the curriculum.

The many meetings necessary for good curriculum planning can give the headteacher frequent opportunities for helping staff to become aware of the major contribution scientific experience can make to children's development, and for pointing out that a curriculum lacking plans for provision of such experience cannot possibly be balanced and therefore cannot be adequate. [. . .]

Communication

The type of curriculum and organization we are considering could only result from much discussion between the headteacher and members of staff and the headteacher is the person who would initiate both small meetings of a few teachers and full staff meetings.

Here is one headmaster's acount of the way in which such meetings were used to develop scientific work in his school.

'Our school, a four-form entry junior type for 550 children aged 7–11 years, serves an area which is mainly industrial council housing.

When I became headmaster, I began to frame school policy through general staff meetings, but soon found this inadequate for all purposes. In addition it soon became necessary to hold informal talks with smaller numbers of teachers, usually those concerned with the same year groups. These meetings, held at weekly intervals, enabled us to exchange opinions and ideas and learn more about personal day-to-day problems. Apart from the many suggested activities that were put forward the need for adequate resources soon became obvious – books, materials, apparatus and information about techniques for using more specialized equipment, such as microscopes or the overhead projector.

Working Parties were formed to prepare assignments and work sheets and for construction of simple apparatus. Self help is essential in building up resources and in our school after a group meeting, details of requirements were posted in the staff room, necessary raw materials were made available and the volunteer teachers from any year group worked during specified days and times. This team effort proved extremely successful. The division of labour required meant that where necessary personal skills could be concentrated, also these skills were frequently disseminated by example. Our interest in each other's work increased considerably and there was the added satisfaction and pleasure from shared company and a job well done.

Scientific studies began naturally with two or three enthusiasts developing work with their own classes. When these teachers were asked to assist with the County's in-service training programme, others who had aided the pioneers in making equipment, found themselves sufficiently confident to encourage their own children to carry out investigations. This development was stimulated by information and ideas drawn from Science 5–13 source books and discussions about them.

At the present time members of staff meet frequently, often on their own initiative, to discuss projects directly related to science, for general interest has been aroused. Our material resources are growing too; special areas have been designated for the purpose of keeping livestock and material. I feel that I am helping and encouraging, particularly by making sure that catalogues, equipment and money are always available.

Our meetings are a dynamic part of school life; it is interesting, therefore, to note changes that are taking place . Originally discussions were pre-arranged, but now individual members of staff or small groups make their own plans for projects or for developing work that has arisen from the children's starting points. Senior teachers, and others with special interests, frequently become involved, and the discussions take place in the dinner hour, at the end of the day or during other odd moments.

The greater measure of co-operation between members of staff and increased knowledge of each other's interests has resulted in the children seeking help and guidance from teachers other than their own. Frequently younger children are to be seen working in rooms with older children or vice versa. Either skilled help is being gained from another teacher or the other pupils are offering themselves as consultants in the investigation being undertaken.

A further benefit is that in offering explanations older children are consolidating their knowledge and increasing their own understanding.

To sum up, it is now quite clear that I regard scientific experience as an essential part of a balanced curriculum, but more than this, all our staff are becoming interested in science and the growth of scientific activities is an integral part of the school programme.

Having reached this stage, the question for us now is "Where do we go from here?".'

In addition to group meetings, there will be times when the headteacher will need discussion with individual teachers. It may be with the deputy or another experienced member of staff when work is to be delegated or jointly planned; or it may be the means by which a headteacher seeks to help a particular member of staff who is enthusiastic about a certain idea, or one who is encountering some beginner's problems. In the latter cases the greatest success may be achieved when the headteacher is, for certain periods of time, prepared to work alongside this teacher, sharing with him or her the handling of a group of children. In such situations the need for joint planning develops naturally and ideas do not have to be imposed. An inexperienced, uncertain teacher can soon gain confidence when somebody else is equally responsible for coping with any difficulties that may arise.

Resources for members of staff

Many teachers in primary schools have had no specialist training for teaching science and their personal education in this subject may have ceased at an early stage, yet such teachers may be good organisers and very successful in encouraging their children to work to capacity.

The heavy demands able children can make on a teacher [. . .] may be demands which his or her personal resources may not be adequate to meet. The headteacher will be called upon to supplement these resources. He or she can give some help by making it possible for members of staff to attend in-service training sessions during school hours and by releasing them to visit other schools. The headteacher will also provide resources within the school, such as notes of guidance and a good staff reference library.

The headteacher could draw his or her staff together to discuss:

- why they want to do science;
- what experiences are to be put before the children;
- how the children's progress might be evaluated and records kept.

Such discussion should result in a documented school policy for science.

The use of a graded post

From all that has been said it is obvious that the headteacher's role in relation to science is heavy and demanding, but assistance is possible.

At the present time headteachers have, in relation to the sizes of their schools, a number of points at their disposal. This allows them to place certain members of their staffs at levels on the salary scale above the minimum in return for promoting certain needs of the school through work other than class or group teaching.

There now seems to be general agreement that there should be no appointment of specialist teachers of science in primary schools. Among a number of disadvantages, the appointment of such a specialist would impose inflexibility on the school organization. If the starting points for scientific work that exist in many indoor and outdoor situations are to be recognized as they arise, the continuous help of *all* members of staff is required.

Furthermore, problems caused by certain teachers doubting their own ability to provide children with scientific experience are being reduced, not only through the availability of better source books and more in-service training, but also through the practice of team teaching in an increasing number of schools. When two or more teachers work together it often becomes possible for an uncertain teacher to make better plans for the children's activities, and to deal with problems as they arise in conjunction with teachers possessing more experience. Also, many local education authorities are now appointing Advisory Teachers for Science. Holders of such posts can visit many schools and work alongside teachers, both in and out of doors. They also advise on the development of scientific work and assist with programmes of in-service training.

It is becoming increasingly common for headteachers to use some of their points for the award of graded posts to teachers who will help to develop an area of the curriculum including science by acting as a consultant to other members of staff [. . .].

Conclusion

In this paper we have tried to show that it is not enough to hope to be able to recruit staff who can encourage children in primary and middle schools to work scientifically. A headteacher has a very positive role to play if appropriate scientific experience is to be readily available to all children in the school.

The effective headteacher will have thought carefully about the objectives such experience should achieve, and the teaching methods and organization required. He will be aware of the value of involving all members of staff in planning and in attempts to find solutions to the problems that are found to arise.

It is a role that requires courage, for it is often very difficult for an experienced, competent headteacher to give members of staff opportunities of learning through their own mistakes, and accept the responsibility for the consequences, rather than to give explicit directions.

Finally, a headteacher's role is essentially continuous. As children develop and profit by the experiences they meet, their knowledge and understanding of ideas grows and this makes them ready for change and more advanced work. This means that teachers must be ready at all times to provide new experience. The headteacher is in the best position for encouraging and helping them to do this.

There is no doubt that when headteachers are successful in encouraging their staffs to help children to learn through scientific experience, they not only enrich the curricula of their own schools, they also acquire expertise worth sharing and so become the best people to help and influence teachers from other schools.

PART TWO

Process versus Content

Introduction

Primary science curriculum projects originating in the 1960s tended to be very child-centred and were based on a philosophy of helping children learn how to learn by 'doing' science. The process of science was all important, and the skills and attitudes required for doing science were to be promoted as children worked at problems they themselves chose to investigate. A major difficulty of this approach was the considerable strain it put upon teachers who lacked sufficient background and experience of science. Subsequent projects have moved towards more structural support for teachers, and also towards the definition of suitable content for primary science lessons and the provision of explicit pupil material. The papers in this part address some of the issues in the process versus content debate.

In 'Why hasn't it worked?', Black examines possible causes for the lack of impact of the major curriculum projects, and concludes that concentrating entirely on the process skills of concept-free science is not necessarily the best way to develop an understanding of science with primary children. He reviews some of the arguments for greater specification of content, and the effect this must have on the direct guidance given to teachers and on the provision of pupil material.

The lack of effective policies for primary science, particularly at school level, and of well-structured pupil materials are two further factors which, it is suggested, contributed to the paucity of primary science reported by the HMI survey. In the second paper in this part, Richards discusses the plans of the now completed Learning through Science project and explains why the project team felt it necessary to move towards the definition of content and the provision of pupil material.

Harlen, in her paper 'Does content matter in primary science?', rehearses the arguments for and against a defined curriculum. She concludes that process aims should still come first but that there is a case for content aims, and she suggests examples of content guidelines grouped under broad headings.

2.1

'WHY HASN'T IT WORKED?'

Paul Black

In the 1978 Primary Survey, the Inspectorate presented a bleak picture of primary science. In their view, serious and effective work was achieved in only 10 percent of schools. Elsewhere, much of the effort was superficial and the teaching in science was less well matched to the capabilities of pupils than in any other curriculum area. Few headteachers appeared to recognize that science could make a significant contribution to the development of young children.

This contrasts sadly with the hopes of curriculum reform in the 1960s. Primary science teaching was due for reform having resisted criticism over many years: in 1913 Henry Armstrong had said of nature study that 'Nature too seldom comes into the work and too often study is the last thing thought of'.

The Nuffield Junior Science Project expressed the following belief in the natural power of children to learn: 'Children's practical problem solving is essentially a scientific way of working, so that the task in school is not one of teaching science to children, but rather of utilizing the children's own scientific way of working as a potent educational tool' and '...their own questions seem to be the most significant and to result most often in careful investigations'. So the project's books gave general advice on how to follow children's leads and how to provide resources to support this strategy; facts, concepts, content were ruled out of order.

The project's successor, Science 5–13, built on this work, but differed in giving teachers a definite framework in the form of a set of over 150

Source: Black, P. (1980) 'Why hasn't it worked?', *The Times Educational Supplement*, 3 October 1980, pp. 31–32

behavioural objectives, divided into three neo-Piagetian levels. This was not to determine a syllabus – the child's motivation and the need for learning to be rooted in experience were still paramount. The objectives were to guide the provision of opportunities for learning and to form a basis for monitoring individual's progress. The project also provided a set of more than 25 books, each giving guidance, and examples of children's work, on a particular theme. This material was interpreted and analysed throughout in terms of the detailed objectives which the proposed activities might serve.

Both of these projects were based on the view that the essentials of scientific work lay in the processes of careful observation, perception of patterns, formation of hypotheses and design of experimental tests. Scientific concepts were inappropriate as a framework for curriculum design because they were too abstract and too little related to children's interests. At the same time, it was emphasized that science is a unique source of intellectual stimulus, being the area in which observation and thinking skills have to be based on direct experience. It was hoped that such work could play a distinctive part in an integrated curriculum where any one pupil investigation could lead to activity in science, art, writing, craft and other skills.

Two further projects succeeded these. Progress in Learning Science concentrated on the appraisal of the progress of individual children by a scheme based on the developmental objectives of Science 5–13. The other Learning Through Science is still in progress.

These four major projects, added to many smaller and local initiatives and to the normal efforts of authors and publishers, have influenced only a minority of schools. Yet if the materials produced have failed, it seems that they fell at the first hurdle – that of convincing teachers to take them seriously. A survey has shown that Science 5–13 has only been studied seriously in 30 percent of schools and is being used by 22 percent while the corresponding figures for Nuffield Junior Science are 20 percent and 7 percent respectively.

Primary teachers almost certainly lack confidence to take up the new philosophy. Muriel Whittaker has pointed out (in the *School Science Review,* March 1980) that most primary teachers probably have a strong aversion to physical sciences, which they last experienced in secondary schools where the didactic and factual approach left them with no experience of the type of work now required. Open-ended activity in which a teacher has to encourage particular skills by careful guidance of the pupils' own interests requires some knowledge, or confidence to learn, about many topics and some first-hand experience of the skills involved. Most primary teachers have neither. When the schemes of work they are offered have a complex rationale, offer a wealth of materials, but leave choice of the specific activities, and decisions about level and pace to them, it may not be surprising if the challenge is refused.

While it is clear that active help for primary teachers is a first priority, it cannot be assumed that the only problem is to help them to use the ideas and materials that exist. These materials themselves raise several problems.

One such problem concerns the view that science is organized common sense, arriving at its theories by intelligent induction. The practitioner works within and through a complex framework of concepts and it took the genius of Galileo and Newton, in defiance of the common sense of generations, to establish such concepts for mechanics.

It is, of course, true that these abstract concepts are beyond the powers of young children and that to channel work towards them risks loss of enthusiasm and meaningless rote learning. But the problems illustrated by the mechanics example will not go away: research with children is now establishing in this area, as in many others, that they construct their own conceptual schemes to cope with the problems of understanding nature and that these, like those of every scientist up to the sixteenth century, are a real barrier to the scientific understanding.

What then is to be made of the plea to encourage children to develop and rely on their own ideas? It is not now obvious, *a priori*, that the best route for developing understanding of science up to age 11 is to concentrate exclusively on the process skills of concept-free science.

Arguments for adjusting the policy about content in primary science were put forward recently by several authors, notably Professor Kerr (reprinted as 'Reading 1.3' in this volume), in the Spring number of *Education 3–13*. Norman Booth recalled another project of the sixties, the Oxford Primary Science Project. This offered a scheme which, although based on children's activities, wanted these planned to serve four broad themes – Energy, Structure, Chance and Life. This too failed, and perhaps one reason was the gap between the grand conceptual design and activities of which children were capable. Wynne Harlen, writing in the *School Science Review* in June 1978, proposed a more modest list of content drawing on her experience in the Science 5–13 and Progress in Learning Science projects. Her article reviewed the arguments for and against some content aims, and concluded that while the process aims must come first, the children's activity had to be about something and it might as well be arranged to cover some common broad themes.

Others have argued that children ought to begin to have access to those ideas which have helped scientists to make sense of the natural world. It is also evident that if children's own interests have to be a prime source for activity, then some interests, such as space travel or nuclear energy, may need a degree of reliance on secondary evidence that is fully acceptable in other areas (such as history) for 10 year olds.

If these various arguments have force, they would lead to a strategy in which children's interests and their needs for first hand experiences are still given first priority, but which also organize problems and materials to channel interest and to ensure that some of the experiences provide a helpful challenge in a few particular concept areas.

Such a strategy would have an effect on another aspect which also needs reconsideration, that of providing materials for pupils and more and more direct guidance for teachers. The experience of the superb work which can be produced when children's own initiatives are guided by the best teachers has led many to the view that any planned provision will be an obstacle to excellence. However, without such provision, teachers can only be given vague advice, and the demands, for decision, anticipation and preparation, become too great.

The recently published series on Teaching Primary Science (produced by the College Curriculum Science Studies Project under John Bird) has tried to provide firmer guidance, giving advice and samples on producing work cards for children and clearer background information for teachers with each of its themes, while also providing a short list of objectives to guide the activity, chosen from the schedule of Science 5–13.

Such designed activity can make the teaching task more manageable, partly because contrived experience raises problems which can more easily be guided to fruitful work than many that appear in the complex world of the natural environment. However, the strategy for choosing such activities will have to take account of a further factor that has been largely ignored hitherto. The science of most successful primary teachers has been pure science. If it had been technology, their philosophy and emphasis might have been different and the work of mechanical and electrical construction might have invaded the classroom.

Many and strenuous efforts are now being made to support and promote primary science. But those tending the feeble plant face the dilemma: does it need just light, air and water, does it need artificial fertilizer, or should we pull it up again and have another look at the roots?

2.2

LEARNING THROUGH SCIENCE

Roy Richards

Initiatives

During the past 20 years a great deal has been done to help teachers promote science in primary schools. The first major British programme pertinent to primary education was the Nuffield Junior Science Project which defined science as '. . . essentially a practical investigation of the environment. It makes use of some of the young child's most outstanding characteristics, his natural curiosity and his love of asking questions'. Directly following this came the Schools Council Project 'Science 5–13'. Again, there was an emphasis on children actively exploring the environment and in so doing 'developing an enquiring mind and a scientific approach to problems'. Some 26 books for teachers were produced which compromised units of work and were linked by objectives, which it was hoped children would attain through their work (Ennever and Harlen, 1972). More recently the Schools Council has fostered another project 'Progress in Learning Science' where Dr Wynne Harlen and team have attempted to show how, by observation of children, teachers can chart and record their progress in science and, in so doing, attempt to match activities to children's stages of development (Harlen et al., 1977).

The materials of these projects and the wealth of commercial publications available, of which it must be said that the best are very good indeed, constitute a rich and valuable resource for teachers. It is therefore an irritation

Sources: Richards, R. (1980) Children's learning through science, *Education 3–13*, 8 (2), pp. 4–7, and Richards, R. (1980) A strategy for a policy, *The Times Educational Supplement,* 3 October 1980, p. 33

to hear critics claim that such materials have not been successful. Many teachers have proved them so through their vital, exciting and worthwhile practice. There is no question that science can be done by primary school teachers, the problem is getting all to do it! Compared with work in language and mathematics, science is much more meagrely treated. It is often thought of as an optional extra. Why? One answer is contained in an observation made in the Primary Survey: 'the general impression given by heads' statements was that only a small minority recognized the important contribution which science could make to children's intellectual development'. This is at the crux of the matter. Those teachers who do science well know how essential it is to a young child's development. They see their children improving in observational skills, asking questions, thinking out ways to find answers, discussing and arguing and putting to the test, perceiving patterns and relationships and communicating often excitedly and vitally with others. They see their children developing in curiosity, prepared to listen and argue and yet maintain an open-mindedness, prepared to co-operate, show responsibility and persevere when things are difficult. They would not want any less for their children. Not only do they help give their charges a greater insight into the world around them and 'tools' for investigating that world but, importantly for this nation, they send on to the secondary school children with attitudes formed and forming that may stay with them throughout their lives.

A school policy

How can we persuade more teachers to be like these? This is a major task facing the Schools Council Project 'Learning Through Science'. The project team made a beginning by involving a large number of teachers (50 regional groups) in thinking out a *strategy* whereby teachers might formulate a policy that was pertinent to their own children, their own school and their own school environment. What should such a policy contain?

In the first instance almost all the groups reported that any guidelines should make clear what was meant by science with children of primary school age. It was a cry from practitioners whose understanding of young children made it abundantly clear to them that the image of science as an activity carried out by white-coated laboratory workers was not applicable to their children. As equally inapplicable was the idea that science was a great conglomeration of facts that their children had to absorb like gluttonous Billy Bunters. Yet what was 'science' if not the stereotyped image that many people hold? Wynne Harlen (1978) captures their views when she argues that 'Our central concern in primary science should be to develop the abilities to observe, raise questions, propose enquiries to answer questions, experiment or investigate, find patterns in observations, reason systematically and logically, communicate findings and apply learning'. There was thus general agreement that school policy should begin by making a clear statement of the aims and objectives or reasons – call them what you will – of why a school staff wants to pursue science with its children.

The next step is to consider how these aims are to be achieved. What experiences can be put before children? Where can teachers get help? This, of course, is where the very large amount of literature available can be put to good use. It is a relatively straightforward matter for individuals or, perhaps better still, small groups of teachers to scrutinize source books and take up the topics they suggest or use them as a source of reference for an original theme decided upon within the school.

Interestingly, a number of the groups of teachers that reported back to the Learning Through Science Project thought that there were major underlying themes that should be tackled during a child's primary school years, though these could not be organized into a tight 4- or 7-year syllabus. Put very simply and briefly, teachers seemed concerned that children should know *about living things*, about the cycle of plant and animal life and should be concerned not only with looking after living things but with making comparisons, measurements and carrying out simple testing procedures where these were appropriate and proper. Certainly everyone seemed convinced that children should know *something about themselves*, about the ways parts of their bodies work, and testing here was thought to lead to many opportunities for discussion and questioning. Again, there was universal agreement that children should *investigate their immediate environment. Weather studies and other seasonal changes* were thought to be of great interest to children and important in involving children in collecting data and looking for patterns and relationships. *Energy and energy studies* took their place not only because world attention has focused on such issues, but because they embody basic scientific experiences that lead to an understanding of important and profound scientific concepts. *Understanding of the nature and properties of materials* (beginning in the infant school with active exploration of sand and water, paint and clay) was felt to be vital, too. Working through topics or setting out basic themes to run through the years of a child's primary education were seen as two feasible ways of proceeding. Other teachers – especially teachers of infant children – often favoured taking their science from everyday situations such as creative play in home bays, cooking or construction work. Yet other teachers reported that an excellent way to consider what experiences to put before children was to make maximum use of the school and the school grounds.

The besetting problem facing many teachers is not the substance of what is to be done, but how on earth can one teacher organize it with thirty or more children? In primary education the class is usually largely or completely taught by one teacher and this can give a flexibility often denied to those operating in the secondary sphere. Teachers can and do use a variety of teaching styles and patterns of organization. Any school-based guidance on organization must recognize this fact. Experienced teachers vary their preparation to suit different patterns of organization. Teachers inexperienced in presenting scientific activities might well be advised when starting off to limit the number and the range of their initial investigations. (The rest of the class can carry on with routine activities that are more easily managed.) With experience, the number and range of activities, simultaneously made available to children, can increase. Certainly, there is much to be said for staff discussion on methods of organization and for teachers to spend some time observing and discussing the ways their colleagues proceed, especially where these differ from their own. Science with its emphasis on 'things' demands careful teacher preparation, but the dividends that come are compounded. There is nothing that acts as a surer catalyst to children at the concrete operational stage of thought than confrontation with an object or objects. It is the 'I, thou and it' of science – teacher, child and 'thing' must interact.

[. . .] There will be those things needed that arouse and maintain children's curiosity. Anything from building blocks, sand and soils to rocks, fossils, bones, clockwork and mechanical toys, batteries, bulbs, wire, wheels, bottles – the list can be legion.

Then there are those things that help children to gather data and specimens as they explore around the school. That is to say: clipboards, pencils, paper, plastic bags, specimen boxes, hand lenses, and perhaps plastic spoons for picking up small creatures such as woodlice. Living things will need cages so that they can be properly looked after and means will have to be found and devised for displaying and storing the non-living materials.

Equipment such as measuring sticks, stop watches, thermometers, balances, strength testing devices and so on will all be necessary to help children develop inquiry skills. There may be a good case for making collections of materials for inter-disciplinary studies. For example, 'Homes and Houses' is a common topic and there would be good reason to have a box containing a variety of floor coverings and another box with a variety of fabrics. In both instances these boxes would yield useful material for practical investigation.

Much more can be said about resources for the school. For example, the school grounds can be a useful resource for scientific investigation if there are plant tubs, chequer-board gardens, a weather station, bird tables and a pond. Of course, resources need to be organized and used and this is an important aspect for staff discussion and implementation.

[. . .] One last but important aspect of any policy should be a proper consideration of how to evaluate children's progress and how to keep records of such progress (Harlen et al., 1977). The main question about the form of record kept seems to be whether it should list *activities or development*. Keeping records of activities is useful as an 'aide-memoire' to prevent unnecessary repetition during a child's school career. It is, however, not sufficient on its own, for it gives no indication whether a child is improving in observational skills, getting better at devising tests and identifying variables, attaining basic concepts, and so on. The subject is not a simple one and points to keeping different records for various purposes.

Thus the way forward, the project team suggests, is for a school staff to sit down and thrash out its own policy for science and get it implemented. In all this, the role of the headteacher is crucial. He or she is the main provider of support, encouragement and guidance in the development of scientific education. Our new publication (Richards et al., 1980) lays down a strategy whereby any primary or middle school can determine its own policy for science. Our hope is that this national initiative will be complemented by action at local level and that all schools who have not so far done so will now seriously consider forming a school science policy. It is also hoped that LEA inspectors and advisers will use the text on their in-service courses.

Pupil material

The other main aspect of the project's work has been the production of pupils' materials. The challenges in writing such material have been many! It would have been relatively easy to write prescriptions of things to be done, but this would scarcely have been conducive to getting children to show initiative, to think out good and fair ways to test things, to challenge ideas and interpretations with the purpose of reaching deeper understanding. In other words, it would probably have negated the whole idea of getting children to 'develop an enquiring mind and a scientific approach to problems' as spelled out by the Science 5–13 Project. It would even have been dubious whether such a prescription would teach facts about science, since tasks carried out by rote often lack the basic understanding that intellectual involvement brings. We accepted that children needed to develop certain abilities, attitudes and concepts, but many questions went through our minds as we began to write the first pupil material: What core of experience do we include? What concepts is it to embody? How can such experience help children develop abilities and attitudes? What is a reasonable amount of material to offer children at any one time? Should there be an order of presentation? How can we stretch the able and the less able child?

A start was made by delineating certain areas of experience commonly featured in schools teaching primary science. Of these we have produced or are currently producing material for the themes 'Ourselves' and 'Colour'. To illustrate by reference to the first two of these themes, each has been presented as a series of assignment units, each unit consisting of a four-page A5 folder. The material helps put problems in the paths of children and gives help to the teacher on ways of encouraging and guiding the enquiries. In essence each assignment unit presents a mini topic for children to pursue which is so written as to be very flexible in use. Any one page tries to keep to one basic idea, but the aim of each four-page unit is to try and present a unit of work which allows children flexibility in the way they tackle the task in hand. Often it leaves scope for children to bring in new ideas. Our intention has been to present each assignment unit in such a way that the work could be attempted at many levels and leave scope for children at varying stages of development to take things as far as they could. In practice this has worked. Children of all abilities seem both able and willing to take up the starting points. In no cases have there been any real difficulties with the experiences suggested; this is not surprising since we have seen them work in schools in the past. The units have not been presented in any set order, nor has there been any intention that a child or group of children should necessarily complete everything set out on an individual unit. The teachers' notes explain the aims of particular assignment units, discuss where children may find difficulty, tell how the tasks in hand may be taken further and give additional information. Feedback from the trials has been positive and very encouraging. The difficulty – and it is true to say that it has diminished as the trials have proceeded – has been with methods of organization. Interestingly, these have changed in many classrooms during the course of the trials, and will probably stay changed. Involvement of teacher and children with things has seen to that. Organization is, however, a fundamental matter that schools may well want to give more attention.

Our task is now to rewrite these initial units in the light of comment from teachers and to proceed with the production of further units. We hope to constitute a core of material suitable for primary schools. Certainly we can bring basic experiences before the notice of teachers and children in this way; and bring them in a readily acceptable form. We have been most encouraged by those teachers who wished to alter our material to bring it 'closer' to the children in their classroom. People who realize that curriculum development material has this flexibility and above all realize that there is nothing to beat developing your own material for your own children, are well on the way to promoting good practice in their own classrooms.

References

Ennever, L. and Harlen, W. (1972) *With Objectives in Mind.* MacDonald Educational.

Harlen, W. et al. (1977) *Match and Mismatch.* Oliver and Boyd.

Harlen, W. (1981) Does content matter in primary science? *School Science Review,* 209, 59, 614.

Richards, R. et al. (1980) *Learning through Science: Formulating a School Policy with an Index to Science 5–13.* MacDonald Educational.

Publications

Since the foregoing was written the project has come to fruition. The 'Guide and Index' to *Learning Through Science* (Macdonald Educational, 1985) fully describes the work of the project. The following table reproduced from this book outlines the publications of the project and shows how they interlink to form a cohesive strategy for carrying out work of a scientific nature in primary and middle schools.

The *Learning Through Science* publications

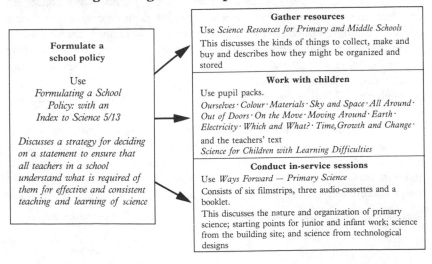

Formulate a school policy

Use
Formulating a School Policy: with an Index to Science 5/13

Discusses a strategy for deciding on a statement to ensure that all teachers in a school understand what is required of them for effective and consistent teaching and learning of science

Gather resources
Use *Science Resources for Primary and Middle Schools*
This discusses the kinds of things to collect, make and buy and describes how they might be organized and stored

Work with children
Use pupil packs.
Ourselves · Colour · Materials · Sky and Space · All Around · Out of Doors · On the Move · Moving Around · Earth · Electricity · Which and What? · Time, Growth and Change ·
and the teachers' text
Science for Children with Learning Difficulties

Conduct in-service sessions
Use *Ways Forward — Primary Science*
Consists of six filmstrips, three audio-cassettes and a booklet.
This discusses the nature and organization of primary science; starting points for junior and infant work; science from the building site; and science from technological designs

2.3

DOES CONTENT MATTER IN PRIMARY SCIENCE?

Wynne Harlen

The reader expecting a straight answer to the question posed in the title
should be warned that I do not intend to give one. To do so would in any case
be foolish without first discussing the various factors on which an answer
would depend; for instance, which parts of the primary age range are being
considered, how the content would be chosen, by whom and in what form it
would be expressed. The discussion of these factors seems more helpful than a
simple answer, and indeed it does lead to an answer, but not a simple one.
To some it may seem surprising to question whether content matters, for if it
is assumed that primary science is all about learning content then of course it
matters what is learned. But an alternative view, which has held sway in many
parts for the past 15 years at least, is that primary science is not concerned
with learning a certain content but with learning skills of enquiry, fostering
attitudes and developing basic concepts. In this view the most useful content
is any that interests the child or arouses his curiosity – whether it is finding
out if food dyes affect the taste of homemade sweets, or how quickly snails can
travel across different surfaces. According to this opinion, what is important
is the way a problem or enquiry is tackled, not the knowledge that comes out
of it.

What is attempted here is an examination of the reasons given in various
circumstances for the importance or otherwise of choosing a certain content
for primary science work. This seems best done by looking at the arguments
given in various programmes or projects which have taken one or the other
view. From these we can perhaps draw out the pros and cons of having a

Source: Harlen, W. (1978) Does content matter in primary science?, *School Science Review*, 59,
pp. 614–625

defined content and can find some guidelines for avoiding the errors of both extreme positions.

In Britain the main curriculum development projects in primary science have been the Nuffield Junior Science Project (1964–6) Wastnedge (1967) and the Schools Council Science 5–13 Project (1967–74). The move which gave rise to these began in the early 1960s when teachers attempting more than the traditional nature study in primary schools found support from Inspectors (Ministry of Education, 1961) and the Association for Science Education, which established a Primary Schools Committee in 1963. The Ministry of Education[1] and the Froebel Foundation[2] sponsored projects to study the development of scientific ideas in children, which overlapped with the Nuffield Junior Science Project. The ideas which all the groups working on these projects held in common were that for children to learn with understanding it was essential for them to have first-hand experience of manipulating objects and materials; they rejected any idea of a simplified version of the science taught in secondary schools, and stressed the importance of science as a way of working rather than a body of knowledge to be mastered. As such this blurred the distinction between science and other areas of the curriculum and an integrated approach to learning was advocated, removing subject boundaries and timetable limitations. Statements made in the Policy Statement prepared by the ASE's newly formed Primary Schools Science Committee clearly supported the emphasis upon *how* rather than *what* children should learn: 'At this level we are concerned more with the developing of an enquiring attitude of mind than with the learning of facts' and again 'at no time is the imparting of factual knowledge to be regarded as an end in itself' (ASE, 1963).

Echoes of this statement can be found in many parts of the Nuffield Junior Science Project (Wastnedge, 1967) and in the Science 5–13 units for teachers (1972–5). But since there has to be *some* content that the children study, what was the basis for selecting it? The Nuffield Junior science project's answer was that the children should tackle problems of significance to them, their own problems, ones they find themselves, not those handed to them by others. Science 5–13 replied in similar vein: 'In general, children work best when trying to find answers to problems that they have themselves chosen to investigate' (Ennever and Harlen, 1972). With these convictions it was impossible for these projects to produce anything like a course, a list of experiments, or a programme of work. Instead they have produced guides for teachers, giving ideas and suggestions but leaving teachers to make their own selection from these to suit their own pupils. There are no pupil books and no kits of equipment, since these would necessarily restrict the freedom of pupils to work on problems of their own finding.

The main differences between the Nuffield project and Science 5–13 are that the latter provides background information for teachers about topics and activities described, gives an explicit statement of objectives, and provides a structure for building up skills and concepts progressively. The Nuffield project team held that stating objectives might needlessly set limits to the children's achievement rather than assist it, whereas Science 5–13 considered that the statement of objectives was necessary for teachers to guide children's work effectively. Many of the Science 5–13 objectives are clearly content-free and can be achieved through pursuing practical investigations in a very wide range of subjects, for example:

Ability to predict the effect of certain changes through observation of similar changes;
Ability to investigate variables and to discover effective ones;
Ability to choose and use either arbitrary or standard units of measurement as appropriate.

Others, however, while not indicating particular activities, can only be achieved if certain kinds óf materials are encountered and certain problems pursued. For instance some objectives relating to living things are:

Awareness of internal structure of living and non-living things;
Ability to construct and use keys for identification;
Knowledge of conditions which promote changes in living things.

The teacher is still left the choice about *which* living things are studied as an aid to achieving these objectives. The objectives are intended to be in the teacher's mind so that she can take any opportunities which arise to work towards them, and thus their statement does not conflict with the project's child-centred philosophy.

One exception to the British projects' whole-hearted embrace of process as opposed to content mastery was the Oxford Primary Science Project, which was supported by Ministry of Education funds from 1963 to 1967 (Redman et al., 1969). This group started from a definition of four basic scientific ideas, energy, structure, life and chance, and then set out to find ways of helping children learn them. Thus they began from the subject matter, not from the child as the other British projects did. The project did not have much impact on primary science outside its trial schools.

The approach through considering *what* children should learn before *how* they should learn has much in common with some US elementary science projects, particularly the Science Curriculum Improvement Study (SCIS, 1970). SCIS defined content, process and attitude objectives, but the basic form of the programme was set by the content objectives. There were also four main scientific ideas determining the content of this programme: matter, energy, organism and ecosystem. The process objectives refer to the process of organizing the content – by property, reference frame, system and model – and not the process of finding out – by observation, experiment and discerning patterns, etc. Nevertheless, the method of working involves practical investigation and first-hand experience and is structured to provide experience of exploration, invention, and discovery, described as the three stages in a child's learning cycle.

In order to enable children gradually to build up the basic scientific ideas identified by SCIS, the programme consists of units geared to each year of elementary school, each unit comprising work books for pupils, a teacher's guide and a kit of equipment. Though there are 'optional activities' the basic experience of science provided by the programme is of working through a carefully devised series of experiments, or watching demonstrations, and reporting observations or answering questions in a work book.

There are many similarities between SCIS, taken as representative of programmes which prescribe a given content, and Science 5–13, which is typical of projects which do not provide a course to follow. They, and similar projects, acknowledge that young children must have *concrete* experiences to help their learning, that they must *see* for themselves, *do* for themselves and form their own ideas rather than memorize those provided by others. I do not wish to deny these similarities in focusing on one of the main points of difference, the question of selection of content. The questions to ask next are about why this difference exists and what are the advantages and disadvantages as seen from each side.

The case against a common content

Those who hold that the content of science activities for young children is less important than encouraging the skills and attitudes of enquiry and experiment give five main reasons for this view.

1. The strongest point is that some of the important aims of primary science cannot be achieved if children are constrained to work on particular problems or investigate phenomena in a given way. Aims relating to children's ability to

raise questions and find out answers for themselves, pursue an investigation until they are satisfied – these are difficult to achieve if a programme is, in effect, telling children to be curious and enquiring only about the things presented to them.

2.   Another point is a reflection of a general reaction against a fixed content in science, because ideas change and what is important to know today may not even be regarded as true, much less important, tomorrow. Rather, it is felt, it serves children better to equip them with skills of learning and finding out that will later enable them to master a variety of content as required.

3.   A syllabus of work which is centrally devised does not cater for regional and local environmental variations; it thus often results in city children learning about things of the country which have no immediate relevance and interest for them, and *vice versa*.

4.   If the content of science activities is determined by the programme being followed then it is difficult to integrate with work in other areas of the curriculum. This means that many opportunities to inculcate scientific attitudes or develop enquiry skills may be lost because of association of science with a certain content and not with the solution of any problems which occur.

5.   The motivation for learning skills and developing concepts is very strong when children are working on what interests them, and it will not be the case that all are interested all the time in the content chosen by someone else. Thus much activity in a prescribed programme will be desultory, lacking purpose as far as the children can see and will not result in a grasp of the ideas intended. This will often happen even though teachers try their hardest to interest the children in the work. In contrast, the work which starts from children's interests, and itself develops new interests, will engage their mental powers more readily and result in a firmer learning.

Before looking at the points for the opposite case it is perhaps as well to acknowledge straightaway the disadvantages of the kind of approach implied in the case against a common content. We can see that, however attractive and worthwhile in theory, it is very difficult in practice to follow the interests of a whole class of children. Teaching in this way is extremely demanding and must be a style a teacher adopts throughout her work, otherwise it will not be effective in only one part of her teaching. Then it must be faced that some children never seem to be interested in anything sufficiently to want to investigate or experiment, and these pupils have to be given problems in any case.

Another set of disadvantages arises from the problems children face if they have to move from one primary school to another, or even from class to class in the same school. Where teachers are responsible for the content, there may be repetition of experiences or large gaps left in building up certain ideas. This would not be a serious matter if teachers really were able to 'start from where each child is' but, as we have said, this makes great demands on a teacher's flexibility and not all feel able to allow children to take the lead in science, where they often feel insecure themselves about pursuing certain enquiries.

Most teachers who work in a child-centred way and take advantage of children's wide-ranging interests find they do in any case cover the content that would be included in any prescribed 'core'. But what of the children of those teachers who do not manage to do so? The argument goes that we cannot leave it to chance, but should make sure that all children have the opportunity to gain basic ideas that lay a foundation for a gradually more sophisticated understanding of their world.

The case in favour of a common content

1. A first point links with what has just been said. There are certain ideas and facts that scientists have to use and there is a body of knowledge which helps not only the scientist but would be of benefit to all who wish to be scientifically literate. Children need knowledge of some scientific ideas and facts to help them make sense of their world, just as do scientifically literate adults. It is therefore our duty in education to make sure that the children encounter the content from which they can gain this knowledge. What actually is the knowledge would be decided from experience of what is, and is not, useful to children at different stages.

2. A second argument uses a different criterion for selecting content. It begins from the same point, that is, from the ideas and facts which are needed by a scientifically literate adult. On the theory that the development of these ideas and mastery of facts depends upon the earlier grasp of ideas which are basic to them, and these in turn on yet more elementary ideas, then a case can be made for laying a foundation of basic ideas chosen so that they contribute to future understanding and knowledge. Thus, for instance, it could be claimed that knowledge of electrical conductors and insulators was important at a certain point, so that ideas which depend on this information can be developed.

3.   Those who advocate or develop programmes with a prescribed content to be learned do not necessarily dismiss as less important the development of enquiry skills and certain attitudes. However, they point out that in order to encourage development of these skills and attitudes it is more effective to work on some kinds of problems than on others, and to use structured materials rather than unstructured ones. For instance, the number of variables in a problem chosen by a child may be so great that there is no chance of controlling them and the result may be dissatisfying. With structured equipment, however, the greatest degree of control can be built in and the investigation carried out satisfactorily. The point is, therefore, that we can avoid too much failure and develop skills more easily by providing activities which have been carefully tried out and for which the right equipment is available.

4.   It has been said that 'knowledge is control' in all fields, and so even in the primary school knowledge of their environment helps children to make sense of what is around them and to control it. But children are immature, and faced with such a multitude of things they could come to know what should they choose? Hence the argument that it is the duty of adults to pass on to children – in this case through experimental activities and investigations – the knowledge which is most likely to be of use to them.

5.   Finally, some points of a more practical nature are often part of this case. One relates to teachers, and though the point is often wrapped up delicately, what it really says is that teachers are not able to see that children encounter a balanced content and so this has to be laid down for them. The second counters a possible objection to the first that it does not matter whether there is a balanced content in the primary years in any case because there is time in the secondary years to provide this balance. It suggests that in fact there is not enough time in the secondary years to build up the necessary body of knowledge and therefore this has to start earlier. In some cases this is true, for instance in developing countries, where compulsory schooling lasts only until the age of 13, or where early specialization cuts a number of pupils off from science after only two or three secondary years. However, true or not, the argument that primary education should make up for the deficiencies of secondary education cannot be pressed too far.

Again, we can easily see objections to some of the points of this case. The greatest is probably to the implied ignorance that we know what the 'best' content is to be. We do not know with any certainty what are the prerequisite ideas or facts which provide a basis for a particular concept to develop and thus we cannot, by analysis only, determine the content which at the primary level will lead to later more sophisticated notions. Even if we could do this, that content is unlikely to meet the other criteria, of being interesting to children and relevant to their understanding of what they see in their immediate surroundings.

Despite the advantages of structured activities which 'work', they lack flexibility and can bring a stagnation to science lessons. The same things are done each year, with the same apparatus, and because they do 'work' they may remain in use long after the knowledge which they yield has become unimportant or obtainable more readily in other ways. Moreover, the common content for all children generally means that they do the same things, regardless not only of differences in interest but also of differences in ability. The self-instructional programme is not necessarily the answer, since time for working is only one variable which affects learning; the presentation of the problem, the materials used, the amount and kind of help given are also important. In the end it may be that a variety of content is needed to get the same ideas over to different pupils and the virtues of a common content are lost.

Is there a middle way?

It is evident that there are advantages and disadvantages on both sides of this argument and the decision to take one course or another is often swayed by circumstances which lend greater weight to some points. Thus in England, where the ethos of primary education is child-centred and the decentralized system gives teachers freedom and responsibility for making decisions about children's learning, the circumstances favour a local choice of content. In countries where the system is centralized there is a tradition of accepting that many decisions are taken out of teachers' hands and thus less tendency to question the merits of a detailed programme of work being laid down.

It may be possible to find a compromise by looking at what happens in practice in the two situations. A teacher enjoying the freedom to decide the content for herself, and being very successful in promoting lively science in her class, nevertheless expressed a worry: 'I'm not asking for a list of things to be "covered", but since there is such a wide field of content I would like to know if it is better for the children if we took up one subject rather than another. We can go to the wood time after time and do really exciting work, but I sometimes wonder if this means they are missing out on other things.' Again a successful teacher using a structured programme: 'We go through the activities, many of which are intriguing and they all "work", but it is difficult to avoid a kind of dull routine creeping in. I feel that I am teaching them to use words in relation to the particular things we do but they don't have any real significance for the children. There we are, surrounded by things they are curious about, but we feel guilty if we don't "get back to the book".'

What seems to be required are content guidelines that are firm enough to ensure that children encounter the range of ideas and facts which are relevant to understanding their environment, yet are loose enough to enable teachers to use a variety of routes to arrive at them. It is the range of possibilities in relation to the meaning of 'content' that makes for difficulty in giving a straight answer to the question posed in the title of this paper.

My position would be that if by content we mean things like 'observing how broad beans germinate', 'separating sand and salt from a mixture of the two', 'connecting light bulbs in series and in parallel', then the answer to the question would be 'no'. There is other content through which the important ideas which could come from these activities might also be arrived at. Thus, in this meaning of the word, whichever items of content are covered does not matter. However, if by content we mean a set of ideas, generalizations and facts which children should encounter, then the answer would be 'yes'. Among the many ideas which children *could* encounter there are some that they *should* encounter. We do not need to prescribe specific activities but we should make sure that these ideas are conveyed through *some* activities.

What I am suggesting are content objectives which can be treated in the same way as process and attitude objectives. When, for example, we wish to encourage powers of observation, or ability to identify variables, we do this not by giving specific exercises in these skills but by using observation and by looking for variables as part of any investigation. So with content objectives; we can express these as ideas and items of knowledge to be achieved not through one set of activities but potentially from any of a variety, none having a greater priority than others.

The form in which such guidelines are stated is critical; if too vague they would be useless, if too specific they could be restrictive. They should also, in their wording, convey the tentative nature of some of the 'facts' and ideas that children pick up, based on their limited experience. Many early ideas are incomplete or ill-defined and later have to be modified and refined as children's experience widens. It is this gradual change towards ideas of greater applicability and generalizability that constitutes their progress. Thus one should expect somewhat different ideas in relation to particular phenomena or explanations from a 9-year-old or an 11-year-old, and the guidelines should reflect this difference.

The conclusion here is an attempt to suggest examples of guidelines to content to meet the criteria just suggested. The items have been arrived at by asking the question: While children are investigating problems they find and developing scientific skills and attitudes, what is the core of generalizations that they should at the same time acquire?

The words 'at the same time' cannot be emphasized too much. The content objectives must not be allowed to replace the process and attitude objectives. So it is perhaps necessary to state explicitly that our central concern in primary science should be to develop the abilities to:

observe, raise questions, propose enquiries to answer questions, experiment or investigate, find patterns in observations, reason systematically and logically, communicate findings, apply learning

and the attitudes of:

curiosity, originality, co-operation, perseverance, open-mindedness, self-criticism, responsibility, independence in thinking.

These aims must influence teachers' guidance of *how* children carry out their activities. In addition, what is suggested is that content guidelines influence decisions about *what* activities they carry out.

Although the answers suggested here, for 9–10-year-olds and 11–12-year-olds, are based on reflection and discussion with teachers over many years, nevertheless they constitute a personal statement and should be regarded as no more than an example. It is important that any set of guidelines should be produced by discussion between the teachers who are to use them and others with relevant expertise in the education of children. Any list should always be under review, for content in any form is only useful in so far as it helps the understanding of the world around at a particular time. In a rapidly changing world for our children our objectives must change accordingly, not lag behind as has happened in the recent past.

The following is a minimal statement and it is intended that the children's ideas should *include but not be restricted to these.* The statements are worded so as to avoid indicating that particular activities must be carried out or specific materials used. Thus the activities through which they come to form these ideas can be chosen to reflect the children's environment and interests.

Examples of content guidelines _kids should have some idea about how_

By the age of 9 or 10 the ideas which children have should include the following:

About ourselves and other living things
- living things have the capability of reproducing themselves and this takes place in different ways in different plants and animals, but for each the pattern is the same in each generation;
- living things grow and develop, and this requires food;
- human beings must have certain kinds of food for growth, energy and to fight disease;
- human beings gain information about their surroundings through their senses; there are limits to the range and sensitivity of the sense organs, but these can be increased by using tools, or instruments.

Here at the age of 8 + 9 this can be justified.

About the physical surroundings
- patterns occur in weather conditions and cycles in the apparent movement of the sun and moon and in changes in plants in the immediate environment;
- the materials described as stone, wood, glass, plastic, metal, have certain sets of properties which help to identify them;
- there are definite differences in the way matter behaves when it is solid, liquid or gaseous;
- some substances dissolve in water very well, others only a little and some not at all;
- some substances float in water, others sink; substances which sink can be used to make things which float.

About forces, movement and energy
- to make anything move (or change the way it is moving) there has to be something pushing, pulling or twisting it;
- when a push or pull makes something move it requires energy which can come from various sources: food, fuel, electricity, a wound spring, etc.;
- all things are pulled down towards the earth; the amount of this pull is the weight of an object;
- the speed of an object means how far it moves in a certain time.

Basic concepts
- the length of an object remains the same when only its position is changed even though it may look different;
- the area is the amount of surface across the face of an object which is unaffected by moving or dividing up the surface;
- the capacity of a container is the amount of space within it which can be filled; the volume of an object is the amount of space it takes up;
- a quantity of matter which exists at a certain time will still exist at a later time either in the same form or in different forms;
- objects or events can be classified in several ways according to their features or characteristics;
- certain actions always have the same consequences and this relationship can often be used to predict the effect of changes.

By the age of 11 or 12 the ideas which children have should include the above together with the following:

About ourselves and other living things
- the basic life processes are growth, feeding, respiration, excretion, reproduction, sensitivity to the surroundings, and some mechanism for movement and support;
- there is a great variety in the ways in which these life processes are carried out by different living things;
- in the human body organs are grouped into systems, each concerned with one of the main processes;
- energy is needed by all living things to support life processes; animals take in food, plants use the sun's energy to produce food they can use and store;
- living things depend on each other for their survival and all animals depend ultimately on plants for their food;
- living things have changed very gradually through time by the process of adaptation to various external conditions; the most successful animals at any time are those best adapted to the present conditions.

About the physical surroundings
- air fills the space around us and contains oxygen, which living things need;
- air contains water vapour, some of which condenses out in various conditions to give rain, dew, mist, snow, hail, ice or water;

- soil is composed of small fragments from rocks, air, water and decayed remains from living material which provide substances needed by growing plants; these substances have to be replenished to keep soil fertile;
- all non-living things are made from substances found in the earth; their supply is not endless, so they must not be wasted;
- pollution of the air, water or land by waste, smoke, or noise can harm both living and non-living things;
- the earth is one of nine planets so far known to be circling the sun, which is our source of heat and light energy;
- the moon circles the earth, reflecting light from the sun;
- melting or evaporating requires energy in the form of heat;
- a complete circuit of conducting material is needed for electricity to flow.

About forces, movement and energy
- a force is needed to accelerate or decelerate a thing which is moving or to change the direction of its movement;
- when an object is not moving (or moving at a constant speed) the forces acting on it are equal and opposite;
- all things which are moving have energy and when they slow down some of their energy is changed into another form;
- friction is a force which commonly opposes motion;
- energy is changed from one form to another in a variety of processes; it is never lost, but what disappears in one form reappears in another.

Basic concepts
- the total volume of an object is not changed by dividing it up or changing its shape;
- the process of measurement is the repeated comparison of a quantity with an agreed unit of the quantity; all measurements, however careful or fine, are inexact to some degree;
- all changes in objects or substances are caused by interaction with other substances or by adding or taking away energy.

Notes

1. The DES supported the Oxford Primary Science Project. The project team produced *An Approach to Primary Science*, by S. Redman, A. Brereton and P. Boyers, Macmillan Educational, 1969.
2. The Froebel Foundation, supported by the British Association, ran a research project into scientific development in children, directed by Nathan Isaacs. A

report, *Children Learning through Scientific Experience*, was published by the Froebel Foundation in 1966.

References

Association for Science Education (ASE) (1963) Policy Statement prepared by the Primary Schools Science Committee

Ennever, L. and Harlen, W. (1972) *With Objectives in Mind*, MacDonald Educational.

Ministry of Education (1961) *Science in the Primary School*, London, HMSO.

Redman, S. et al. (1969) *An Approach to Primary Science*, Macmillan Educational.

Science Curriculum Improvement Study (1970) Rand McNally.

Science 5-13 (1972-5) units for teachers, MacDonald Educational.

Wastnedge, R. et al. (1976) *Teacher's Guide 1, Teacher's Guide 2, Animals and Plants, Apparatus*, Collins.

Acknowledgement

I am grateful to Norman Booth (formerly Staff Inspector for Science DES) for helpful discussion and comments.

PART THREE

Piagetian Influences

Introduction

This part of the Reader contains papers on the psychological basis of primary science programmes. Since the rediscovery of his ideas in the early 1960s, Piaget has been the most influential thinker in this area, and so we have devoted considerable space to an in-depth study of his ideas.

The first paper, 'Children's development', provides a brief description of the main points of his theory, and is a useful introduction for those unfamiliar with his work. It also contains some examples of the type of Piagetian activities which can be used to categorize children's responses as examples of particular stages of development. The second paper, by Driver, discusses the influence of Piaget's view on science education schemes. In the third paper, Lovell discusses Piaget's work since he altered his views, and describes the content in which this work was performed. This exhaustive and scholarly account by a leading authority should provide a starting point for those who wish to pursue a deeper study of Piaget's work.

The last paper in this part is extremely critical of the influence of Piagetian views on the teaching of science. McClelland presents a description of the work of Ausubel, the leading alternative theoretician, and describes how Ausubel's theory, with its concern for the structure of the subject matter, produces different conclusions about what to teach and when to teach it.

3.1

CHILDREN'S DEVELOPMENT

United Nations Educational, Scientific and Cultural
Organization

Introduction

Do science lessons always turn out just the way you planned them? Can you
always predict how your pupils are going to react in every situation? The
answers to these questions are almost certainly 'no', even for very experienced
teachers. One reason for the unpredictability of science lessons is that the
pupils are individuals who differ from one another, so you cannot expect
everyone to act in the same way in every situation. Another reason is that as
children grow older, they develop physically, intellectually and emotionally.
The intellectual and emotional development, however, is not like the physical
development, where the body grows larger and the muscles and bones grow
stronger. Intellectually and emotionally, the child develops through a
sequence of stages. In one stage he thinks and acts differently from how he
will think and act in another stage. In any one class, different pupils are at
different stages of development. They think and act differently from each
other, and also differently from adults.

In this chapter we will show how knowledge about the intellectual and
emotional development of children can be used to solve some of the problems
faced by science teachers. The following example illustrates two familiar
problems related to pupils' development that can arise in a typical science
class.

Source: United Nations Educational, Scientific and Cultural Organization (1980) Unesco Handbook for
Science Teachers. Paris, Unesco/London, Heinemann, pp. 35–44. Reproduced by permission of Unesco

Suppose that you have a group of pupils about 11 years old, who are carrying out an activity in which they dissolve some potassium permanganate in water to make a deep purple solution. They then dilute this solution by adding nine times its volume of water, to make a 'ten times' dilution. A portion of this solution is also diluted ten times, and this process is continued until the purple colour is so pale that it no longer can be seen. The following difficulties could easily arise in this activity:

> While many pupils carry out this activity with obvious interest, and try to find out what happens with repeated dilutions, others do only what they see others doing.
>
> Some pupils continue diluting after there is no longer any visible colour in the water. They seem not to be aware of the changes that have taken place.
>
> After discussion of the activity, when pupils are asked what they learned, many say only that they saw the colour go away. Few say that they can conclude that particles of potassium permanganate must be very, very small, since some remain after repeated dilutions.

Such problems as those mentioned above probably would be less serious with older pupils. With younger pupils trying the same activity, there would be more problems. Problems of these sorts, which all teachers have encountered, do not necessarily mean that the pupils are bad, or lazy, or dull. Many such difficulties are simply a normal feature of the stage of development that the pupil has reached. For example, the first problem may arise when attitudes of curiosity and originality are not well-developed, or when suitable motivation is not provided. In the second case, most 11 year olds will be able to draw conclusions only about things they have experienced directly. They will not easily understand ideas concerned with more abstract concepts, such as the size of particles that cannot be seen.

The main purpose of this chapter will be to help you to:

1. Understand better the ways in which the thinking and emotions of pupils develop.
2. Be able to recognize the stage of development that a pupil has reached.
3. Be able to organize appropriate learning experiences for pupils.
4. Be able to use your understanding of pupils' development to improve your effectiveness as a teacher.

Intellectual development

Pattern of development

Much of our knowledge about how the thinking of children develops we owe to the Swiss psychologist Jean Piaget. From his experiments with children, Piaget has been able to classify their thinking into a series of stages. The main pattern of thought at each stage has its own characteristic features. Other workers have found that children in many different countries all progress through the same stages of thought. These stages are identified in the scheme below. The figures given show the approximate ages at which children first display the characteristics of that stage of thinking. (More will be said later about the variation in rates of development, so the ages should be taken as only very rough estimates. Those for formal operational thought, in particular, are probably too low for most children.)

1. Period of sensori-motor intelligence *0–2 years*
2. Period of representative intelligence:
   (a) pre-operational sub-stage *2–7 years*
   (b) operational sub-stage (often called stage of concrete operations) *7–11 years*
3. Period of formal operational thought:
   (a) organizational sub-stage *11–15 years*
   (b) achievement sub-stage *from 15 years*

According to Piaget, the thought and action of the child always has an underlying organization, or structure. Even the actions of an infant in grasping a toy or searching for the mother's breast are related to each other in ways that are characteristic of the child's stage of development. As the child grows older, he constantly interprets everything he sees, feels, or hears, in terms of his own mental organization. At the same time, this mental organization is constantly changing as a result of the child's exposure to new experiences. Intellectual development at all stages depends on the child's mental organization and how he responds to and interprets all new experiences.

Sensori-motor period. During the period of sensori-motor intelligence, the child's intellectual world is limited to building up sets of actions on objects. Through these actions the child develops the idea that an object continues to exist even when he is not playing with it or looking at it. Another important idea at this stage is the realization by the child that he can decide to take an action which can cause a desired result. For example, by pulling a string, he can draw a toy closer to himself. He also realizes that events can have a cause other than his own actions.

Representative intelligence. During the next period, lasting about 10 years, the child develops an ability to represent things by symbols, such as language and mental images, and also develops operations of thought. These operations of thought are still based on the child's actions, but during the stage of pre-operational thought they progress from the simple, direct actions typical of the sensori-motor period to actions which involve changes such as joining, separating, putting into order and classifying. From about 7 years of age, the stage of concrete operations, these operations of thought become co-ordinated with each other in a way that allows increasingly flexible and general thought. Until that time, the child's thought has been limited by his tendency to consider external reality from the standpoint of his own body, actions and views.

The following descriptions of two activities that can be carried out with young children illustrate how responses differ greatly from one stage of development to another. Each activity will be described, together with responses typical of the pre-operational and concrete operational levels. If you can carry out these activities yourself with several children whose ages range from about 5 to 10 years, you will gain a better appreciation of how children can respond in unexpected ways. These responses will also illustrate characteristics of thought at each stage of development.

Activity 1: Pouring water

Show the child two identical containers, such as drinking glasses, which are filled to the same level with water, or perhaps some coloured drink. Adjust the levels until the child agrees that they are the same in both containers. Then pour the liquid from one of the containers into a large, shallow dish or bowl. Then ask the child which container has more liquid, or if both have the same amount. He should also be asked how he knows. The liquid should then be poured back into the original container. Show the child a tall, narrow container, and ask him to predict where the liquid would come to if it were poured into that container from one of the original glasses. Then pour the liquid, and ask the same questions as before. The following sorts of containers could be used:

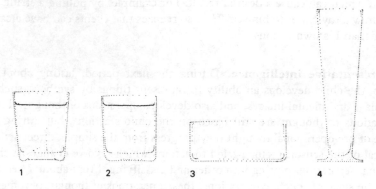

(a) Pour from 2 to 3, and then back to 2.
(b) Predict where the liquid would come to if poured from 2 to 4.
(c) Pour from 2 to 4.

Older children immediately realize that the amount of water remains constant throughout all of the changes, and may give reasons such as, 'It's the same water. You haven't taken any away or added any to it'. They may say that the amount of water has decreased on pouring, but will point to drops left in the original container. Younger children are just as certain that the amount of water changed when it was poured into a container of a different shape. Some may say that there is less water in the wide container, because it is low, while others may say that it is spread out, and so there is more. An intermediate stage may also be observed, where the child may solve part of the problem, but become confused and uncertain, and fail on other parts.

Activity 2: Time and velocity

This activity requires a pair of toy cars, or small dolls. The cars or dolls race as in the diagram below. They start from A and A' at the same time, and this moment of starting is indicated with a click or some such noise. One car moves faster than the other, and they reach B and B' at exactly the same time, also noted by a click.

Ask the children questions such as:
Did the cars start moving at the same time?
Did the cars stop moving at the same time?
Did both cars travel the same distance?
Did one car move for a longer time than the other?
Did one car move faster than the other?
The last question can also be asked when the paths of the cars are such that B and B' are directly opposite each other, so that the cars do not pass each other:

The child who is at the level of pre-operational thought may deny that the cars stop at the same time, or that they move for the same length of time. He may claim that the car moving from A' to B' took longer and stopped later. If this car passes the other, as in the first diagram, he probably realizes that it is moving faster. In the second case, where the faster car does not pass the slower, he is likely to claim that the speeds of the two cars are equal. About midway through the stage of concrete operations, these mistakes no longer are made.

Some of the limitations of pre-operational thought are illustrated by the responses to these activities. The pre-operational child reasons from one particular instance to another, and may be unaware that his conclusions contradict each other. His conclusions may also contradict his observations, as when he denies that the cars stop at the same time. He often is misled by visual appearances, because he pays attention to only one aspect of the situation at a time. Thus when the water has been poured into a container of a different shape, the child says that the amount has changed. Even though he has seen that both height and width of the liquid have changed, his explanation of his answer often indicates that he has taken only one of these changes into account. In the second activity, inadequate answers appear when the child pays attention only to the end points of the race and does not consider both distance and time.

As the structures of concrete operational thought develop, children outgrow these earlier limitations, and develop abilities to classify objects and to arrange them in order, and to understand ideas of number, time, space, speed, causality and chance. They also realize that in many transformations some feature of the system remains constant, despite visual appearances, such as in the activity of pouring water. At this stage, however, the child can apply his reasoning only to concrete objects and the relations between them, experienced at first-hand. Consideration of a wider range of possibilities that does not include first-hand experiences must await the development of formal operational thought.

Period of formal operations

Activity 3: The pendulum

This activity should be carried out with older pupils, from about 10 to 15 years of age. Each pupil should have a pendulum, in the form of a string which can be varied in length from its point of attachment, and several objects of different weight to be attached to the lower end of the string. Discuss factors which might influence the frequency of oscillation (not the speed), such as the length of the string, the weight of the attached object, the height from which the pendulum is dropped to start its motion, and the force of any push given to it. [. . .] The factors involve: height of drop; force of push; length of string; and weight of object.

The point of interest to the observer is to see how the pupil goes about solving the problem and finding that only the length of the string affects the frequency of oscillation. Only at the level of formal operational thought can the pupil realize the importance of changing one factor at a time, while holding all others constant. Thus he may test the effect of the height from which the pendulum is dropped by using two different heights, but the same length of string, weight of object and force of push. A pupil who has not yet reached that stage of thought will probably carry out tests in which the variables are not separated. For example, he may start the pendulum from different heights, but also use different lengths of string for the pendulum. He cannot tell from this whether both of the factors, or only one, are responsible for any differences observed. The abilities associated with concrete operational thought are not adequate for problems of this sort.

Thinking at the stage of formal operations, which usually starts in adolescence, makes use of the same mental operations that were available at the concrete operational stage, but now they are integrated into new structures of thought. These new structures allow a person to reason without directly referring to concrete objects. He can draw conclusions from statements which are possibilities and not merely observations of reality; he can consider a number of possibilities simultaneously, and in combination with each other; he can deal with relations between relations, such as proportions. Where several variables must be considered, he is not restricted to dealing with them one at a time, as in the stage of concrete operations. He can experimentally or mentally cancel out the effect of all other factors, while systematically varying one to determine its effect, as is required in activity 3.

Variations in development. In the sections above, we outlined the ways in which thought develops. [. . .] The application of these ideas is complicated by two aspects of development: (a) for an individual, the change from one stage of thinking to another occurs gradually, rather than abruptly; and (b) different individuals develop at different rates.

In the first case, individuals do not enter a particular stage of thought all at once, but gradually develop, over a period of several years, a range of abilities which are associated with that stage. In activities 1 and 2 described above, successful solutions require concrete operational thought. In activity 2, however, success may be achieved 2 years or even more after the child has succeeded in activity 1. Even an ability such as classification, once developed, may be applied more readily in one situation than in another, depending upon familiarity and interest in the material to be sorted. Thus when we say that an individual is at the level of concrete (or formal) operational thought, we mean that he shows *mainly* those aspects of thinking that are characteristic of that stage. In some areas of thought, he may be at a different stage.

Not only does an individual move gradually from one stage to another, but individuals progress at different rates and may follow different patterns of development. The exact reasons for these differences are not known, but they depend on the nature of the physical and social experiences that the child has had. It is widely believed, for example, that experience in manipulating and transforming a large variety of materials promotes intellectual growth. The culture in which the individual has been brought up will also influence the development of his thought. Through observation and instruction from older members of the society, the child learns the beliefs, values and accepted forms of behaviour in the society. These influences on his patterns of thought may well cause him to interpret a problem, and therefore respond to it, according to his culturally conditioned ways of thinking. Even the teacher who is aware of these patterns of thought may be taken by surprise by answers from pupils, as their thinking may influence their responses in unexpected ways. The teacher may misinterpret the pupil's response unless he is careful to find out the reason behind the answer. For example, Kamara in Sierra Leone gave equal balls of plasticine, representing equal portions of rice cake, to Themne children. A child would claim that one of the balls contained more to eat if he were asked to think of sharing it with an older child, since fair distribution of food in Themne culture requires that an older person must receive a larger portion than a younger. Here the concept of equality was interpreted in the context of the traditional culture.

While groups of children from one type of background may, on average, develop more rapidly than those from another background, they still progress through the stages in the same order. There are no guidelines that allow a teacher to predict, exclusively from their backgrounds, that one individual pupil will be ahead of another. What can be said is that where the pupils in a class come from a variety of backgrounds, they are unlikely to be all at the same stage of development, but will show a rather wide range of abilities. This will be true even where the children in the classroom are all of roughly the same age. If the class contains children of very different ages, the range of abilities will probably be greater than if the children are of similar ages, but perhaps not much greater. Intellectual development depends on the number of years the individual has spent in school, as well as on his or her age. This means that a 14-year-old in the sixth year of school may be closer in ability to an 11-year-old in the sixth year of school than to another 14-year-old in the ninth year.

Other views of intelligence. In addition to Piaget's theory of intellectual development, there are other points of view about the nature and development of intelligence, and the processes by which learning takes place. Only a few of these theories, however, have any immediate relevance to science education.

One psychologist who has written extensively about education is Jerome Bruner, His ideas are similar to Piaget's in that he views intelligence as developing through a series of stages. Bruner gives more emphasis than Piaget to the process of thinking, and stresses the role of language. He characterizes three ways in which an individual displays or represents his knowledge: by action; image; or symbol. These form a developmental order, like Piaget's stages of intellectual growth. The implication of this theory is that the pupil probably learns best if the material to be learned is presented to him by the processes which correspond to his stage of development. Thus a child at the second stage learns by means of his own actions and perceptions, and represents what he has learned through actions and visual images. The use of language, which is symbolic, comes later.

Most of the major contributions to the psychology of thinking have been by those concerned specifically with learning. Most of these theories are concerned with the processes involved in learning and the conditions which promote it. They do not take into account the child's intellectual development. Much of this work is of limited use to science education because it can be applied only to tasks which are very much less complex than those faced by pupils in a science class.

One attempt to specify the conditions for learning complex tasks has been made by Robert Gagné. Gagné claims that what a person can learn depends on what he already knows. He identifies eight different types of learning, and arranges them in a hierarchy from the simplest to the most complex. Learning at any level depends on having learned all of the relevant material at the lower levels. In principle, any task can be analysed in terms of all of the steps in learning which must precede the final step. This analysis may be very complex, even for relatively easy tasks, but Gagné's ideas are useful in reminding us that problems may be simplified for pupils by breaking them down into their component parts, and making sure that the basic ideas are understood before proceeding to the more complex.

Piaget claims that learning depends on the child's own actions, so learning simply by verbal statements is not likely to be effective until the pupil has reached the stage of formal operations. David Ausubel, on the other hand, claims that activity is not necessary for learning, and that learning can be efficient and effective for young children as well as for adolescents when only verbal methods are used. Ausubel proposes that meaningful verbal learning can occur when new ideas can be incorporated into a structure of thought that has already been established by previous learning. He specifies the necessary relations of the new knowledge to the existing structure. In broad terms, he claims that general principles should be presented first to the pupil, followed by more detailed and specific information. This information will be retained in the pupil's mind if he can relate it readily to the general principles that he already has learned. At the level of formal operational thought, these ideas are consistent with those of Piaget.

We still have a greate deal to learn about children's thinking, but at this stage Piaget's theory seems more useful than any other for possible application to science education. No other theory about children's thinking is so comprehensive and has at least its major aspects so well-supported by experimental evidence from many parts of the world.

3.2

PIAGET AND SCIENCE EDUCATION: A STAGE OF DECISION

Rosalind Driver

Introduction

This paper attempts to review the main areas where Piaget's work has made a significant contribution to science education in order to indicate problem issues and outline fruitful areas for future development.

Few people in the field of science education would dispute the influence that the work of Jean Piaget and his collaborators has had on the curriculum and teaching in primary and more recently secondary school science. In the curriculum development period of the 1950s and 1960s, science educators were looking for a useful framework to use in developing science materials: a framework which would give some guidance from a psychological point of view on fundamental issues such as what to teach, when to teach it and how. Many saw in Piaget's writings a coherent basis on which to build.

As a result, his work has been used explicitly as a basis and rationale for several science programmes: The Science Curriculum Improvement Study (SCIS) in America, Science 5-13 in England and the Australian Science Education Project (ASEP); and undoubtedly it has influenced many others.

Of course, Piaget is not an educator. It is not until recently that he himself has written about the application of his work to education (Piaget, 1970a). Nor does he consider himself primarily a psychologist. His major underlying concern, one which his early works demonstrate and to which he has recently returned, is that of genetic epistemology. It should not be surprising, however, that science educators have found and continue to find his work of immense interest and value.

Source: Modgil, S. and Modgil, C. (eds) (1982) *Jean Piaget: Consensus and Controversy.* London, Holt, Rinehart and Winston, pp. 351–363

He and his collaborators have systematically collected data on the performance of children and adolescents on several hundred tasks. The majority of these involve the manipulation of physical materials and yield information on How children develop their understanding of the physical world: how they structure their ideas about such factors as time, space, matter and motion. The results of these investigations by themselves would provide the science educator with rich and useful insights into the ideas children may bring to formal school learning, and what to expect in their development.

However, there is, of course, a more significant aspect of Piaget's work which is of interest: that is the underlying mental operations which these tasks are designed to elucidate.

The large number of studies undertaken by Piaget and his collaborators in Geneva between 1930 and 1950 formed a basis for his elaboration of the development of underlying structures or operations of thought. The operations of interest in the school years being those identified as characteristic of the thinking of 5 to 11 year olds, the logical groupings concerned with seriation and classification, and the infralogical groupings concerned with space and time. The operations he identified as developing during adolescence differ essentially from the earlier ones in that they are not now performed on concrete objects or representations of them, but on the operations themselves. As is well known, Piaget suggests that operations of this kind, i.e. second order operations, enable a child to think hypothetico-deductively, to see reality as a subset of possibilities. He has represented such operations by a mathematical model or metatheory involving the complete combinational system and the operations of the INRC group.

These sets of concrete and formal operations are held to characterize two major stages in children's thinking. The underlying assumptions behind the stage theory being that as children develop, the operations characteristic of that stage become better articulated and integrated and form a 'structured whole' (Pinard and Laurendeau, 1969). As will be outlined later, there is currently some debate about this aspect of the theory, specifically whether it is children or operations which should properly be ascribed to a stage.

If such a model can be shown to represent the development of children's thinking skills, then it can be seen why it should be of interest to science educators. The operations Piaget identifies are ways of thinking which underlie much of scientific thinking: classification, ordering and use of hypothetico-deductive thought. Conversely, if children have not developed such operations, this, too, will have implications for their achievement in school science classes.

Equilibration and the process objectives of science education

Underlying his theory of the development of operations, and prior to it, is his view about the nature of learning, which contrasts with the views of classical psychology.

> 'For classical psychology, intelligence was to be conceived of either as a faculty given once and for all, and susceptible of knowing reality, or as a system of associations mechanically acquired under the pressure exerted by things. Hence, we have seen the importance attributed by older educational theories to receptivity and the furnishing of memory.' (Piaget, 1970a, p. 157)

The contrasting views of Piaget are well known. He distinguishes between learning and development, that is, development of the operations referred to earlier. In an important paper (Piaget, 1964) he suggests four factors that influence the development of operations: *maturation, experience* of the efforts of the physical environment, *social transmission* including linguistic transmission and education, and, lastly, what he calls *equilibration*.

This concept of equilibration derives from Piaget's biological ideas of man as an adaptive organism.

> '. . . this adaptation is a state of balance . . . between two inseparable mechanisms: assimilation and accommodation. We say, for example, that an organism is well adapted when it can simultaneously preserve its structure by assimilating into it nourishment drawn from the external environment and also accommodate that structure to the various particularities of that environment: biological adaptation is thus a state of balance between an assimilation of the environment to the organism and an accommodation of the organism to the environment. Similarly, it is possible to say that thought is well adapted to a particular reality when it has been successful in assimilating that reality into its own framework while also accommodating that framework to the new circumstances presented by the reality. Intellectual adaptation is thus a process of achieving a state of balance between the assimilation of experience into the deductive structures and the accommodation of those structures to the data of experience.' (Ibid., pp. 153–154)

It is clear that such a view implies an active approach to learning:

> '. . . adaptation presupposes an interaction between subject and object, such that the first can incorporate the second into itself while also taking account of its particularities; and the more differentiated and the more complementary that assimilation and that accommodation are, the more thorough the adaptation.' (Ibid., p. 154)

Man is therefore seen from his earliest days as an active, goal-seeking problem-solving organism. This view perhaps underlies the prime influence that Piaget's work has had on education as a whole and science education in particular. It hàs given support and credibility to the idea that the child learns naturally, through interaction with its environment. This view underlies much of the developments in primary science in this country, and elsewhere.

Of course, Piaget is by no means unique in his ideas. Many educators including Rousseau, Froebel and Dewey have espoused this view. The special contribution that Piaget has made to 'modern methods' in education is to move beyond the statement of principles or polemics to outline in some detail the nature of the developments which children undergo; thus laying a foundation for practical educational programmes based to a greater extent on empirical findings.

When we look at the recommendations that Piaget himself makes for science education, we see the major emphasis he would place on science as a process, an active engagement in enquiry:

'. . . the repetition of past experiments is still a long way from being the best way of exciting the spirit of invention, and even of training students in the necessity for checking or verification . . . if the aim of intellectual training is to form the intelligence rather than to shock the memory and to produce intellectual explorers rather than mere erudition, then traditional education is manifestly guilty of a grave deficiency.' (Ibid., p. 51)

As he indicates in his writings, the operations children develop between the ages of 11 and 16 provide them with the necessary tools of thought for undertaking such an investigatory approach.

Several science curriculum projects have specified process objectives for their courses based on Piagetian operations. The Science Curriculum Improvement Study (SCIS, 1974) has a main objective to develop formal thinking structures. Karplus (1977) has outlined a three-phase learning cycle involving exploration, concept introduction and concept application which purports to encourage such development.

The Australian Science Education Project (ASEP) also includes process objectives:

'A child makes sense of his environment through the organization of his experiences into some stabilized, internalized structure which, once it has been built up, enables the student to process more effectively and more quickly information received. If the new experience does not fit the child's established mental structure, then the structure must be modified or new ones built. We believed that the exploration of the environment using the processes of science would assist in the establishing of the necessary structures.' (ASEP Handbook, p. 5)

Piaget's ideas about equilibration are clearly reflected here. Science 5–13 is also a project that outlines its process objectives around a Piagetian stage framework.

Such courses are therefore using Piaget's operations as specific curriculum objectives. They have become the 'what' in 'what to teach'. Many attempts to evaluate the effectiveness of such programmes, especially the SCIS programme, in accelerating development have been undertaken. Linn and Thier (1975) report particularly encouraging results of the effect of SCIS materials in developing pupils' ability to control variables.

Nussbaum (1979) also reports positive results in using the relativity unit in developing pupils' spatial reasoning. He does report, however, that it is the pupils who are at a transition stage already who are most likely to improve as a result of instruction.

So far we have considered the concept of equilibration in terms of the educational support it has given to 'natural learning' or 'enquiry teaching' methods. Much educational research and practice accepts the equilibration model as a premise. But what empirical evidence is there for the equilibration model itself? There have been few critical experiments reported which compare Piaget's equilibration or cognitive conflict theory with that of classical learning theory. One notable exception is an experiment on learning in infants reported by Bower (1974), which does give support to the Piagetian model.

The idea of provoking cognitive conflict to encourage learning has its appeal. Palmer (1965) outlines the implications of the cognitive conflict model for science education. Smedslund (1961) reports how children have acquired conservation of substance and weight through practice in a conflict situation. Murray (1972) reports the use of conflict through social interaction as promoting the development of conservation concepts. He grouped one non-conserver with two conservers and required the group to come to a consensus on a conversation task. Bredderman (1973) compared training with external reinforcement with conflict training on the development of pupil's abilities to control variables. His results indicated no significant difference between the groups. A recent experiment reported by Johnson and Howe (1978) compares conflict training involving one-to-one contact with an adult, with conflict training between peers on an area conservation task. The results indicate that peer interaction gives the most beneficial results. These studies do give some support to Piaget's claim that social interaction affects development. They also indicate what may be fruitful approaches in teaching methods, giving some guidance on the question not simply of 'what' and 'when' to teach, but 'how' to teach it.

Epistemology and conceptual development in science

Developing skills in the process of scientific enquiry is not the only stated aim of many science courses. The development of an understanding of scientific principles and ideas gains more importance with older pupils. Piaget does not place these two goals in simple opposition. For him, the development of major scientific concepts comes as a consequence of the development of operativity. The two are closely related.

We can comprehend his position if we consider that his main concern is for epistemology. Piaget is a genetic epistemologist, and as such his concern is for the 'epistemic man' and the development of knowledge, specifically that of the physical world. It was this interest that motivated his early work in the 1920s and lately he has returned to give it particular attention. His book, *Biology and Knowledge* (1971), outlines his ideas concerning man the knower, his environment and the central importance of the logical operations in the development and communication of knowledge. Briefly, Piaget puts forward the theory that our knowledge develops through an active interplay of experience and the developing structures which process and order our perceptions. In addition, similar structures or operations have developed throughout the human species through interaction with common elements in the environment; because of these shared structures knowledge can be communicated.

In fact, Piaget clearly sees these cognitive structures and their development as a continuation of the evolutionary process of adaptation:

'these cognitive mechanisms are an extension of the organic regulations from which they are derived, and these mechanisms constitute organs of such regulation in their interaction with the external world.' (Piaget, 1971, p. 346)

We are left in little doubt about Piaget's main focus of interest in this passage from his book, *Genetic Epistemology* (1970b, p. 13):

'The fundamental hypothesis of genetic epistemology is that there is a parellelism between the progress made in the logical and rational organization of knowledge and the corresponding formative logical processes. Of course, the most fruitful field of study would be reconstituting human history — the history of human thinking in prehistoric man. Since this field of biogenesis is not available to us, we shall do as biologists do and turn to ontogenesis.'

With the considerable insight into the development of operational thought behind him, Piaget returned in the 1960s to reconsider the problem of causality. In an extended series of tasks he attempts to trace out the development of children's understanding of a range of physical concepts (mostly on dynamics but including aspects of heat, light and the structure of matter) in an attempt to understand the development of the subject matter itself (Piaget, 1974).

The underlying claim in these studies is that the development of causal or conceptual explanations by individuals reflects a dialectic between the developing logico-mathematical operations of the knower, which structure observations and events in certain ways, and the experiences that are assimilated. An example is given of the operation of additive composition being fundamental to the development of children's construction of the idea of atomicity. For example, children from the age of 8 or 9 infer that matter is conserved, and that dissolving involves an initial visible substance disintegrating into little pieces ending in an invisible form, and that these parts can be brought back again adding up to the initial whole. (More details about these studies can be found in a review by Driver and Easley, 1978).

Underlying this work is a very optimistic assumption. Piaget suggests that his studies on causality show that pupils are capable of developing an understanding of physical principles without instruction, through interaction and physical systems, and even that formal instruction obstructs learning (Piaget, 1973). Here I would not dispute that children do impose meanings on events of their own accord and that they construct implicit theories as ways of handling novel or familiar situations. What I would dispute is that by experience alone children will come to develop the conceptual framework of accepted science (Driver, 1979). Children can be given experiences and practical materials to manipulate, but they may then impose meanings on them which are at variance with the accepted scientific view.

Two pupils in a science class had been heating blocks of different metals using an electrical heating coil. They had plotted graphs of the temperature of each block against time and noticed that the thermometer readings went up at different rates. When asked how they interpreted this one of them said:

'that different . . . um . . . that different materials and that see how heat could travel through them . . . heat went through the iron more easier than it did through the aluminium.'

Here, an activity that was designed to develop the idea of variation in thermal capacity was interpreted instead in terms of thermal conductivity.

Piaget himself has indicated the importance of social transmission in development. The arguments he has put forward for it are in terms of enabling pupils to discuss ideas to help them decentre by listening to other points of view. A further function of social transmission, and one which is significantly different from that presented by Piaget, is the transmission by the teacher, or through the written materials provided, of the agreed conventions of the scientific community. When Galileo was conducting his investigations into falling bodies, his first formulations of accelerated motion were in terms of changing speed over a given distance. It took him considerable time before he found his data was much more elegantly handled if he adopted what we now accept as a conventional way of computing acceleration.

Those who found Piaget's work useful as a basis for science teaching would not dispute this position either. Atkin and Karplus (1962) make a useful distinction between discovery and invention in teaching, and the approach is used as a basis of the learning cycle recommended as a foundation for using SCIS materials.

The stage theory and matching the curriculum to the learner

As was outlined earlier, this aspect of Piaget's theory speicifies the operations that children develop as a result of the action of four factors: maturation, experience, social transmission and equilibration. It also specifies the general order in which operations develop. Lastly, it suggests that rather than taking the form of a gradual build-up of operations in a child's repertoire, development occurs in stages; the operations characteristic of each stage become integrated and consolidated so they have an internal coherence before significant development takes place in the operations characteristic of the next stage.

Currently, there is considerable debate among science educators about aspects of the theory. The most fundamental criticisms come from those who adopt a traditional, learning-theory approach which does not hypothesize the existence of internal structures of operations guiding behaviour, but instead interprets behaviour as a response to external reinforcements. If reinforcement patterns change then behaviour changes. More complex behaviours or skills can be built up by careful programmes integrating prior-learned behaviours.

The distinction between these two positions is not merely an academic one. They do have significantly different implications for educational practice in terms of the selection and ordering of teaching experiences. In a much quoted passage Ausubel writes:

> 'If I had to reduce all educational psychology to just one principle, I would say this: The most important single factor influencing learning is what the learner already knows. Ascertain this and teach him accordingly!' (Ausubel, 1968, vi)

It is probable that either developmentalists or classical learning theorists would agree with this statement, but the meaning they would each ascribe to it would be significantly different. If learning a new idea depends primarily on what has been acquired previously, then any idea can be taught to a child of any age provided a carefully sequenced teaching programme of necessary subordinate ideas is used. Developmental theory, on the other hand, would also take into account what the learner already knows, but in this case it would be in terms of the cognitive operations he has available to him. If there is a great mismatch between the logical demands of what is to be taught and the operations available to the child, little permanent learning may take place.

Experiments have been undertaken on various occasions to put the two theories to the test (e.g. Anderson, 1968). So far results obtained by traditional learning techniques have not been as dramatic as might have been expected, thus lending support to the developmental position.

Important replication studies of many of Piaget's tasks have shown his results to be repeatable (Elkind, 1961; Smedslund, 1961), such studies are too numerous to cite individually: they have been surveyed by Lovell (1961a). The studies do indicate, however, that the ages at which specific operations appear may differ from Piaget's results. It is also recognized that the time of their appearance may vary from child to child and depend on the context in which the task is set.

Although empirical studies tend to confirm Piaget's results, there is some dispute over their interpretation. The logical metatheory Piaget constructed to give coherence to his stage descriptions has been critically reviewed and found wanting (Parsons, 1960; Bynum, Thomas and Weitz, 1972).

Alternative models to Piaget's structuralist model have been suggested to account for the development of operations based on cybernetic principles (McLaughlin, 1963; Pascual-Leone, 1969; Case, 1974). Such studies are not questioning the existence of the operations Piaget has identified, but are offering a different interpretation of them.

Another aspect of the stage theory that is a current focus of research is the question of the internal coherence of the stages. This is a matter of some practical concern in science education. If attempts are made to match the logical demands of a curriculum to the operational capabilities of the learner, it is important to know how generalizable any assessment of a pupil's stage of thinking will be. If a pupil is tested to see whether he can control variables using, for example, the pendulum task, will this mean he will be able to control variables in other situations? Or, more generally, will an assessment of his stage of thinking based on the pendulum task generalize to problems involving other formal level operations such as proportionality?

The question of the homogeneity of the stage of concrete operations has been reviewed by Lunzer (1965), who confirms the unitary nature of concrete operations. A review by Ennis (1975) presents a more sceptical interpretation. Studies on the coherence of the operations involved in formal thinking have been undertaken by several people. One of the earliest replication studies was undertaken by Lovell (1961b). He used ten of Piaget's tasks described in the *Growth of Logical Thinking* (Inhelder and Piaget, 1958). His results suggested general internal coherence within the stage.

More recently, factor analytic studies have been undertaken by Lawson and Renner (1974), Lawson and Nordland (1976), and Shayer (1978a), which give support to the underlying unity of the formal operational schemes. Lawson, Karplus and Adi (1978) also report a factor analytic study using tasks involving proportions, probability, correlations and propositional logic. Their results indicate the possibility of a developmental link between the first three types of task but not the fourth.

Other investigators report less homogeneity within formal level tasks (Berzonsky, 1978). Further critical studies are reviewed by Brown and Desforges (1977). Lunzer (1976) indicates his scepticism in the existence of all underlying processes in formal operations, and suggests instead types of development in reasoning beyond the concrete level. One point he makes that is supported by the recent study by Lawson, Karplus and Adi, is that propositional logic has little to do with the development of higher forms of thought during adolescence.

One factor which has been shown clearly to affect the level of pupils responses to a task is the content or context in which it is set. Wason and Johnson-Laird (1972) report an important series of experiments on adult thinking. They gave subjects tasks with similar logical structures but set in different contexts. They conclude that: 'Content is crucial, and this suggests that any general theory of human reasoning must include an important semantic component' (ibid., p. 245). According to their study the way the content affects the subject's responses is also interesting:

> 'The experiment confirmed our view that the individual tends naturally to think in a causal fashion and that if this tendency is set into opposition with the logical requirements of an inference, it is extremely difficult for the correct deductions to be drawn.' (Ibid., p. 74)

Useful reviews of other studies indicating the relative importance of content over form are reported in Wason (1977) and Donaldson (1978). These findings obviously have important implications for science education which we will return to later.

In this brief review of research related to the stage theory the following issues have emerged:

1. The developmental, or stage, theory differs from that of traditional learning theory in the implications that can be drawn for educational programmes.
2. Although Piaget's metatheory, which accounts for the existence of the operations he identifies in the concrete and the formal stages, is questionable, the actual results appear to be replicable.
3. Studies on the coherence of operations within a stage indicate some conflicting results.
4. The content of a task is at least as important as its logical structure in determining a subject's success at solving it.
5. The results of research on the coherence of stages has implications for science education on what might be called the *matching model*.

Two curriculum projects already mentioned, Science 5–13 and ASEP, organize the material to be presented to pupils according to the underlying cognitive demands it makes. Both schemes have prepared materials appropriate for pupils at these stages of development. Suggestions are given to teachers in the guides on how to diagnose the level of thinking a pupil is capable of and hence how to select material which is matched so as to stimulate development but not to be completely beyond the capabilities of the pupil. The emphasis in both approaches is to place the teacher in the role of diagnostician. Such programmes suggest that pupil learning depends on developmental level but it has been left to later studies to indicate this empirically.

A study by Lawson and Renner (1975) identified the degree of possible mismatch between the demands of secondary science courses and the developmental level of the learners. Sayre and Ball (1975) assessed the level of thinking of 14- to 18-year-old pupils using interviews and showed the scores obtained on the tasks correlated with grades obtained in science courses. Both studies drew attention to the low number of students who operate on the tests at a formal level. This matching model has been considered in greater detail with secondary-school pupils in a sequence of work by Shayer.

In a series of papers, Shayer analysed the cognitive demands of a range of secondary science courses in terms of Piagetian levels (Shayer, 1970, 1972, 1974). He and his team have devised group forms of some of Piaget's tasks and have undertaken a major survey of the level of operation of British school-children (Shayer, Kuchemann and Wylam, 1976). The purpose behind the work is to enable a better match to be made between the logical demands of the curriculum and the cognitive capabilities of the students. It is argued that learning best occurs where the match is appropriate. Shayer reports results of an empirical study in which pupil performance on tasks assessed to be at a late concrete level is predicted from their performance on group-administered Piagetian tasks. The correlation coefficient reported is 0.77 indicating that about 60 percent of the variance in the attainment scores is predictable on the basis of the Piagetian tests (Shayer, 1978b). The study is of value in showing the current problem in our secondary schools of the mismatch between the courses we offer and the capabilities of the pupils. In addition, it does give some support to the matching model. However, there are reasons for being cautious before allowing such studies to have a prescriptive influence on the school science curriculum. The first concerns the reliability of the analysis of the cognitive demand of the curriculum materials themselves. The level to which any topic or lesson can be ascribed does depend on the teacher's interpretation of the materials and the approach used, in other words, it is a pedagogical, as opposed to a curricular, matter. A prescribed topic may be treated in a way that possibly demands formal operations as outlined in a teacher's guide. However, in practice the teacher uses an approach which only requires concrete reasoning.

Earlier in the paper, it was indicated that the content as well as the form of a task affects the pupil's response. Pupils will perform at different levels depending on the content or topic under consideration. Various studies report different levels of correlation between levels of performance on different formal level tasks by the same pupils (reported results vary between 0.3 and 0.7). Even taking the highest reported level, any prediction based on a diagnostic test that the teacher may make about a pupil's level of operativity in a given situation would only be a weak guide.

Group diagnostic tests of the level of operativity of learners may have some part to play in guiding teachers in a broad way to select material and approaches that are appropriate. There is a danger that the results will be interpreted in too narrow and prescriptive a way. Instead of being an aid to the teacher, guiding his expectations and helping him to be sensitive to the differences between individuals, it will interfere with teachers' own professional judgments.

Although there is reason to be cautious about the application of a general matching model, information on the articulation of logical operations within the learning of specific concepts may be a more profitable line of enquiry.

Raven (1974) gives evidence that training in the logical operations can enhance learning of concepts such as force, speed and work. Wheeler and Kass (1977) report that there is a significant relationship between students' ability to apply general proportional reasoning and their achievement in the four areas of chemistry that depend on it. Boulanger (1976) reports a small but significant effect between instruction in proportional reasoning in relation to the concept of speed and parallel development of proportional reasoning in a more general set of tasks.

This section has attempted to outline the contribution that the stage theory has made and can continue to make to science education. Although knowledge of the development of general logical operations is an important consideration in planning and ordering a science teaching programme it is not the only consideration. Information about the way children's causal thinking develops is also an important consideration and one we will now give attention to.

Children's causal thinking

If, as Wason's studies suggest, causal thinking acts as a control on the logical operations employed, then it should be of interest to science educators to consider the development of pupils' causal thinking in its own right.

Here I am not suggesting as is fashionable in the current literature a pro- or anti-Piagetian position. This I think is misleading. There is evidence for the age dependence of a range of logical operations that are important in science.

What is suggested here is that another dimension, and one just as important, needs to be considered and that is the development of pupils' sets of beliefs about natural phenomena in the world around them.

These two concerns are not mutually exclusive but may be viewed as orthogonal axes when considering children's conceptual developments (see Figure 1). From the earliest age children have constructed implicit theories or beliefs about natural phenomena and the way they work. As some studies show, those implicit theories or conceptual frameworks influence the way pupils tackle problems, the variables they consider significant and the factors they observe and pay attention to (Driver, 1973; Karmiloff-Smith and Inhelder, 1976; Kuhn and Brannock, 1977).

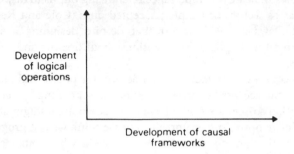

Development
of logical
operations

Development of causal
frameworks

Figure 1

Piaget's early causality studies (Piaget, 1929, 1930) are a source of information for some beliefs children have about the natural world. In his recent research on causality, already mentioned, Piaget and his collaborators study the development of a range of children's ideas. It is unfortunate that in interpreting the extensive number of tasks undertaken in this study, Piaget was looking for evidence for the articulation of children's causal thinking with their operational development. In this way much information concerning the development of the causal or conceptual frameworks themselves has not been reported.

Other researchers are using Piaget's method of clinical interviewing to investigate pupils' conceptual frameworks in a range of areas. In these studies pupils are probed to assess their underlying conceptualizations, the interview data from children of a range of ages are then subjected to analysis not to determine the underlying logical operations that are embodied in the thinking, but to categorize different and developing sets of beliefs or conceptual frameworks used by the pupils in responding to the tasks.

Studies of this kind have been reported by Delacôte and his team on the topics of heat (Tiberghien and Delacôte, 1976a), light (Guesne, 1976) and electricity (Tiberghien and Delacôte, 1976b). Nussbaum and Novak (1976) report on the development of children's concept of the earth in space. Erickson (1979) reports on what he calls conceptual inventories concerning children's conceptions of heat and temperature. Viennot (1974) has studied the reasoning of university students about dynamics problems and has identified Aristotelian thinking even at that level.

All these studies indicate that pupils may have conceptual frameworks developed from their own experience which can differ fundamentally from those presented to them in science lessons.

Some studies indicate the importance of allowing pupils to disprove already existing ideas as well as confirming accepted ones (Cole and Raven, 1969). Rowell and Dawson (1977) report that despite designing a sequence of instruction to refute pupils' misconceptions about floating and sinking, some still persisted.

Changing conceptual frameworks is not easy for pupils and takes time. In fact, learning the accepted conceptualizations in school may place pupils in a parallel position to scientists who have to undergo a paradigm shift in their thinking. We are optimistic or unrealistic if we think we can programme it to happen at the time in the order and at the rate at which our teaching takes place.

Just as educators are currently concerned about the possible mismatch between the logical demands of school science and the logical capabilities of pupils, so similar consideration may need to be given to the problem of mismatch in conceptual frameworks. As mentioned before, the most important single factor influencing learning may be what the learner already knows. However, we may need to ascertain this not to build on it but to challenge it.

As a final comment on the contribution of Piaget's work to science education, I would like to mention his methodology.

The very method by which Piaget has worked, i.e. the clinical interview, is itself a contribution to research methods and, indeed, to education. The clinical interview enables the elucidation of the subject's way of thinking without prior knowledge of what that might be. It makes the important assumption that another person may think about and structure a problem differently from that conceived initially by the researcher and enables this structure to be elaborated. Training in this method of listening and talking to children can make a useful contribution to teacher education. Several of the science courses developed over the last 20 years place some emphasis on the teacher as a diagnostician. If this is to be effective, teachers need to learn to listen to and probe children's ideas without asking leading questions, so they can understand better the child's way of thinking about a problem or reveal underlying difficulties from the child's point of view.

Learning to do this effectively is not easy. Piaget himself comments

> It is hard not to talk too much when questioning a child, especially for a pedagogue! It is so hard not to be suggestive! And above all, it is so hard to find a middle course between systematization due to preconceived ideas (on the part of the interviewer) and any directing hypothesis. (Piaget, 1929, p. 9)

There is some concern about the mismatch between science courses in secondary schools and pupils' ability to comprehend them. One of the most important ways of avoiding this is to have teachers who are able to listen and to reflect on pupils' learning, as well as structure and present their own teaching materials.

References

Anderson, R. C. (1968) *An Analysis of a Class of Problem-Solving Behavior*. Report to US Dept of Health, Education and Welfare, Office of Education, Bureau of Research.

ASEP A Guide to ASEP: The ASEP Handbook.

Ausubel, D. P. (1968) *Educational Psychology: A Cognitive View*. New York, Holt, Rinehart and Winston.

Atkin, J. M. and Karplus, R. (1962) Discovery or invention? *Science Teacher*, 29, 45–51.

Berzonsky, A. (1968) Interdependence of Inhelder and Piaget's model of logical thinking, *Developmental Psychology*, 4 (3), 469–476.

Boulanger, F. D. (1976) The effects of training in the proportional reasoning associated with the concept of speed, *Journal of Research in Science Teaching*, 13 (2), 145–154.

Bower, T. G. R. (1974) *Development in Infancy*. San Francisco, Freeman.

Bredderman, T. A. (1973) The effects of training on the development of the ability to control variables, *Journal of Research in Science Teaching*, 10 (3), 189–200.

Brown, G. and Desforges, C. (1977) Piagetian psychology and education: time for revision, *British Journal of Educational Psychology*, 47, 7–17.

Bynum, T., Thomas, J. and Weitz, L. (1972) Truth functional logic in formal operational thinking: Inhelder and Piaget's evidence, *Developmental Psychology*, 7 (2), 129–132.

Case, R. (1974) Structures and strictures: some functional limitations on the course of cognitive growth, *Cognitive Psychology*, 6, 544–573.

Cole, H. and Raven, R. (1969) Principle learning as a function of instruction on excluding irrelevant variables, *Journal of Research in Science Teaching*, 6, 234–241.

114   Piagetian influences

Donaldson, M. (1978) *Children's Minds*. London, Fontana, Collins.

Driver, R. (1973) The representation of conceptual frameworks in young adolescent science students. Ph.D. thesis, University of Illinois, Urbana, Illinois.

Driver, R. (1979) *The Role of Science in General Education: A Critical Review of some Claims*. Paper delivered at London Institute of Education Seminar, January, 1979.

Driver, R. and Easley, J. (1978) Pupils and paradigms: A review of literature related to concept development in adolescent science students, *Studies in Science Education*, 5, 61–84.

Elkind, E. (1961) The development of quantitative thinking: a systematic replication of Piaget's studies. *Journal of Genetic Psychology*, 98, 37–46.

Ennever, L. and Harlen, W. (1972) *With Objectives in Mind Guide to Science 5–13*. London, Macdonald Educational.

Ennis, B. (1975) Children's ability to handle Piaget's propositional logic: A conceptual critique, *Review of Educational Research*, 45 (1), 1–41.

Erickson, G. L. (1979) Children's conceptions of heat and temperature *Science Education*, 63 (2), 221–230.

Guesne, E. (1976) Lumière et vision des objets: un exemple de representations des phénomènes physique pré existant à l'enseignement. *Proceedings of GIREP*.

Inhelder, B. and Piaget, J. (1958) *The Growth of Logical Thinking from Childhood to Adolescence*. New York, Basic Books.

Johnson, J. K. and Howe, A. C. (1978) The use of cognitive conflict to promote conservation acquisition, *Journal of Research in Science Teaching*, 15 (4), 239–247.

Karmiloff-Smith and Inhelder, B. (1976) If you want to get ahead, get a theory, *Cognition*, 3, 195–213.

Karplus, R. (1977) *Workshop on Science Teaching and the Development of Reasoning*. Berkeley, California, Laurence Hall of Science.

Kuhn, D. and Brannock, J. (1977) Development of the isolation of variables scheme in experimental and 'natural experiment' contexts, *Developmental Psychology*, 13 (1), 9–14.

Lawson, A. E. and Nordland, I. (1976) The factor structure of some Piagetian tasks, *Journal of Research in Science Teaching*, 13, 461–466.

Lawson, A. E. and Renner, J. W. (1974) A quantitative analysis of responses to Piagetian tasks and its implications for curriculum, *Science Education*, 58 (4), 545–559.

Lawson, A. E. and Renner, J. W. (1975) Relationships of science subject matter and developmental levels of learners, *Journal of Research in Science Teaching*, 12, 347–358.

Lawson, A., Karplus, R. and Adi, H. (1978) The acquisition of propositional logic and formal operational schemata during the school years, *Journal of Research in Science Teaching*, 15 (6), 465–478.

Linn, M. C. and Thier, H. (1975) The effect of experimental science on development of logical thinking in children, *Journal of Research in Science Teaching*, 12, 49–62

Lovell, K. (1961a) *The Growth of Basic Mathematical and Scientific Concepts in Children*. London, University of London Press.

Lovell, K. (1961b) A follow-up of Inhelder and Piaget's 'The Growth of Logical Thinking', *British Journal of Psychology*, 52, 143–153.

Lunzer, E. A. (1965) Problems of formal reasoning in test situations, in Mussen, P. H. (ed.) *European Research in Cognitive Development*, Mon. Soc. Res. Child. Dev., 30 (2), 19–46.

Lunzer, E. A. (1976) *Formal Reasoning: a Re-appraisal*, Paper presented at the meeting of Jean Piaget Society.

McLaughlin, G. H. (1963) Psycho-logic: a possible alternative to Piaget's formulation, *British Journal Educational Psychology*, 33, 61–67.

Murray, F. (1972) Acquisition of conservation through social interaction, *Developmental Psychology*, 6 (1), 1–6.

Nussbaum, J. (1979) The effect of the SCIS 'Relativity' unit on the child's conception of space, *Journal of Research in Science Teaching*, 16 (1), 45–51.

Nussbaum, J. and Novak, J. (1976) An assessment of children's concepts of the earth utilizing structural interviews, *Science Education*, 60 (4), 535–550.

Palmer, E. L. (1965) Accelerating the child's cognitive attainments through the inducement of cognitive conflict. An interpretation of the Piagetian position, *Journal of Research in Science Teaching*, 3, 318–325.

Parsons, C. (1960) Inhelder and Piaget's 'The Growth of Logical Thinking'. II: A logician's viewpoint, *British Journal of Psychology*, 51, 75–84.

Pascual-Leone, J. (1969) Cognitive development and cognitive style: A general psychological integration. Unpublished doctoral dissertation, University of Geneva.

Piaget, J. (1929) *The Child's Conception of the World*. New York, Harcourt, Brace.

Piaget, J. (1930) *The Child's Conception of Physical Causality*. London, Routledge and Kegan Paul.

Piaget, J. (1964) Cognitive development in children: Development and learning, *Journal of Research in Science Teaching*, 2, 176–186.

Piaget, J. (1970a) *The Science of Education and the Psychology of the Child*. New York, Orion Press.

Piaget, J. (1970b) *Genetic Epistemology*. Columbia, Columbia University Press.

Piaget, J. (1971) *Biology and Knowledge*. Edinburgh, Edinburgh University Press.

Piaget, J. (1973) Comments on mathematical education, in Howson, A. G. (ed.) *Developments in Mathematical Education*. London, Cambridge University Press.

Piaget, J. (1974) *Understanding Causality*. New York, W. W. Norton.

Pinard, A. and Laurendeau, M. (1969) 'Stage' in Piaget's cognitive developmental theory: Exegesis of a concept, in Elkind, D. and Flavell, J. H. (eds) *Studies on Cognitive Development: Essays in Honor of Jean Piaget*. New York, OUP.

Raven, R. J. (1974) Programming Piaget's logical operations for science inquiry and concept attainment, *Journal of Research in Science Teaching*, 11 (3), 251–261.

Rowell, J. A. and Dawson, C. J. (1977) Teaching about floating and sinking: An attempt to link cognitive psychology with classroom practice, *Science Education*, 61 (2), 245–253.

Sayer, S. and Ball, D. (1975) Piagetian cognitive development and achievement in science, *Journal of Research in Science Teaching*, 12, 165–174.

SCIS Teacher's Handbook (1974) Berkeley, California, Lawrence Hall of Science.

SCIS Science Curriculum Improvement Study, University of California, New York, Rand McNally.

116 Piagetian influences

Shayer, M. (1970) How to assess science courses, *Education in Chemistry,* 7 (5), 182–186.
Shayer, M. (1972) Conceptual demands in the Nuffield O-level physics course, *School Science Review,* 54, 26.
Shayer, M. (1974) Conceptual demands in the Nuffield O-level biology course, *School Science Review,* 56, 381–388.
Shayer, M. (1978a) *Is Piaget's Construct of Formal Operational Thinking Valid?* Paper given at British Educational Research Association Conference, Leeds, September, 1978.
Shayer, M. (1978b) The analysis of science curricula for Piagetian level of demand, *Studies in Science Education,* 5, 115–130.
Shayer, M., Kuchemann, D. E. and Wylam, H. (1976) The distribution of Piagetian stages of thinking in British middle- and secondary-school children, *British Journal of Educational Pyschology,* 46, 164–173.
Smedslund, J. (1961) The acquisition of conservation of substance and weight in children. V Practice in conflict situation without external reinforcement, *Scandinavian Journal of Psychology,* 2, 156–160.
Tiberghien, A. and Delacôte, G. (1976a) Conception de la chaleur chez les enfants de 10 à 12 ans. *Proceedings of GIREP.*
Tiberghien, A. and Delacôte, G. (1976b) Manipulations et représentations de circuits electrique simples par des enfants de 7 à 12 ans, *Review Francaise de Pedagogie,* 34.
Viennot, L. (1974) Sens physique et raisonnement formel en dynamique elementaire, *Encari Pedagogique,* II, 35–46.
Wason, P. C. (1977) The theory of formal operations – a critique, in Geber, B. A. (ed.) *Piaget and Knowing.* London, Routledge & Kegan Paul.
Wason, P. C. and Johnson-Laird, P. N. (1972) *Psychology of Reasoning.* London, B. T. Batsford.
Wheeler, A. E. and Kass, H. (1977) *Proportional Reasoning in Introductory High-school Chemistry.* Paper presented to the fiftieth Annual Meeting of the National Association for Research in Science Teaching, Ohio.

3.3

SOME ASPECTS OF THE WORK OF PIAGET IN PERSPECTIVE

Kenneth Lovell

The scope of his work

When the history of twentieth century developmental psychology is written it is likely that the name of Piaget will stand, like the body of a giant, head and shoulders above all the others. His work is so fundamental that most papers now published in the field of child psychology refer to his views in some way or another. Note, however, that Piaget may not regard himself as an expert developmental psychologist. He is more likely to look upon himself as the founder of a particular branch of psychology, namely genetic epistemology. This is an important point, for while thousands of persons around the world regard him as an outstanding child psychologist, it is his own conception of his aims which gives the vital key to his life's work. He became a developmental psychologist in order to find out how knowledge is constructed. In short he wanted to know if knowledge results from the accumulation of small bits of information or whether there must already be a mental structure or reference frame inside which some new piece of knowledge can be meaningful.

For more than 50 years he and his colleagues have reported a mass of observations on aspects of child and adolescent developments and from these he has elaborated important hypotheses relating to the growth of knowledge. He used the clinical or 'critical' method of individually interviewing children, and thereby attempted to build a bridge between his early love of biology and his enduring passion of epistemology. Piaget and his colleagues have

Source: Floyd, A. (ed) (1979) *Cognitive Development in the School Years.* London, Croom Helm/The Open University Press, pp. 13–28, 32–33

published more than 40 books and a much larger number of articles. Further, his work has generated an enormous amount of research by other workers – a true sign of the greatness of his own efforts. The compilation of Piagetian research by S. and C. Modgil (1976), which is in eight volumes and includes some 3,500 references, gives some idea of the extent of the research by the Genevans and others to the end of 1975.

His work may be divided up into four broad periods. First the period up to about 1930 in which the empirical data was obtained wholly by verbal methods. This period includes his classic studies of the language and thought of the child, and the moral judgement of the child. Piaget later admitted (Piaget, 1953) that his method of studying logic in the child was much too verbal at first. The second period involved his observations of his own children, and from these he developed his views on the origins of intelligence and the construction of reality (Piaget, 1936, 1937). Indeed in this phase it was the study of the sensori-motor phase of his own children's development that provided much of the basis for his theoretical work (Piaget, 1947).

Some of the best known of Piaget's work occurred in the third phase in which he studied the move from pre-operational thought to concrete operational thought and from the latter to formal operational thought. Here we have the many and well known studies of conservation, classification, seriation; together with the growth of understanding of number, space, geometry, time, chance and others. In this period he was investigating, because of his epistemological interests, the origins of the concepts with which we structure the world. Without doubt it is the studies of this period which have greatly coloured the teacher's view of the work of Piaget. Much, but not all of this work in this period, is briefly summarized by Piaget and Inhelder (1969).

The fourth period of his work extends to the present time. In this period we find the many volumes of Etudes d'Epistemologie Genetique (written with the help of others) as well as books on structuralism, memory and intelligence, mental imagery and thinking, causality, on the growth of the child's conceptualization of his own actions, and a further volume dealing with the problem of equilibration (Piaget, 1975).

We have already indicated Piaget's philosophical interests, namely how knowledge comes to be constructed. A brief word now is given on his philosophic stance. Of genetic epistemology he writes, 'The fundamental hypothesis of genetic epistemology is that there is a parallelism between the progress made in the logical and rational organization of knowledge and the corresponding psychological processes' (Piaget, 1970, p. 13). Put more simply, what he calls genetic epistemology is the study of how knowledge has progressed from early simple forms to more complex and indeed, more powerful constructs. To pursue this study, genetic epistemology employs three broad sources of data. First, the study of the cognitive development of the child through investigating the slow construction of his basic conceptualizations (rather than the build-up of particular skills or the acquisition of specific pieces of information). A second source is the history of science, from the viewpoint of how one level of knowledge gave way to a higher level. The important point here is what it is in the one theory held that paved the way for the creation of new scientific knowledge. A third source resides in formal models of the state of some specific piece of scientific knowledge at a given point in time. Such models assume or presuppose experimentally determined regularities; on the other hand such models also allow the discovery of new relations between regularities. However, these formal models are mainly structured models and therefore have limitations from the point of view of genetic epistemology or developmental psychology, for these require process models, that is, frameworks which model the processes which move the knowledge from one stage to the next.

Thus, if Piaget's philosophical interest is in knowledge construction, his philosophical viewpoint involves a form of structuralism. His critics have often pointed out that he, like everyone else, looks at evidence from 'a point of view', and that there could be other conceptual frameworks elaborated to cover the same ground. This argument is accepted, but it is pointed out that in the natural sciences too, it is not unusual for alternative frameworks to be elaborated to explain the evidence. Other critics object to his work because of the non-observable and non-measurable nature of the main concepts which he employs such as schemes, assimilation, accommodation. True, many of these do not lend themselves to clear hypotheses which experimental evidence can support or refute. On the other hand many of his ideas are testable.

It has been assumed in this section that readers already have some knowledge of at least some areas of his work. This brief historical treatment is to give no more than a sketch of the vast scope of his work over more than 50 years, and merely to indicate the philosophy that informed it.

The present position of Piaget on some issues

It is a great mistake to think that Piaget considers his theory to be either complete or all embracing. Rather it is constantly being modified either by himself or others. Indeed, he has referred to himself as 'one of the chief "revisionists of Piaget" ' (Piaget, 1970, p. 703 footnote). Again in a special issue of *Archives de Psychologie* published in 1976 in honour of his eightieth birthday he himself wrote,

> 'I have the conviction, illusory or well founded . . . and only the future will tell whether this conviction is partly true or only the result of my obstinate pride . . . that I have laid bare a more or less evident general skeleton which remains full of gaps so that when these gaps will be filled the articulations will have to be differentiated but the general lines of the system will not be changed.'

We cannot, of course, be sure how much the general lines of the theory will have to be changed in the future, but we can speak of some changes that have been made in his own views on specific issues over the period, say 1958 to 1978. It must be remembered that in many areas of the natural sciences too, for instance physics, theories elaborated 20 or 30 years ago have had to undergo many changes since then. Below there is a brief discussion of just four issues on which Piaget has changed his mind in recent years. Space does not permit further discussion.

Equilibration is perhaps Piaget's most important, yet most controversial, concept and we begin by considering this. In a recent book on this subject (Piaget, 1975) he points out that the earlier writings on this subject were quite inadequate. Some 40 years ago he intuitively formulated his ideas that cognition was a self-regulatory or self-referential system. In such a system interactions between different parts of the system interact with interactions between other parts, this wholeness of the system giving it its stable properties. In biological organisms there are certainly simultaneous interactions between, say, perception and action which maintain an internal equilibrium. For Piaget, cognition shares with biological organizations this self-regulatory quality which establishes whatever levels of activity that have to be maintained for equilibrium, and thus the interactions of interactions.

Now if such systems merely compensated for perturbations and re-established a pre-existing equilibrium, one would merely be maintaining the status quo. Piaget argues that cognitive systems do not operate in this fashion. Rather they operate, as it were, in an ever widening spiral fashion. This reflects the ability of the systems to deal with more and more disturbances which arise from both inner reflection and outside contradictions as the child's experience of the world grows. The widening spiral also reflects the ability of the systems to integrate disturbances into wider and more powerful structures as, for example, when early concrete operations are slowly replaced by later concrete operations and when the latter gradually give way to formal operations. That is to say, not only does the compensation of perturbations get the system back to an equilibrium state but it attains a higher order of equilibrium. Piaget is now particularly concerned (Piaget, 1975) to be able to give an account of what he calls 'equilibration majorante' or 'augmentative equilibrium'. This contrasts with his earlier interest which lasted over many years in giving more weight to a structural description of the main stages of equilibration as in concrete and formal operational thought.

This change in outlook leading Piaget to give a new account of the mechanisms of equilibration has led him to change, slightly, the observational and experimental methods employed. There is now an even closer look at individual children, and more attention paid both to the experimental situation and to the dialogue with the child. These changes are reflected in his work on correspondences discussed below.

While Piaget's views on the processes of equilibration have changed he remains as firmly as ever an interactionist. While for the empiricist, discovered knowledge was already an existence in external reality, and for the naturist or apriorist forms of knowledge were predetermined inside the subject, for Piaget the cognitive structures involved in knowing are given neither in the object nor in the person, but in the interaction between them.

A second important change in Piaget's outlook concerns his views on the role of correspondences and morphisms in cognitive growth. As is well known he holds the view that knowledge involves essentially systems of transformations. We can only know something if, and only if, we can construct and transform it. Although he did not invent this viewpoint he has held to it consistently. However, more recently, he has become interested in correspondences as well as transformations. This is linked to his current interest in the child's growth in understanding of the mathematical concept of category.

Transformations can be arranged in the manner in which they follow on from one another. In correspondences, however, there is no transformation. Here we are comparing terms or states as they are. One can of course compare transformations, for a transformation produces a state, but in making the comparison, as such, there is no further transformation. We can find examples of correspondences at every level of intellectual growth (Piaget, 1976). For example, he argues that at the sensori-motor level each assimilation into a specific scheme is a correspondence. Thus if the infant when touching one hanging rattle to make it swing sees another similarly hanging, he will make a correspondence between the second and the first and set the second one swinging too. At the operational level it is not just a case of assimilating through physical action whatever can be perceived; rather there is now a mental action and thus a *necessary* correspondence. For example, every direct operation (say, addition) corresponds to an inverse operation (subtraction).

In the last few years the Genevans have been experimenting to establish the relationships between correspondences and transformations. This new work cannot be discussed in any detail but one experiment (Piaget, 1976) will indicate that their findings change some of their earlier views. Consider the well known experiment in which two balls of plasticine are judged by the child to be equal in amount. A piece of plasticine is taken off one of the balls and the young child is asked if there is now the same amount of plasticine in the ball. Young children invariably answer correctly. Then the piece is put back on the other side of the ball and the child again appropriately questioned. Once more they answer correctly. This process goes on until the same sausage shape is obtained as when the plasticine in the traditional experiment is rolled. The interesting thing is that with this 'taking off' and 'adding on' process, 75 percent of $5\frac{1}{2}$ year olds conserve giving correct answers like 'You took the piece away but put it back again so it's now OK'. Moreover the conservation is stable because if the classic experiment is carried out and the ball rolled into a sausage, conservation is still maintained and good reasons are given.

Piaget's view now is that rapid learning has taken place because use was made of the correspondence of the isomorphism between what was taken off and what was replaced (Inhelder, Sinclair and Bovet, 1974). This new type of conservation experiment focuses the pupil's attention on the fact that whenever there is one correspondence there must be the other. In another sense here we have an experimental situation that emphasizes the functional aspects of transformations. Now at the operational level there are, as stated earlier, necessary correspondences between every direct operation and its inverse. Piaget is thus giving emphasis to correspondence as an aid in cognitive development, at the same time, of course, maintaining the importance of transformations in knowing.

The relationship between language and thought is another issue about which Piaget seems to have changed his mind in recent years. His views in the late 1950s are given by Inhelder and Piaget (1958). In general terms we may say that he had often stated that language was not a sufficient condition for the formation of intellectual operations. Similar views were held in the early 1960s. Again we find him saying in respect of younger children (Duckworth, 1964): 'The level of understanding seems to modify the language that is used, rather than vice versa . . . Mainly language serves to translate what is already understood . . .' In 1967 we find Sinclair-De-Zwart (1967), a colleague of Piaget in Geneva, giving details of fresh studies carried out by her. In essence she stated that up to and including the level of concrete operational thought, logical structures determine the nature of the linguistic structures rather than the other way round. Language may play a role in the growth of such thought; language can, so to speak, prepare an operation; language helps in the selection, storage and retrieval of information; but it does not play a central role in the elaboration of concrete operational structures.

In the early 1960s, Piaget (1963) had a more open mind about the role of language in the elaboration of formal operational thought. In respect of the structures of such thought he wished to reserve his judgement on the role language played, whether it was 'truly conservative or merely indirect and supportive'. However, by 1970 Piaget seems to make language less dependent on cognition for its structure (see Ferriero, 1971). There is no longer the emphasis that cognitive operations (or pre-operations) direct language or language acquisition, rather than the other way round. The view now held is that both cognitive, linguistic and non-linguistic structures (such as those involving imagery) derive from a more abstract logical system of regulations and organizations common to all domains. Linguistic structures may well be affected by cognitive structures and vice versa through this more general abstract system. This allows both cognitive and linguistic structures to influence one another and at the same time for each to have a degree of autonomy. The partial autonomy of the linguistic structures suggests that it may be possible under certain circumstances to construct operational structures by verbal means; the suggestion having already been experimentally confirmed in the case of conservation.

A fourth change in outlook may be briefly noted. By the late 1960s Piaget and his colleagues came to the view that by the later part of the pre-operational period of thought, say, 5 to 7 years, children's thinking did in fact possess some kind of logic. But it is semi-logic compared with the thinking of the concrete operational period for it does not possess the property of reversibility. Thus we find Piaget et al. (1968a) describing their work on *identities*. These are essentially qualitative in nature in that the child recognizes that an object is the 'same thing' even when its appearance, form or size changes; as for example, when a piece of straight wire is twisted to form 'spectacles'. In other words the wire is still the same entity as before, although the child will not yet conserve its length (a quantitative invariant).

Piaget et al. (1968b) also maintain that children of this age have some understanding of functions in the sense of grasping that the value of a depends on the value of b, or $a = f(b)$. Using apparatus a child is able to relate, say, changes in the length of a spring to changes in the weights attached to it. But the changes the child notes are only qualitative correspondences in respect of objects or situations, in the sense that changes in one object tend to be associated with changes in another. The functional relationship is only qualitative and there is no precise quantitative relationship.

These identities and functions reflect the young child's increasing awareness of associations, consistencies and invariants in his world, thereby rendering it a more predictable place to live in. This is an important step for him.

Some comments on, and criticisms of, Piaget's theory

It will be appreciated that the present writer must be highly selective in respect of the issues chosen for discussion in this section. We begin by mentioning two questions raised in a recent publication which bear on his theoretical position and then discuss some of the experimental evidence which either amplifies or runs contrary to some of his views.

Mention has already been made of a book by Piaget on structuralism (Piaget, 1971). In a recent publication entitled *Structure and Transformation* edited by Riegel and Rosenwald (1976) there is a comprehensive description of the basic principles of the structuralist paradigm. However, while Piaget considers himself a structuralist his views differ at times from those of the contributors to this recent volume. For example, he writes 'If it be true that all structures are generated, it is just as true that generation is always passing from a simpler to a more complex structure, this process, according to the present state of knowledge being endless.' This is strictly in keeping with the structuralist paradigm which argues that as the individual changes – as for example in middle and old age – so does reality for the individual, and in turn as reality changes so does the individual. Yet in Piagetian theory, structural development stops at mid-adolescence when the INRC structure is elaborated, and so the contributors ask for new conceptualizations by Piaget about changes of structure in adulthood.

In studying cognitive development one frequently encounters the term 'stages'. This is used in two ways. First, to indicate the increase in understanding of some specific idea. Thus Lovell (1971) and Thomas (1975) indicate the stages through which pupils pass in their increasing understanding of the concept of mathematical function. Second, the term is used by Piaget to indicate the increasing ability of pupils to solve tasks which demand more and more complex logical mathematical operations for their solutions. It is in this sense that the term is used, and briefly discussed, in this paper. It must, of course, be made clear that the 'stage' of thinking as used in the second sense of the term, underpins the 'stage' at which pupils are in understanding some specific idea (the first sense of the term).

We next consider an important issue in the 4- to 7-year-old period. A very large number of training studies have taken place in an effort to accelerate the growth of children's thinking mainly from pre-operational to concrete operational thought. Various techniques have been used in, say, conservation training: for example, conflict-equilibration (proposed by the Genevans themselves because of their theory); constituent structure training (the child is trained in one of the constituent skills held by Piaget to be critical to conservation training); verbal rule instruction (verbally presented rules are co-ordinated with experimental manipulations); and a number of others. All these differing approaches have shown that operations can be trained and this seems to be the case whether strong or weak criteria are used to test for operational thinking.

It might be thought these findings are at variance with Piaget's teaching. This is now only partly true for the Genevans themselves have, in recent years, carried out a number of training studies and come to the same broad conclusions (Inhelder, Sinclair and Bovet, 1974). The argument now is whether such training is effective unless there are at least some of the relevant constituents present. The Genevans, for example, argue that when training is successful there is evidence of partially attained structures before the training begins, and are uncertain what happens when the child is completely pre-operational. It must be admitted, of course, that there are difficulties in defining precisely the behavioural manifestation of cognitive structures. However, since learning takes place using methods not necessarily based on conflict-equilibration this does leave Piaget with a problem his theory has not resolved.

A number of workers such as Bruner, Bryant, Gelman and others argue that many cognitive functions such as, say, conservation, are available to the child much earlier in life and are not constructed in the 5- to 7-year period as indicated by Piaget. The child is said to be unable to give evidence of these contructions or use them because of, say, conflict among alternative hypotheses, failure to remember initial conditions, or for other reasons. Some of the relevant studies by these workers have still to explain how the cognitive functions originally arose and make clear how experience changed the strategies the young child used. Moreover, the views of these workers do not necessarily deny Piaget's views on the need for progressive construction.

Finally it should be noted that far fewer training studies have been carried out at the interface between concrete and formal operational thinking. To date the number would be something in excess of twenty (cf. Siegler, 1977). Moreover, as far as this writer knows, none, to date, has followed up the effects of such training for longer than 4 months after training ceased. Thus our knowledge of the effects of training at this interface is limited.

When we consider concrete and formal operations more broadly a number of issues arise. First, Piaget is sometimes criticized for apparently holding the view that 'stages' are found in cognitive growth; and that such growth is discontinuous rather than continuous. In reply to the attack on stages as such, it must be stated that he is not an empiricist with 'stages out there' to be discovered. Rather he set up tasks which demanded for their solution increasingly complex logical-mathematical operations which were relevant to his philosophical position, and children progressed through 'stages' as they showed an improvement in solving the tasks. In respect of the discontinuity/continuity argument he has clearly stated that the research techniques are tasks used to restrict the number of identifiable intermediate steps that can be detected. Thus we can never be sure whether discontinuity or continuity best describe the phenomena being studied since the number of intermediate steps can never be complete or exhaustive (Piaget, 1960). Rather he takes the view that within an open system we find phases of relative) stability, as in the case of concrete and formal operational stages, punctuated by unstable periods of transition. In connection with this issue the longitudinal study of average grade school pupils by Neimark (1974) using an information processing approach should be considered. She tested pupils twice a year over at least 3 years in respect of their problem solving strategies. The task was novel, language free (except for the instructions), and involved simple patterns of black and white on card. Thus to pupils in a developed society the task could be regarded at least as content-familiar. Her findings suggest two qualitatively different levels of approach corresponding to concrete and formal operations, the move from the lower to higher level proceeding through discrete steps. This was also true, with advancing age, using a cross-sectional approach. However, nothing that has been written in this paragraph necessarily implies that the concept of stages will be of lasting value.

Second, Piaget's notion of *structure d'ensemble* has been questioned. The completed elaboration of such structures could not, of course, be expected before the end of the relevant developmental period. But if at the end of, say, the concrete operational period there was established empirically an asynchronism among the constituents of a *given concept*, his notion of *structure d'ensemble* would be in great jeopardy. There is some evidence (cf. Hooper and Sipple, 1975) that in the age range 5 to $7\frac{1}{2}$ years or so the development of classificatory abilities may sometimes lag behind rational abilities, contrary of course to Piagetian theory. But in pupils aged 9 to 12 years the position is by no means clear. After a review of the relevant literature, Hooper and Dihoff (1975) made a thorough study of synchrony in this age range. In order to avoid possible criticisms of their data analysis they used multi-dimensional scaling, clustering and factor analytic procedures. They concluded that, on the basis of their evidence, developmental synchrony cannot yet be abandoned, but this does not preclude asynchrony being established in the future. At the level of formal operations there is no evidence as yet for a unitary concept even at 17 to 18 years of age; indeed there is some evidence against it. The question of synchrony must not, of course, be confused with that of horizontal decalage (the same structure applied to adjoining cognitive areas), or oblique decalage (Inhelder, Sinclair and Bovet, 1974).

At this point it must be made clear that some psychologists are quite opposed to Piaget's notion of operatory structures. Instead they prefer to regard the acquisition of a particular piece of knowledge as dependent on the learning of a set of skills which are then practised and perhaps combined into new combinations. Such skills will most likely arise from the cumulative learning of prior skills. However, the skills or the new combinations of skills are then activated and used by the individuals when perhaps they are suitably motivated by the task and appropriately cued into it. When considering this viewpoint one must remember that the question of the 'narrowness' or 'width' of the intellectual skill must be considered. A skill could be narrow in the sense that it enabled the individual to assimilate a particular piece of knowledge but did not transfer to new knowledge. On the other hand an intellectual skill could be wide enough to be an operation and thus a part of an operatory structure. For psychologists who take a narrow view of intellectual skills it is obvious that the question of synchrony of the constituents of an operatory structure does not arise.

Third, there is the important question of whether the required strategies of thought will be invoked to solve a given task when the same strategies are indeed used by the individual in the solution of other problems. By the early 1960s it was known (cf. Lovell, 1961) that there were only moderately sized correlations between the level of responses to tasks given by Inhelder and Piaget (1958). This is an issue which traditional Piagetian theory has not seriously considered at the level of formal operations.

Piaget and Inhelder (1969) certainly maintain that concrete operations are not content-free and are thus subject to variability due to stimulus differences. When Inhelder and Piaget (1964) gave a classificatory task involving pictures of animals the task was found to be much harder than when beads or flowers were used. Their rationale was that children are more familiar with beads and flowers. This may well be true, but it is likely to be only part of the story.

At the level of formal thought Inhelder and Piaget (1958) consider that the content of the problem is subordinate to the form of the relations in it. This is not the case in fact. The response which a child or adult gives to the task depends on the social context of the task and the meaning that the task has for him in his world. So it is not just a question of familiarity with the content, although that certainly plays a part.

There is now much evidence to support the view just expressed. For example, the work reported by Wason and Johnson-Laird (1972), or Wason (1977) shows that reasoning is affected by the content of the problem and in a systematic way. Indeed most people realize that the content of a problem which they have to solve in everyday life affects the ease with which they solve it. The studies reported by Luria (1976), also Cole and Scribner (1974), show that the types of concept formed (functional relational rather than categoric concepts) and the ability to use specific strategies in reasoning, do depend upon the content of the problem and the meaning it has for the individual. Again Tulkin and Konner (1973) report hypothetico-deductive thinking among Kalahari bushmen in relation to animal tracking. Yet if the same bushmen were suddenly taken into a physics laboratory and asked to solve a problem involving, say, the separation of variables – an analogous task – it is most unlikely that hypothetico-deductive thinking would be available until after a long period of study which would give meaning to the task and provide familiarity with the variables.

The problem of the availability of reasoning skills in diverse situations is an important issue for psychology and education. There is now much evidence that, in Britain and elsewhere, 3-year-old children from some homes use language less often to report on past experiences and predict the future, to give explanations, to justify behaviour and to reflect on feelings, compared with children from professional homes. The former children more often use language to communicate the 'here and now' events. By 7 years of age these working-class children when talking to peers, can make as long and as complex sentences as children from professional homes, but their families less often encourage them to make comparisons, to recall the past, anticipate the future, to look for similarities and differences, and to offer 'logical' explanations (Tough, 1977). Because of this children from different families enter school with a different set of meanings or constructions about the world.

In some families then, in Britain or in any other country, the life style is such that thinking is more frequently rooted in the perceptible or tangible, the concrete, the practical. But there is by no means a one-to-one relationship between this kind of life style and socio-economic status.

Some families of limited income do encourage their children to think of possibilities and hypothetical situations, thus divorcing themselves more often from the tangible and concrete, to subject themselves to more long-term planning, to reflect on their actions and the likely outcomes, and to think and find solutions to problems for themselves rather than have them transmitted merely by rule or routine sequence. Many professional families do this too: some do not. But studies of language use, also of concept formation and reasoning in a number of countries, suggest that family life style, as defined, has implications for cognitive development.

Children from families where there is no attempt to move them from thinking in terms of the immediate present may sometimes be better at assessing the perceptual cues of objects or situations. Moreover, we must never belittle such thinking; it may be appropriate for certain life styles. But they have a greater tendency to use functional relational concepts, and they have more difficulty in handling verbal-logical relations where the form of the argument is divorced from the content – as is often the case in formal schooling. The reasoning of everyone is, of course, affected to some extent by knowledge of, and familiarity with, the content; but certain life styles make it easier for the pupil to handle verbal logical relations independent of content. Life styles which do not help the children in this way put children at something of a disadvantage in formal schooling in a developed or developing society. These differences in family life styles are found in all countries, regardless of whether their economic system is capitalist or socialist. Much could be done by families (often regardless of income) to help their children acquire and use in diverse situations, those thinking skills which are now increasingly demanded by developed and developing societies throughout the world.

Piaget's failure to consider content and meaning in his traditional theory of formal operations is well expressed by Halford (1972) when he points out that Wason's work had shown that: 'If adults have what Piaget calls formal operational thought, then Piaget does very little to specify the conditions under which this will be observed.' While human reasoning is no doubt rule governed, its rules are not those of traditional propositional logic and the appropriate calculus has not yet been formulated.

Fourth, we have already explained that there are difficulties over the problem of stages. It remains to be seen to what extent Piaget's more recent views on equilibrium (Piaget, 1975) can provide a satisfactory and generally agreed account of the processes involved in the transition between stages. In other words, will it indicate the strategies children adopt in response to the changing child-environment interaction? An information processing approach may also help in the testing out of the steps in cognitive development. The most frequently used models now used in information processing are probably the production system models made possible by using computers. Well known workers in this field are Klahr and Wallace (1975) and Baylor et al. (1973). All information processing approaches are well concerned with a detailing of the processes of reasoning and concept formation, a detailing that Piagetian theory has lacked. But to date it must be said that information processing is of limited value for the teacher (although of value to the researcher) for it is time consuming to tease out the micro-processes, and there is limited experience of teaching the processes found and establishing the outcomes of such teaching.

Aspects of Piaget's work likely to be of lasting value

Much could be written on this topic but the writer's judgement must be summarized briefly. Some of the points listed below overlap to some extent, but they do separately suggest some of Piaget's work and ideas are likely to be of long term value.

1. The sheer amount of factual knowledge established which shows at least some of the broad outlines of cognitive development. This in no sense implies that Piaget's notion of stages will be of permanent value. Nor does it set approval on the theoretical framework he elaborated, but the framework did enable him to get a mass of data.
2. His strong approval, through use, of an age-long approach, namely, the clinical method. Although this method has marked strengths, it also has weaknesses. But in Piaget's hands it has been very productive in many areas of cognition. Moreover, it has been adopted, as a result of Piaget's influence, by innumerable research workers in studying pupils' ideas in areas of knowledge not covered by him. It will continue to be used in this way for a long time.
3. The extensive research that has been generated, and will go on being generated, by Piaget's research. Some studies involve testing his results, some developing new lines of research based on his ideas. Eventually this research

will lead to new and lasting knowledge even if the findings are at variance with his.

4. Piaget's emphasis on organization, for without this there can be no adaptation. From this follows, for him, the importance of cognitive organization. This means that new knowledge will be internalized and structured, and in time will determine the strategies used in future encounters with the environment. This is a very different stance from that of linking particular behaviours with specific aspects of the environment and specific learned skills.

5. The position Piaget adopts in respect of the progressive construction of knowledge resulting from the interactions between subject and objects. If new knowledge is not progressively constructed by the individual himself, with the aid of teaching, action, observation, the use of materials and/or language, and social interaction, as required, it remains imperfectly understood. This view does not necessarily lend support to what is broadly known as 'discovery learning' in certain educational circles.

6. His perspective which maintains that knowledge is constructed out of the interaction between the person and reality, for the cognitive structures involved in knowing are given neither in the object, nor in the person, but in the interaction between them. While he may not have been the first person to advance this general view, he did relate this to the idea of decentration and its relation to objectivity. For example, Piaget (1950) wrote: 'It is impossible at any level to separate the object from the subject. Relations exist between the two only, but these relations may be more or less centred or decentred, and it is this inversion of direction which makes up the transition from subjectivity to objectivity.'

7. The importance given to the role of cognitive conflict as a means of bringing about improved cognitive adaptation and hence a higher level of thinking. [This is not to deny the place of verbal rule learning. One way in which such learning may act is through being able to mobilize unintegrated structures through generating conflict.] In the school situation his notion of cognitive conflict argues that the curriculum or task presented to the pupil should demand cognitive skills slightly more advanced (+1 level) than those available in order to induce conflict.

8. Just one detailed study (Piaget, 1977) may perhaps be mentioned where the insights obtained are likely to be of lasting value. This relates to the time lag between a child having the requisite strategies or programmes to carry out an action (e.g. walking on all fours) and being able to reflect on his actions and describe what he is doing. The cognisance, or act of becoming concious of an

active scheme (i.e. of a repeatable and generalizable action), or of an internalized scheme for that matter, is a pre-requisite for generalization and for tackling new problems in which the same strategies are involved.

It is likely to be a long time before the lasting insight which Piaget has produced together with those established by others, can be brought together into a theory which subsumes or replaces his own. In the special issue of the *Archives de Psychologie* already mentioned he writes: 'When a theory succeeds another theory the first impression is often that the new theory contradicts the older and eliminates it. But later research often shows that more has to be retained of the older theory than could be foreseen. The better theory turns out to be the one that retains most of the preceding theories.' It is in this light that we should regard Piaget's work. It is not that he has been proved wrong or right. An effort has been made in this paper to show that he is incorrect in respect of some matters while other aspects of his work are likely to have lasting value. His theory will certainly have to be amended but it is too early yet to say what form the new one will take.

References

Baylor, W. et al. (1973) An information processing model of some seriation tasks, *Canadian Psychologist*, 14, pp. 167–96
Cole, M. and Scribner, S. (1974) *Culture and Thought*. Wiley, London.
Duckworth, E. (1964) 'Piaget rediscovered', in Ripple, R. E. and Rockcastle, V. N. (eds), *Piaget Rediscovered*. Cornell University School of Education.
Ferriero, E. (1971) *Les relations temporelles dans le language de l'enfant*. Librairie Droz, Geneva.
Halford, G. S. (1972) The impact of Piaget on psychology in the seventies, in Bodwell, P. C. (ed) *New Horizons in Psychology*, vol. 2. Harmondsworth, Penguin.
Hooper, F. and Dihoff, R. E. (1975) *Multidimensional Scaling of Piagetian Task Performance*. Wisconsin Research and Developmental Centre for Cognitive Learning, Madison.
Hooper, F. and Sipple, T. S. (1975) *An Investigation of Matrix Task, Classificatory and Seriation Abilities*. Wisconsin Research and Development Centre for Cognitive Learning, Madison.
Inhelder, B. and Piaget, J. (1958) *The Growth of Logical Thinking from Childhood to Adolescence*. London, Routledge & Kegan Paul.
Inhelder, B. and Piaget, J. (1964) *The Early Growth of Logic in the Child*. London, Routledge & Kegan Paul.
Inhelder, B., Sinclair, H. and Bovet, M. (1974) *Learning and the Development of Cognition*. London, Routledge & Kegan Paul.
Klahr, D. and Wallace, J. C. (1975) *Cognitive Developments: An Information Processing View*. New York, Lawrence Erlbaum Associates.

Lovell, K. (1961) A follow-up study of Inhelder and Piaget's *The Growth of Logical Thinking*, Brit. *J. Psychol.*, 52, pp. 143–54.

Lovell, K. (1971) 'Some aspects of the growth of a concept of a function', in Rosskopf, M. F. et al., (eds.), *Piagetian Cognitive Development Research and Mathematical Education*. National Council of Teachers of Mathematics, Washington.

Luria, A. R. (1976) *Cognitive Development*. London, Harvard University Press.

Modgil, S. and Modgil, C. (1976) *Piagetian Research: Compilation and Commentary*. Windsor, National Foundation for Educational Research.

Neimark, E. D. (1974) 'Intellectual development during adolescence', in *Child Developmental Research*, vol. 4. London, University of Chicago Press.

Numero special en hommage à Jean Piaget (1974) *Archives de Psychologie*, no. 171, p. 44.

Piaget, J. (1936) *The Origins of Intelligence in Children*. London, Routledge & Kegan Paul, translated into English 1953.

Piaget, J. (1937) *The Construction of Reality in the Child*. London, Routledge & Kegan Paul, translated into English 1955.

Piaget, J. (1947) *The Psychology of Intelligence*. London, Routledge & Kegan Paul, translated into English 1950.

Piaget, J. (1950) 'Introduction à l'epistemologie genetique, II. La pensée physique' Presses Universitaires de France, Paris.

Piaget, J. (1953) *Logic and Psychology*. Manchester, Manchester University Press.

Piaget, J. (1960) 'The general problems of the psychobiological development in the child', in Tanner, J. M. and Inhelder, B. (eds), *Discussion in Child Development*, vol. 4. London, Tavistock Publications.

Piaget, J. (1963) 'Le langage et les operations intellectuelles', in J. de Ajuriaguerra et al. (eds), *Problemes de psycho-linguistique*. Paris, Presses Universitaires de France.

Piaget, J. (1970) *Genetic Epistemology*. Columbia University Press.

Piaget, J. (1971) *Structuralism*. London, Routledge & Kegan Paul.

Piaget, J. (1975) *L'equilibration des structures cognitive*. Paris, Presses Universitaires de France.

Piaget, J. (1976) On correspondence and morphisms, *The Genetic Epistemologist*, May issue.

Piaget, J. (1977) *The Grasp of Consciousness*. London, Routledge & Kegan Paul.

Piaget, J. and Inhelder, B. (1969) *The Psychology of the Child*. London, Routledge & Kegan Paul.

Piaget, J. et al. (1968a) *Epistemologie et psychologie de l'identité*. Paris, Presses Universitaires de France.

Piaget, J. et al. (1968b) *Epistemologie et psychologie de la fonction*. Paris, Presses Universitaires de France.

Riegel, K. F. and Rosenwald, G. C. (1976) (eds.) *Structure and Transformations: Developmental and Historical Aspects*. London, Wiley.

Sieler, R. S. (1977) 'Formal operational reasoning', *The Genetic Epistemologist*, October issue.

Sinclair-De-Zwart, H. (1967) *L'acquisition du langage et développement de la pensée sous-systèmes linguistiques et opérations concrètes*. Paris, Dunod.

Thomas, H. L. (1975) 'The concepts of function', in Rosskopf, M. F. (ed.), *Children's Mathematical Concepts*. London, Teachers College Press.

Tough, J. (1977) *The Development of Meaning.* London, George Allen and Unwin.

Tulkin, S. R. and Konner, M. J. (1973) Alternative conceptions of human functioning, *Human Development,* 16, pp. 33–52.

Wason, P. C. (1977) The theory of formal operations, in Geber, B. A. (ed.) *Piaget and Knowing.* London, Routledge & Kegan Paul.

Wason, P. C. and Johnson-Laird, P. N. (1972) *Psychology and Reasoning: Structure and Content.* London, Batsford.

3.4

AUSUBEL'S THEORY OF LEARNING AND ITS APPLICATION TO INTRODUCTORY SCIENCE

J.A.G. McClelland

Introduction

A central reason for teaching science is that, through science, children can gain understanding of a large part of their environment. By learning science they can put on conceptual 'spectacles' through which pattern and order may be imposed on otherwise chaotic and diverse phenomena and experiences. The more we have a theoretical grasp of how such learning takes place and how it fulfils this function, the better the position we will be in to make decisions about what to teach, when, and in what sequence. I believe that Ausubel's theory of learning (1968) provides a very useful framework for such decision making. To date, the theory is not widely understood nor appreciated, largely, I think, because it has been framed in very careful, but not particularly accessible, language. By re-expressing the ideas almost entirely without this careful, technical, language, I may well fail to do justice to the rigour and subtlety of the original and I shall inevitably distort it, but I hope that I shall convince you of its value and provide a bridge to it.

Ausubel's theory of learning

There is wide variety of changes in behaviour or capability which can be termed learning. Ausubel writes almost exclusively about a very restricted range, that of learning meanings expressed in symbols – mainly words. For

Sources: McClelland, J.A.G. (1982) Ausubel's theory of learning and its application to introductory science Part I Ausubel's theory of learning, *School Science Review*, 64, pp.157–161, and McClelland, J.A.G. (1982) Ausubel's theory of learning and its application to introductory science Part II Primary Science: an Ausubelian View, *School Science Review* 64, pp.353-357

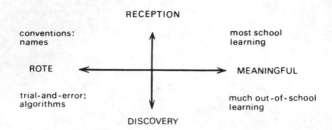

this reason, his theory is particulary relevant to school learning. He distinguishes two dimensions to the learning process, the degree of meaningfulness, and the mode in which the material is encountered. Learning is rote if it forms no link with anything but itself, has no ability to help further learning, and is learnt 'by heart'. Entirely meaningful learning fits into a network of other knowledge, extending both what is already known and what can be learnt. Probably no real learning is entirely rote nor entirely meaningful, but learning of nonsense syllables is very nearly rote, while arbitrary lists of symbols, like telephone numbers, can gain some measure of meaning through their connections with their owners.

Conditions for meaningful learning

For meaningful learning to take place, three conditions must be met:
A. The material itself must be meaningful, that is, it must make sense or conform to experience. (This does not mean that it has to be true. Something untrue can be learnt meaningfully.)
B. The learner must have enough relevant knowledge for the meaning in the material to be within grasp.
C. The learner must intend to learn meaningfully, that is, must intend to fit the new material into what is already known rather than to memorize it word-for-word.

Consider the following sets of words:

Na vlark es grum kerfland
Eu sou estopim da bomba
Hadrons are quarks bound by vector gluons

The first is invented and fails to meet A. It could only be learnt rotely. The second is the first line of a Brazilian song (I am the fuse of a bomb) and has as much inherent meaning as most such lines. It fails to meet B unless you understand Portuguese. The third meets A, but will meet B to different degrees according to how much sub-atomic physics you know. The rest of this article is intended to meet A and B. Condition C is up to you.

None of these conditions is as simple as it may appear at first sight. Material to be learnt may be inherently meaningful, as would usually be the case in a science lesson, but it still might be presented in an incoherent way, or in an unsuitable sequence. Relevant knowledge will vary from individual to individual and will be affected by experience. If your lesson involves dogs, Jane, whose uncle runs kennels, may not get your message because she is eager to display her knowledge or has noticed your misconceptions, while Billy, who was savaged by a dog last year, sits paralysed in silent horror. Learning is an individual, constructive, activity in which new material is related to what is already known, leading to an end product which is different for each person. Ausubel writes 'meaningful learning is not to be interpreted as the learning of meaningful material'. As teachers we may fall into this trap if we think of our teaching material as what the children are to learn. We actually produce as many different effects as there are learners, and this is as true in the sciences as anywhere else.

The intention to learn meaningfully is compounded from a variety of elements, most importantly the perception by the learner that it is worthwhile to make the effort. If word-for-word recall is required, say, in tests or examinations, this will promote rote learning. If the new material does not appear to have any relevance to the interests or needs of the learner (beyond those of achieving a quiet life in school) there will be no motivation to learn it in any form. If we teach sciences as though they were valuable *sui generis*, without making a convincing case for their usefulness, we are likely to face learners who do not meet condition C.

It may be noticed that the conditions do not specify the form taken by the learning encounter. This is seen as a separate dimension. Didactic presentation and discovery methods can equally range across the spectrum of meaningfulness. Something essentially arbitrary and minimally connected to any network of knowledge may be discovered, while highly meaningful material may be learnt through being heard or read. Many of the laboratory exercises which I carried out as a schoolboy and as a student, and which, for a while, I inflicted on another generation, essentially fell into the 'rote learning by discovery' quadrant of the figure.

Concepts

School learning has (or should have) little concern with real objects, but with concepts derived from them at different levels of abstraction. Wheeled trolleys are accelerated and rats are dissected, not because we want children to be knowledgeable about trolleys or the intestines of rats but because they may be used conveniently to exemplify more general ideas. The teacher's problem is to organize learning experiences so as to promote rapid and efficient meaningful learning of the underlying abstractions. Most areas of human understanding may be analysed into hierarchies of concepts of ever greater degrees of abstraction. A simple example is Rover, dog, mammal, vertebrate, chordate.

What is know by an individual is also organized hierarchically, but in this case it is not so neat, for concepts are shared across areas of knowledge, and different individuals have different structures covering the same general areas.

According to Ausubel it is the concepts at the highest level of abstraction in an individual's organized knowledge which are the most stable and useful. That is, they are the most resistant to forgetting and the most valuable for dealing with new situations. It is this ability to create high-level abstractions which gives human thought its power, and it will happen spontaneously if not guided. Children are natural theory-builders. Stable concepts are so because they are useful. Situations in which they are successfully marshalled deepen and extend their base. Situations in which they lead to inappropriate action lead to their modification or to avoidance behaviour. The higher the level of a concept the wider the range of its applicability to new situations and the more useful it becomes. The more common the situations to which it applies, the more it is used and stabilized. If what we teach is not, in fact, useful to an individual, this stabilizing effect will not take place.

High level concepts cannot be pinned down by simple definitions or lists of attributes. Much research on concepts has dealt with trivial examples such as identifying 'blue triangle' from among sets of coloured shapes. The relationship between this and the formation of a clear concept of 'force' or 'adaptation' is tenuous in the extreme. High-level concepts do not, in general, spring, fully armed, into the heads of their conceivers. They are developed, not accepted whole, and they may be more or less clear, cohesive, all-embracing, and applicable to new situations. My concept of energy is probably more elaborated in these respects than yours, since I have spent a great deal of time thinking about it, but your concept of monetarism may be sufficiently elaborated to enable you to appreciate cuts in educational spending which are incomprehensible to me. In both cases, it is a matter of degree, not of absolutes. High level concepts are more than means for coping with existence: they also determine what, of the myriad input of sensory data during waking hours, is perceived and paid attention. People with different concepts inhabit different worlds. Shelley's skylark blithely poured forth profuse streams of unpremeditated art· mine is on red alert defending its territory (which does not prevent me from enjoying the song).

Relatedness of new material to existing knowledge

The degree to which something new is potentially easy or difficult to learn depends on two factors: the internal complexity of the new material, and the relationship which it bears to what is already known and the way in which that knowledge is organized. These can be seen as separate dimensions. Consider the following statements (whose sources are immaterial).

> 'Maxwell proposed to station a demon, whom he endowed with a modest intelligence, at a small trap door in a partition between two gases with instructions to let fast-moving molecules , and only fast-moving molecules, pass through the door one way, and only slow-moving molecules through the other way.'

> 'As the configurational entropy of a solvent increases during an isothermal, isobaric, increase in solute concentration, the difference between the molar entropy of the solvent vapour and the molar entropy of the liquid solvent, with which the vapour was perhaps in equilibrium, decreases.'

These can be compared with the earlier statement 'Hadrons are quarks bound by vector gluons'. Of the three the short statement has least internal complexity, but possibly places the greatest demands on prior knowledge. The first quotation has more, but still low, complexity and demands little prior knowledge. The second, to me, is high on both counts. The direct effect of an increase in internal complexity on ease of learning is to increase the time required to process the information. For an individual there may be a ceiling to the degree of complexity which can be tolerated. In what follows it will be assumed that internal complexity is kept constant, and below such a ceiling.

Six levels of relatedness to pre-existing knowledge can be distinguished, each of which leads to different learning characteristics. The new material:

1. Could be derived or deduced from what is already known.
2. Is an extension, elaboration, or recoding of what is known.

3.   Draws together several concepts into one higher-level abstraction.
4.   Is inherently meaningful but cannot be directly nor specifically related to what is already known.
5.   Is inherently arbitrary and lacking in potential meaningfulness (or the learner approaches it in this way).
6.   Is inherently meaningful but denies or negates an existing stable, high-level, concept.

The characteristics of the learning which takes place in each case are as follows:
1.   Learning occurs rapidly and easily; there is relatively rapid loss of specific recall. This is not the same as forgetting, because, although it falls below a threshold of recall, subsequent relearning is even easier than before. If you have mastered Newton's laws, you must have experienced many examples of their use. Probably you cannot remember these specific examples (unless you recycle them in your teaching). You expect to be able to re-create them from your higher-level knowledge whenever necessary, and they are not retained as jumble in your available memory store. Higher level concepts wax fat and powerful by gobbling up their lower level counterparts.
2.   Not so easy nor rapid to learn: relatively long-lasting. An example is vocabulary learning in a second language.
3.   Provided the initial concepts are clearly held and the new material is successful in drawing them together, learning can be very rapid, with a 'Eureka' effect. The new concept becomes more stable than its predecessors which may become incorporated into it beyond specific recall. I no longer recall Bernouilli's formula, nor Kirchhoff's laws. I reconstruct them, where necessary, from the principles of conservation of energy and charge. I did not learn them that way.
4.   Very difficult to learn and liable to rapid forgetting unless links can be forged to create stability. More extensive comment is given below.
5.   Relatively easy to learn by heart in small amounts but rapidly becomes more difficult as the amount increases. Learning earlier material inhibits later learning, and vice versa, particularly if they are similar in any respect. As a general rule, the phenomenon known as negative transfer of learning is characteristic of, and confined to, this form. Forgetting is initially rapid and eventually almost complete. Relearning is then virtually no easier then initial learning (in sharp contrast to form 1). Longer term memorization requires multiple rehearsal, (overlearning). What constitutes 'a small amount' is variable. Total nonsense can be counted in syllables. Internally coherent

material can be tolerated in larger quantities. However, such material is unlikely to fit the description of form 5, that is, having *no* relationship with existing knowledge.

6. Most difficult of all, even painful, the more so the higher-level and more stable the concept with which the new material conflicts. This is the most powerful argument I can put forward against permitting children always to form their own concepts through unguided experience. I do not think it highly fanciful to argue that children's spontaneous ideas of physical reality are unlikely to be more appropriate to modern theory than those of Aristotle, nor that attempts to replace them, in circumstances where the new ideas do not seem, to the child, to matter very much, may lead to outright rejection of science. It seems to me to be no accident that the biological sciences, where theoretical ideas do not noticeably conflict with naive observation nor with human social behaviour, suffer less than the physical sciences where notions of atoms and forces fly in the face of everyday observation. In my own world-view, parapsychological phenomena are so contrary to its most all-embracing ideas that I have considerable difficulty giving serious attention to articles which are sympathetic to it. If I were forced to accept evidence of, for example, communication with the dead, it would be a deeply painful experience which might well shatter my intellectual self-confidence. If the arguments about learning in this article run counter to your cherished theories, you probably are experiencing a similar reaction.

Implications for teaching

Although children bring to school a great deal of knowledge and experience, the main long-term task is to develop high-level concepts with which to cope with their reality. Initially, in most areas, they will find themselves without an elaborated hierarchy of organized knowledge, and the required learning will fall into category 4.

The Ausubelian strategy for presenting such new material is to develop stable anchorage as quickly as possible by giving the learner a set of statements at a high level of generality, and then using specific instances to develop their meaning. Initially the general statements have little meaning, so the underlying concepts are vague and limited. Experience with the widest possible range of examples, specifically related to the statements, clarifies and refines them to the point where they can take over, putting new examples into category 2, and, eventually, category 1. At first the statements act as a clue that something worthwhile is to be learnt and act as a guide to what that learning will be like. If I wished to introduce 'moral education' into my classes I should attempt to crystallize my concepts of moral behaviour into a few powerful statements. Three which occur to me are 'Do unto others as you would that they should do unto you' (or Do-as-you-would-be-done-by'), 'Maximise the pleasure, minimize the pain', and 'Two wrongs don't make a right'. A wide range of tales and situations could be contrived or chanced upon through which to refine their meanings. If you are horrified by the moral position I imply, do not let this divert you from the point I am trying to make. Following an Ausubelian strategy does not mean that everyone will do the same thing. Your powerful statements may differ from mine, and what intent or serendipity would lead you to use as examples would certainly differ. The important point is that the learner should know the purpose of the examples and should be able to see the links between them. If you like, the learner would see the forest as well as the trees.

Agreeing with the strategy does not stifle arguments about readiness. I should not attempt to introduce quantum electrodynamics to 7-year-old children.

Where the learner already has knowledge to which an analogy can be drawn, the introduction can take the form of statements showing that analogy. In this case, when the concepts are being clarified, part of the process is to distinguish them from their analogues.

Ausubel and Piaget

The main differences, which I feel to be important, between an Ausubelian and a Piagetian view concern the interpretation of children's responses to tasks, and the role of verbally presented material in learning.

The responses of children to a variety of well-known tasks have been widely described (see for example Gruber and Vorèche, 1977). Apart from the fact that people are more strongly affected by the context in which a task is presented than had been realized initially (Donaldson, 1978; Freeman, Lloyd and Sinha, 1980) an Ausubelian interpretation would be in terms of the relevant organized knowledge to which the task could be related, rather than in terms of the attainment or non-attainment of broad stages of cognitive operations. To take the conservation of substance as an example, there may be a quite considerable structure of related concepts needed before a child could realize that plasticine is conserved in changes of shape. Naive observations of liquids evaporating or boiling away, balloons being blown up and bursting, sponges being squeezed, or people eating large meals and looking just the same, could lead to quite different suppositions about matter independently of any logical capabilities. The more directly important difference in this context is that advice to teachers based on Piaget's theories tends to stress action over verbalization and may even make a virtue of 'messing about' (Wadsworth, 1978). (Piaget's own writings include statements which appear to me to be both in favour of and contrary to the position outlined here.) An Ausubelian approach would stress the importance of activities and concrete experiences, not in and of themselves, but to give meaning to verbal propositions. It emphatically would not recommend 'chalk and talk' but would recognize that activity and verbal presentation can be, and should be, complementary.

Science

It is a cardinal principle of teaching that learners should not be misled. This extends not only to the content of what is taught but to the title under which it is taught. Hence, if we are going to tell children that we are teaching them science, we ought to be certain in our minds that we are doing just that. Whatever distinguishes science from other human activities should be present as a central feature of our course. Much of what passes for science at primary, and indeed secondary, level is wide open to criticism in this respect. This does not necessarily mean that I deplore what is taught. On the contrary much of it I find entirely admirable.

Science as an activity overlaps with other human activities, such as the systematic study of phenomena and the solution of technical problems. The overt features of all three of these may be indistinguishable to an outside observer. The unique distinguishing feature is the aim of the activity, and a science, whether physical, biological, social, or any other, aims to create theoretical models for phenomena. Each science involves methods or processes which are chosen for their applicability to the elucidation of the particular theoretical problems being tackled. These processes are the tools of the sciences, not their defining characteristics.

I am not trying to suggest that children should not learn processes such as observing, measuring, hypothesizing, and so on. Far from it: even in societies which would never be considered scientific, people must use many of them to survive. I draw upon them when I wrestle with my aged car, but I do not then feel that I am acting as a scientist nor even scientifically. Any artisan in the Dark Ages would have acted analogously. I use saws and chisels but this does not make me a carpenter not a sculptor. I become a carpenter when I build furniture (etc.) and a sculptor when I shape materials for aesthetic ends. The fact that my skill with either tool is strictly limited does not (I think) detract much from my use and appreciation of furniture and sculpture. Similarly, using the so-called processes of science does not make me a scientist. I become one when I tackle a scientific and therefore theoretical problem. If, like Einstein, I have no laboratory, I am not precluded from advancing science, and certainly not from learning it.

Learning science

If science consists of theories, learning science is learning theories and these theories are the content. It is, of course, entirely open to argument what methods, experiences, examples, and sequences may be appropriate to learning these theories, but if we are not attempting to teach them we are not attempting to teach science. The actual examples and exeperiences used are not the content but the vehicle for learning the content, as was pointed out above. You may well conclude that science, as I conceive it, should not be taught at primary school level. If so, I disagree with you, but, if I cannot persuade you by my arguments, I would ask you to call what remains by some other name.

Learning theories is entirely different from inventing them. Children learning science are not acting as little scientists. Newton modestly claimed that, if he had seen far, it was because he had stood on the backs of giants: children should be helped to reach the same point of vantage.

Applying Ausubel's theory

When any aspect of science is first introduced, its theoretical ideas will be unfamiliar to children. They will not possess organized knowledge and experience to which the ideas can be related directly. That is, it will fall into category 4, for which a general strategy has been outlined. The first task is to reduce it to key statements in language which is accessible to the learners. This does not mean that every word used must be within the existing vocabulary of the learner, nor does it mean that every word must be in common use in the society. A word which is unfamiliar to adults is no more difficult to learn than one which is familiar, if you have never met either of them. It is the concepts they express, and their degree of exemplification through experience, which determines their learnability. The key statements act as signals that something is to be learnt and act as a linking framework for specific examples and experiences.

The second task is to devise means for exemplifying the statements, showing their power to explain and impose coherence on perceptually different phenomena. The third is to alert the learner to examples in the environment, not contrived for teaching purposes, to which the ideas apply.

As the process continues the learner gradually moves from using the examples to give meaning to the key statements, to using the statements to understand new examples.

Primary science

A theory of learning cannot specify what it is that children ought to learn, nor is this self evident. Even if agreement is reached about general areas, there may be disagreement over their expression in key statements and over what experiences would exemplify them suitably. What follows necessarily represents my opinion. I see as important at all stages, three general concepts; energy, the particulate nature of matter, and adaptation, all of which I believe to be accessible to children before the age of 11 in a form which will enable them to impose coherence on much of their environment. The fact that most children would not acquire highly rigorous concepts capable of mathematical expression, does not worry me in the least. Continued quantification and refinement can take place at all stages and levels. Like justice, democracry, or beauty, these high-level but pervasive concepts are useful to all, across the spectrum from the most naive to the most sophisticated. To a large extent this concept of useful science agrees with that described by Booth (1980) and the ASE document (1979) although the detail may differ. Very brief indications of how I would approach the three general areas at primary level follow.

Energy

The following is a summary of a strategy which has been used with children in the age range 7–8 years (McClelland, 1970). The overall concept of energy was conceived as based on the following heirarchy written from high to low level.

conservation of energy
energy as an entity (the ability to cause changes)
class names of forms of energy
class names of properties: moving, elastic, hot, etc.
class names of specific objects used in examples

The key statements used were:

'Energy is the ability to makes changes'
'Energy is never lost or destroyed: it is changed from one form to another'

In addition a list of names of forms of energy; kinetic, potential (used for gravitational effects only), elastic, chemical, heat, light and sound was provided. A very large number of example of changes in which energy is transformed between pairs of these, and in both directions, can be contrived easily, mostly out of familiar objects and circumstances. It was found that, under individualized instruction (audiotutorial) conditions, five lessons each of about 15 minutes' duration could bring about very satisfactory learning outcomes. For example, many children could work out for themselves that, when a motor car is stopped, there must be heat energy produced at the brakes to compensate for the loss of kinetic energy, and I have already relayed an anecdote (McClelland, 1978) which transmits the flavour of what I understand by meaningful learning of a useful concept. Those with a background in physics may throw up their hands in horror at the absence of any mention of work. In attempting to define energy it is common to take work as the starting point. However, work, in its turn, depends on the very abstract and difficult notion of force. (If you think that force is not a difficult and abstract concept, I suspect that you do not know it very well: see for example, Warren, 1979.) The association of the concepts work and energy stems from their history of development and the preoccupations of the industrial revolution. This is not a valid reason for maintaining the link at the level of a definition, and as I have partly argued before (McClelland, 1978) the notion of work is not particularly useful when considering transformations other than between kinetic and potential energy.

Adaptation

There are many very useful and interesting activities which can be carried out using plants and animals but in the absence of a linking framework, these can be experienced as isolated and incoherent. The key statements which I have used with children in the age range 7–8 years to provide such a framework, are as follows:

Plants and animals have to solve three problems:
1. How to get food.
2. How to avoid being eaten.
3. How to breed.

Different shapes, sizes and ways of doing things help them to solve these problems and to live in the places where you find them.

Each of these problems throws up a set of questions which give shape and meaning to even the most naive study of any organism. Children can take them with them and use them, out of school as well as within, to impose pattern on their environment.

Particles

Of the three general areas, this is the one on which I should spend initially least time and effort. It has been shown (Keislar and McNeil, 1961) that quite young children can form usable concepts of molecules, but I consider this area to have the least initial accessibility and explanatory power of the three, because the evidence for it is largely by inference and analogy. However, the terms 'molecule' and 'cell' are widely used and are very likely to be encountered by primary school children so, at the very least, it would appear unwise to ignore them completely.

Examples of key statements would be:

Everything is made up of a very small pieces called molecules.

What we see, feel, and smell depends on what sort of molecules there are, and how they are organized.

Different materials are made up of different molecules.

Living things have special large groups of molecules called cells.

Different parts of plants and animals are made up of different cells.

Mathematics, technology and nature study

At the ASE Annual Conference 1979, Roy Richards gave a talk about primary science, in which as an example, he described how children found a value for the areas of their bodies by cutting and fitting paper shapes which were then flattened out. This is splendid mathematics, but I see no science in it. Indeed, anything which is a measurement for measurement's sake, should it be temperature, volume, weight, or the time taken for snails to cross different surfaces, is mathematics rather than science. I am entirely happy that children should do these things, learn from them, and enjoy them, but unless they are carried out for purposes which are themselves embedded in science, I do not want them carried out under that rubric. In fairness, it may be added that Roy Richards (1973) has written that '. . . discovery science with young children is not science in the usual meaning of the word'. The Schools Council project

Progress in Learning Science has been included under 'Mathematics for young children' in one review (Cooper and Whitfield, 1980). Evans (1977) has described a set of experiences under the general title of technology which, apart from the specificity of the objectives and procedure, might have appeared in almost anyone's recommended primary science course. I very much admire these also, and feel entirely happy that they should be correctly named for once, but I felt, reading the report, that some of the activities cried out for a theoretical framework as I have suggested.

Presst (1976) and Conran (1980) have argued the merits of Nature Study and regret its apparent eclipse. Again, I do not wish to decry its use, in its place, but this I see more as a stimulus to expressive writing and to artwork than to science. An extended and illustrated argument about the use of the natural environment in this way has been provided by Anderson and McQuillen (1980).

Practicalities

What happens in classrooms is both what teachers see as valuable, and what they feel capable of doing. Those who have not achieved success in school science are unlikely to view themselves as qualified to teach it at any level–nor is it easy to pay more than lip-service to the value of what is not understood by one's self. However, an approach which is initially non-numerical and which is accessible to a primary school child should be very much more readily accessible to an adult, so a relatively short course should suffice to satisfy both objections, whether in-service or pre-service. Short courses which put teachers through the same sort of atheoretical and incoherent experiences as have been argued against for children, are unlikely to have more than brief effects on practice.

My own experience, involving both direct classroom teaching and the use of individualized instruction, convinces me that the services of a peripatetic expert are not the solution. Both the success stories I have cited, on energy and particles, involved individualized instruction. I have found, under classroom conditions, that the degree of continuous attention I have been able to obtain, and the number of examples which I have been able to deal with in a short period of time, has been much reduced, to the point where much of the message has not been received. I believe that successful instruction in science at primary level would be best achieved through relatively short bursts of individualized, or at least machine-based, teaching materials, concentrating on development of theory, interspersed with normal classroom activities, both serving to exemplify and further elaborate the theories and giving opportunities for mathematical and technological development. In contrast with what I asserted about science I believe that children solving technological problems can be little technologists. Films and videotapes have an obvious role to play, although direct interaction with real objects is central to the learning process. The greater level and span of concentration reported when children use microprocessors (e.g. *The Times Educational Supplement*, 23 April 1980) fits with my speculation that human contact may sometimes be actually dysfunctional when young children are attempting to acquire abstract concepts. As Donaldson (1978) has reported, children's responses to tasks are affected by context and answers given to adults may differ from those purportedly given to a toy panda. Understanding and coping with adults may be too important to permit concentration on the formation of other high level, abstract, concepts. In contrast, it is quite clearly possible and appropriate to teach skills so there is plenty for the teacher to do.

While the focus of this article has been on primary science, the theoretical framework is applicable at any level. Where pupils enter secondary school without any understanding of theory it has obvious relevance to the design of science courses to be offered to them. The prerequisites for teaching purposes, that the teacher should know in advance the relationship of each learning task to what is known by each student and that the teacher should be able to justify the inclusion of each learning experience in terms of high level abstractions it helps to form, are challenges to all.

References

Anderson, D. and McQuillen, B. (1980) *Mud, Daisies and Sparrows: Exploring Outdoor Environments*. Nafferton Books.

ASE (1979) *Alternatives for Science Education*, ASE.

Ausubel, D.P. (1968) *Educational Psychology: a Cognitive View*. New York, Holt, Rinehart & Winston.

Booth, N. (1980) An approach to primary science, *Education 3-13*, 8, 1.

Conran, R.J. (1980) Nature study: its rehabilitation, *Education 3-13*, 8, 2.

Cooper, K. and Whitfield, K. (1980) Mathematics for young children – a comparison of three Schools' Council projects, *Curriculum*, 2, 1, 35–40.

Donaldson, M. (1978) *Children's Minds*. Fontana.

Evans, P. (1977) Technology in the primary school, *School Science Review*, 205, 58, 635–57.

Freeman, N., Lloyd, S. and Sinha, C. (1980) Hide and seek is child's play, *New Scientist*, 30 October 1980.

Gruber, H. and Vorèche, J. (1977) *The Essential Piaget: an Interpretative Reference and Guide*. Routledge & Kegan Paul.

Keislar, E.R. and McNeil, J.D. (1961) Teaching scientific theory to first grade pupils by an auto-instructional device, *Harvard Educational Review* 31, 71–83.

McClelland, J.A.G. (1970) *An Approach to the Development and Assessment of Instruction in Science at Second Grade Level: the Concept of Energy,* unpublished PhD thesis, Cornell University

McClelland, J.A.G. (1978) The teaching of energy, *School Science Review,* 211, 60, 369–70.

Presst, B. (1976) Science education: a reappraisal, *School Science Review,* 203, 58, 203–9.

Richards, R. (1973) The swinging of a pendulum: discovery science with young children, *Education 3–13,* 1.

Wadsworth, B. (1978) *Piaget for the Classroom Teacher.* New York, Longman Inc.

Warren, J.W. (1979) *Understanding Force.* John Murray.

PART FOUR

Research Approaches

Introduction

This part consists of papers describing research projects into how children learn science.

The first paper describes the results of the Survey of Science in Schools at Age 11 carried out by the Assessment of Performance Unit. This provides a revealing snapshot of the abilities which a typical pupil will have developed by age 11, and as such is a useful document for any teacher of primary science.

The other three papers are examples of the alternative frameworks school of science education research. The Driver paper describes the general approach of research workers in this area. The Watts paper describes the application of an interesting research methodology, the 'interview about instances' approach to studying the alternative frameworks pupils use to interpret the meaning of the scientific term 'force'. The Black and Solomon paper describes the meanings that pupils ascribe to the word 'energy', a core topic in many primary science schemes.

These last three papers do not provide prescriptions for the improvement of teaching of these topics, but illustrate the folly of assuming that pupils who have not received formal teaching of certain topics will not have developed their own notions of their meaning.

4.1

SCIENCE AT AGE 11

Wynne Harlen

1. Introduction

In 1980 and 1981 the Assessment of Performance Unit carried out the first of a series of surveys in England, Wales and Northern Ireland designed to assess children's performance in science at the age of 10-11 years. Full details of the surveys are provided in the reports listed at the end of this paper.

This paper presents a summary of the main findings which are likely to be of most interest to teachers and some conclusions drawn from them which have implications for practice. These form the two sections immediately following this introduction. The categories of performance which were assessed are listed in secion 4, followed by examples of test questions and children's responses in section 5.

The view of primary science which the surveys attempt to reflect is that it is

● a rational way of finding out about the world, involving the development of a willingness and ability to seek and use evidence;
● the gradual building of a framework of concepts which help to make sense of experience;
● the fostering of skills and attitudes necessary for investigation and experimentation.

Source: Harlen, W. (1980) Science at Age 11: APU Science Report for Teachers. London, Assessment of Performance Unit, pp. 5–32. Reproduced with permission of the controller of HMSO

The process skills, attitudes and concepts which are implied in this description were identified (and are given in section 4) and tests were devised to assess them.

Practical tests were used to give information about the children's:

- ability to perform investigations;
- skill in observing
- ability to use simple measuring instruments and equipment;
- reactions to science-based activities.

Written tests were used to assess the children's ability to:

- plan investigations;
- interpret and explain information given in the question, by making use of patterns in the data or suggesting hypotheses;
- use graphs, tables and charts.

When children carry out practical tests it is possible to observe what they can actually do rather than what they can express in writing. Thus special importance is attached to these results.

2.   Main findings

The surveys provide information about children's performance in the tests, about their reactions to science activities and about the provision for science in the schools. The main results under each of these headings are summarized below.

Children's performance

Most 11 year olds
— set about practical investigations in a relevant manner
— observed broad similarities and differences between objects
— read the scales of simple measuring instruments correctly
— classified objects on the basis of observed properties
— read information from flow charts, tables, pie charts and isolated points from line graphs.

About half 11 year olds

— reported results consistent with the evidence from their investigations
— were more fluent at observing differences than similarities between objects
— made predictions based on observations
— suggested controls in planning parts of investigations
— used given information to make reasonable predictions
— applied science concepts to solve problems
— proposed alternative hypotheses to explain a given phenomenon
— added information to a partially completed graph or chart.

Few 11 year olds

— repeated measurements or observations to check results
— controlled variables necessary to obtain good quantitative results
— recorded the observation of fine details of objects
— produced an adequate plan for a simple investigation
— gave good explanations of how they arrived at predictions
— described patterns in observations or data in terms of general relationships.

Children's reactions

In practical tests the children showed that they like and are interested in science activities. They were very willing to be involved in all types of investigations with both living and non-living things. They appeared equally willing to tackle written tests. On the other hand there was little evidence of children considering their own work in a critical, reflective way.

The survey results suggested that, at this age, differences in performance between the sexes were not marked and did not follow a clear pattern. Girls were slightly ahead in using graphs, tables and charts and in making observations of similarities and differences. They were also better at planning investigations and in recording descriptions of events during investigations. This could be related to girls' greater fluency in written language at this age. Boys, on the other hand, were ahead in using measuring instruments, in applying physical science concepts to problems and in recording quantitative results in investigations.

Provision for science activities

Schools taking part in the surveys were asked to complete a questionnaire which included questions about the provision for science activities. The replies showed that 85 percent of schools included science activities in the curriculum, spending, on average, about 5 percent of lesson time on them. The topics covered range from nature study and other biological topics such as 'ourselves' to physical science including electricity and the properties of air and water. An impression of the material resources available to support the work may be gained from the information that schools spend an average of 5 percent of their capitation on science. About 50 percent of the schools overall (78 percent of middle schools, 42 percent of junior and 22 percent of junior with infant) reported that a member of staff had a post of responsibility for science. Most schools organized the work so that all of the children in a class were engaged on science activities at the same time, though working in groups and often on different problems.

Two separate lists in the questionnaire were used to collect information about the degree of emphasis which the schools give to various science-based activities and the goals which teachers consider to be most important. The schools were given a list of 18 science-based activities and asked to select eight which they emphasized most in their work with 10–11 year olds. What was found is shown on the following page.

Similar results were obtained when the schools were asked to select the goals which they thought were most important. The greatest emphasis was given to making observations, recording them and drawing conclusions. Those goals concerned with the identification of variables, designing experiments, the need to repeat measurements and the critical examination of experimental methods generally received much lower priority.

3.   Implications for practice

The general picture emerging of children's performance is that they seem to be doing better in the general skills which are important in all parts of the curriculum but less well in the skills more specifically related to science activities. The close relationship between the kinds of activities most frequently emphasized in schools and performance of pupils, suggests that high performance in the general skills may be the result of emphasis on activities which promote these. At the same time the low performance in the more science-specific skills may well result from lack of opportunities to develop these skills.

There are many ways in which the same topic can be pursued, leading to different kinds of learning experiences for the children, which are illustrated by the following example of work reported by one of the survey schools. It began with a visit to the docks and led to children designing and making their own balsa wood boats. These children had opportunity to observe the similarities and differences between boats and to try to explain these observations in terms of size, weight and function of different boats. Back in school they discussed their observations with each other and with their teacher as a preliminary to designing their boats. To test their ideas they had

What teachers emphasise in science-based activities with 10/11 year olds (1980 results)

% schools

	0	10	20	30	40	50	60	70	80	90	100
Make careful observations at first hand											
Make a satisfactory written record of their work											
Make notes of observations/results during work											
Draw conclusions from results or make generalizations based on observations											
Follow carefully written instructions											
Use scientific words correctly											
Estimate a measurement before taking it											
Apply scientific knowledge to different problems											
Pay careful attention to demonstrations											
Check results using reference books where possible											
Decide on the problem they wish to investigate											
Repeat any measurements/readings to reduce error											
Identify variables operating in certain situations											
Design their own experiments											
Choose what kind of record to make of their work											
Examine work critically for flaws in experimental method											
Incorporate controls in experiments											
Read about experiments which it is not possible for them to carry out											

to consider what factors might affect the result, how to make the test 'fair', what they would measure to make a comparison and how the result would be found out.

This planning might not have taken place before starting to do anything; more likely it went on whilst the boat-making was in progress and even when tests on the boats were under way. Tests may well have been begun again because someone pointed out that the comparison was not fair (there were variables not controlled). During these activities the pupils would gain experience in observing, interpreting and using equipment – that is, in most of the process skills being assessed – and probably more besides. They would also have had a chance to learn from experience about how to carry out an investigation.

By contrast the school might have decided to follow up the visit with only limited involvement in scientific acitivities. A description of the docks, a picture, an account of where ships were coming from and going to, what they were carrying, imaginative writing about life on a ship – there is so much to pursue that the scientific aspects can easily be squeezed out. If this happens, of all the science process skills which might have been developed through the topic, the children's experience reduces to 'observing'.

The survey results would support the belief that this narrowing of potentially rich science experience to observation and recording often does happen.

To guard against this schools might review their teaching methods by asking how the work can best be presented to develop science process skills. A school might develop its own list of questions to guide its planning. For example, it might ask 'How far will the teaching approach enable the teacher to:

- encourage children to design their own approaches to solving problems and allow them to try out their ideas;
- discuss with the children the progress of their investigations and encourage them to discuss with each other;
- discuss the children's results and challenge them to show how they were worked out from the evidence;
- listen to children's ideas and probe their 'wrong' responses; encourage them to explain their reasons for their ideas; use this knowledge in planning further activities for the children;
- help children to review critically their practical procedures and to consider alternative strategies for solving problems or investigating?'

The help which individual children require will vary according to their development of science process skills, concepts and attitudes. However the survey findings indicate that it may be useful to bear in mind that:

- girls may need more encouragement to take an *active* part in science activities, especially in using equipment and making measurements;
- boys may need guidance in recording their procedures systematically and describing their experiments so that others can follow what they have done.

When considering the content of work it is helpful to recognize that some of the process skills can be used in relation to a wide range of content, in topics in many areas of the curriculum. Observation is an obvious example. Other process skills are likely to be more specifically related to science topics, where the natural and physical environment is being explored. Design and performance of investigations are examples here. In all cases, however, the content of the activity and the process skills interact. Through using process skills children build up ideas about what they are observing or investigating. These ideas are the ones they use in further observation or investigation and will affect the use of these process skills; for example, children 'observe' not everything that is in a certain situation but that which their present ideas suggest to them is relevant – if details are not thought important, then they don't 'see' details – and in their investigations they will control as variables in a 'fair' test those things which past experience has suggested to them may affect the result.

So process skill, attitude and concept development proceed hand in hand. The foundations of process skills can be – and the APU results suggest that they are being – laid in practical activities across the curriculum. As children get older, however, it is important for them to apply the process skills to content from which science concepts can be formed as well as in other topics. Through using the process skills the ideas will be learned with understanding and, at the same time, the ideas will enable the skills to develop into science process skills.

4. Assessing science process skills, attitudes and concepts

To find out about children's performance in the various skills, attitudes and concepts involved in science activities the APU surveys divide science performance at the age of 11 into separate categories and sub-categories as follows:

Category	Sub-categories
1. Symbolic representation	Reading information from graphs, tables and charts. Representing information as graphs, tables and charts.
2. Use of apparatus and measuring instruments	
3. Observation	Making and interpreting observations.
4. Interpretation and application	Interpreting presented information. Distinguishing degrees of inference. Applying science concepts to make sense of new information. Generating alternative hypotheses.
5. Design of investigations	Planning parts of investigations Planning entire investigations Identifying or proposing testable statements.
6. Performance of investigations	

This is only a framework for *assessment*; as discussed in the previous section, it is important that in *teaching* the different skills and ideas are developed in unison. It is also recognized that in a nationwide survey not everything that is important can be included, though what is included must be important.

The examples of test questions which follow illustrate the types of question used to assess some of these categories and sub-categories. They are just a few of the many questions used in the 1980 and 1981 survey, which in turn are a sample only of the large bank of test questions which have been developed. More examples are published in the full reports of the surveys listed at the end of this paper. The description of the children's responses provide some illustration of the kind of evidence from which the findings summarized earlier were drawn.

5.   Examples of test questions and children's responses

Practical tests

Performing investigations. Six practical investigations were used in each survey. The children were assessed individually, each carrying out three investigations. The testers (who were teachers released from school and trained by the survey team) used check-lists to note down details of what the children did and how they reacted to the activity. As part of the individual testing the children were also assessed in the use of certain simple measuring instruments and equipment, such as a thermometer, a stop-clock and a hand lens. Thus information was gathered about performance in category 2 as well as category 6.

The example below outlines briefly the administration and results for one of them. The pupils found this the easiest and the quickest investigation to carry out. The pupil was handed three balls and told:

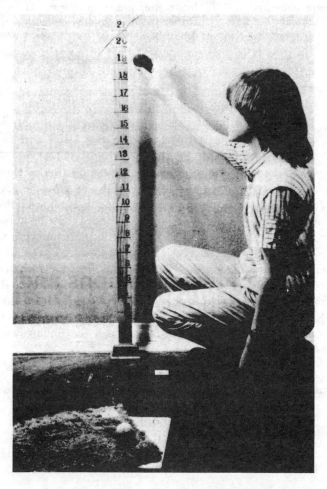

'In this question you will be finding out how well these balls bounce on different surfaces. Would you like to try to see how well they bounce on the floor first of all?'

The pupil tried bouncing the balls on the floor and then discussed with the tester whether they all bounced equally well.

Three squares of material were then shown and the tester said:

'Now I wonder if the balls rebound the same amount on these three different surfaces. This is something you can find out. Here is a carpet tile, a sheet of rubber and a sheet of plastic foam. Try all of these and see if the ball that bounces best on one is also the best bouncer on all of them. You may find this ruler on the stand useful and you can use it if you want to'.

When the tester was satisfied that the pupil had understood the problem, the practical work began. The tester observed the child and used the check-list to note features of the general approach, the attention to variables, and the recording of results. After the investigation had been completed the tester discussed it with the pupil to clarify some aspects of what he or she had done.

Generally a very large majority of the children found an appropriate way of tackling the problem by applying similar tests to each of the materials. Many recorded the results on the paper supplied. When the aspects of performance relating to a more specifically scientific approach to the problem were necessary the level of success was much lower. Few pupils correctly controlled variables or repeated observations or measurements as a routine check.

The children's reactions were noted during the investigations. About three-quarters of the pupils showed real interest and approached the tasks with deliberate and thoughtful actions. Less than 5 percent of the pupils appeared 'bored, uninterested or scared'. The level of the children's interest was broadly similar in all six of the investigations which were used and there were no consistent differences between boys and girls in this respect.

The children's 'willingness to be critical of procedures used' in the investigation was assessed. About one quarter suggested ways of improving their investigation to make it 'fairer'. Forty percent seemed uncritical of what they had done even after the discussion during which hints about possible improvements might well have been picked up. A possible explanation is that these children did not have the experience of carrying out an investigation in a scientific manner and so had no basis for criticizing what they had done. However, relationships between school experience, performance in investigations and willingness to be critical are still being explored.

Pupils' Paper

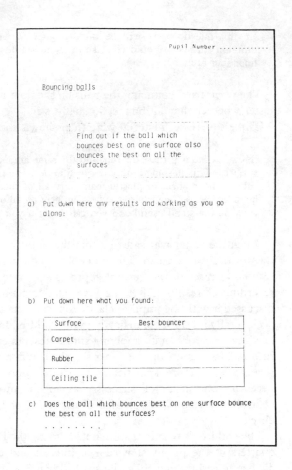

The care which children take in handling living things was noted in two investigations in 1981 using snails and woodlice. Only a small proportion (3 percent for snails and 7 percent for woodlice) treated the animals as if they were inanimate and the large majority handled them with care and without dislike. About half of the girls, but only a quarter of the boys, avoided touching the woodlice.

Observation. The tests concerned with making and interpreting observations were given to children in small groups. The children were provided with objects to handle or asked to look at drawings, photographs or moving film.

In the example below children had to use their sense of touch by putting their fingers through a slit in a box to feel the pieces of material glued inside. The illustration (extracted from the report of the 1980 survey) shows the question page on which the pupils wrote their answers.

Materials given to pupils

Results

(a) 90% correct
Most common error
'metal'

(b) 15% mentioned two or
more properties. 71%
mentioned one property.
5% gave no response to
this part

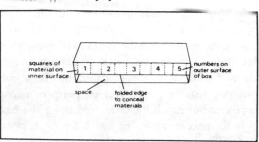

Inside the box behind each number there is a thin square
which may be made of:

glass
metal
wood
leather
rubber

Put your fingers in the box and feel the squares.

a)   Decide which is <u>rubber</u>.
Write down the number in front of the one
you think is rubber:

b)   How did you decide it was this one?

. . . .

. . . .

. . . .

. . . .

Question page

The tester showed the pupils how to put their fingers into the box through the slit to touch the squares of material on the inside of the numbered surface. The tester then presented the question in the following words:

'For this question you use your fingertips to feel the surfaces inside the box behind the numbers, like this. Stuck on the inside there are thin squares of five different things: glass, metal, wood, leather and rubber. By feeling them only (don't try to peep!) decide which one is rubber. When you have decided put down the number which is in front of the one you think is rubber. Then write down at (b) how you decided it was this one'.

In this and similar questions the pupils tended to make broad general observations rather than observations of finer details. In questions where explanations of observations has to be given as well as noting the observations, the children performed better in making the observations than in explaining them. Similarly, in questions about classification, where objects had to be grouped together, the level of performance was high in *grouping* objects correctly but much lower in *explaining* the basis of the classification.

In the next example, for which a short film excerpt was shown, the children had difficulty in selecting the correct group and *explaining* their reasons for their choice. The film showed objects being sorted into three groups, A, B and C:

A	B	C
Paperweight	Wooden cube with hole	Die
Coaster	Flat wood with hole	Wooden cube
10 p	Plastic bead	Metal cube
Draught	Bracelet	Wooden triangle
Metal cylinder	Wooden circle with hole	Cassette box

At the end of the sorting a ball and key were left. The children had to say where these fitted best and to give a reason.

Results

(a) 43% chose B which was the group of objects with the holes in them. 23% chose 'none of these groups'.

(b) 9% gave a complete and acceptable answer. Other responses were 'There is nothing else of the same shape in any of the groups', 'It is not a regular shape', 'Because most of the groups had 1 2 3 4 or 6 sides something like that'.

(c) 50% chose A. 9% chose 'none of these groups.'

(d) 1% correct. Other responses were 'It fits into Group B because it is round', 'It begins with the letter B and most of the things which begin with B were put into group B', 'It is a solid shape', 'Group C has plastic things in it'.

a) The key fits into:

    Group A
    Group B
    Group C
    None of these groups

key

b) Because ·
· ·

c) The ball fits into:

    Group A
    Group B
    Group C
    None of these groups

ball

d) Because ·
· ·
· ·

Question page

Written tests

Planning investigations. The planning of investigations was assessed for the first time in 1981 so the results have to be regarded as rather more tentative than those obtained in other categories, where they are based on the evidence of two surveys. The questions tested the ability to plan, wholly or in part, an investigation to solve a problem or test an hypothesis.

In questions concerning the general way of approaching an investigation the performance was higher than in questions asking about controls or for criticisms of investigations which lacked controls. Performance was low where children were asked to propose a whole plan, rather than parts of one, and again there was a pronounced difference in success in the more general parts of the plan than in attention to controls and explanation of how results might be found.

One example was:

During a lesson at school some children put a ring of salty water around a snail on a desk.
They noticed that the snail would not move across the salty water.

> Bill said: The snail will not cross
> because of the water.
> Mary said: The snail will not cross
> because of the salt in the water.

What tests would you do to find out who was right?
You may draw if it helps.

An acceptable approach was proposed by half of the children, but most failed to add those details of controls and interpretation which would be needed to make the test fair. Only a small proportion accepted the invitation to 'draw if it helps' and the drawings were usually additional to the words rather than a substitute for them. For example:

I would put water on it's own
round the snail and see is it
would move, then I would put
salt on it's own and see is it
would move.

water on it's own.

Salt on it's own.

In marking the scripts, three types of approach which the children proposed were regarded as acceptable ways of tackling the problem. In order of popularity these were:

Put a ring of water round the snail and then a ring of salt and see
   which it crosses   33%
Put a ring of water round the snail and then a ring of salty water
   and see which it crosses   8%
Put a ring of water round the snail   5%

A very low proportion (4 percent) suggested repeating the trials to confirm the results, as in the following example:

put the same snail in a ring of
pure water and find out if it crosses
if it does Mary will be right. But if
it does not cross Bill will be right.
To Put different snails in a ring of salt, then
pure water.

Very few possible variables were controlled in the pupils' answers and half of the answers made no mention at all of keeping anything the same in successive trials. Only one or two pupils mentioned the radius and/or the width of the ring of water or salt and a few mentioned keeping the surface on which the snail was moving the same. The one control that was frequently suggested (by 47 percent) was that the snail should be the same when different substances were tried. Two percent of pupils said that the snail and the surface should be the same.

The interpretation of the result of the investigation was an area in which children's answers were weak. About 10 percent indicated that, having set up two different rings round the snail, they would be able to find their result by seeing which it would go across. Seven percent made more elaborate statements showing how the matter would be decided by reasoning based on observations:

put a ring of salty water round
the snail if the snail does not move
across put a ring on normal water
around the snail if it moves across its
because of the salt. If it doesn't move across
it because of the water

Many answers were not expressed clearly enough to show what interpretation would follow (e.g. 'see what it does', 'see if it crosses'). Some who proposed placing the snail directly on water and salt, or salty water thought they would be able to judge which the snail liked or disliked more. Almost 60 percent of pupils failed to make any suggestion as to how the results would be found from the situation they had set up.

Interpreting information. In these tests the children were presented with information which they had to use to define patterns, to make predictions or to draw conclusions. The results showed that children could more easily use information to make or select a prediction than to explain how they used the information in their answer.

Question page

Results

(a) 73% were correct (stones), 5% ticked swing, 2% field, 6% tap, 2% slide.

(b) 30% gave full explanation, mentioning 'dampness and darkness'. Many mentioned only damp or dark.

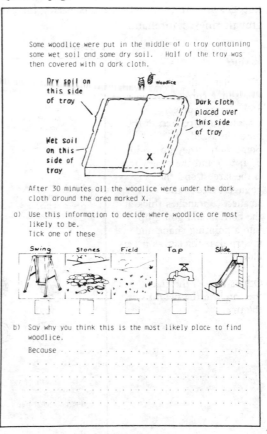

Some woodlice were put in the middle of a tray containing some wet soil and some dry soil. Half of the tray was then covered with a dark cloth.

Dry soil on this side of tray

Woodlice

Dark cloth placed over this side of tray

Wet soil on this side of tray

X

After 30 minutes all the woodlice were under the dark cloth around the area marked X.

a) Use this information to decide where woodlice are most likely to be.
Tick one of these

Swing   Stones   Field   Tap   Slide

b) Say why you think this is the most likely place to find woodlice.
Because . . . .

This is illustrated in the findings for the question above. All the information required for answering the question is given, apart from the everyday knowledge that woodlice are living things which can move about. The illustrations in part (a) of the question page contain relevant information and need to be examined carefully. For example, it is made clear that the tap could provide dampness but little shade, whilst the slide, not being on grass, could provide shade but not dampness. However the mark scheme did allow for credit to be given if a pupil selected a place other than the stones *and* gave a good reason for doing so in part (b).

A question on growth rings presented information through diagrams about tree growth rings. It was not necessary for pupils to know anything about growth rings beforehand.

Question Page

Results

27% related all relevant data in a single correct response. 19% gave a 'correct' response, not related to the question asked.
Some were: 'they go up in 3, 4, 5, 7 and the oldest tree is the largest and the youngest tree is the smallest', 'branches thick at the bottom and going up into a pointing shape and the trunk is thicker as it gets older'.

Others related the size of the trunk to the height of the tree.

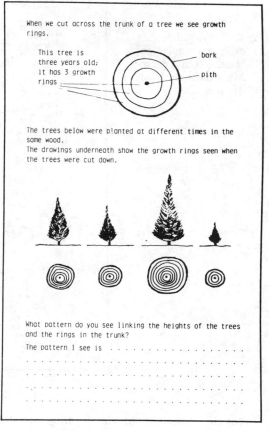

When we cut across the trunk of a tree we see growth rings.

This tree is three years old; it has 3 growth rings

bark

pith

The trees below were planted at different times in the same wood.
The drawings underneath show the growth rings seen when the trees were cut down.

What pattern do you see linking the heights of the trees and the rings in the trunk?
The pattern I see is . . . .
. . . .
. . . .
. . . .
. . . .

Only a small proportion of pupils described the pattern in the data in terms of a general statement covering all the information.

Applying science concepts in interpreting information. In these tests the emphasis was on *applying* concepts to help in the interpretation of information. None of the questions asked for the straight recall of scientific knowledge or concepts. In the following example the concept concerned the type of information detected by the various senses.

This was one of the few questions where the context of the question was the pupils themselves. They had to apply the general idea that different senses detect different kinds of information about the environment.

Results

(a) 59% were correct (the pie)

(b) 36% gave the correct answer – they could feel it with their hands.

Incorrect responses varied from 'three of them can smell it, three can see it and that is why I chose this one', to 'the hot drink with no steam rising' (he chose the incorrect response for (a)).

Others answered that 'soap is normal scented', missing the point of the question.

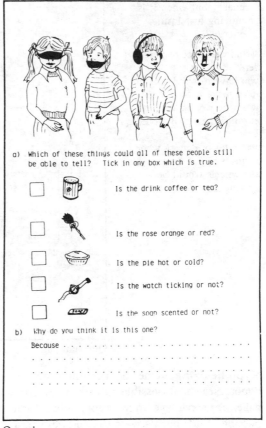

a) Which of these things could all of these people still be able to tell? Tick in any box which is true.

☐ Is the drink coffee or tea?

☐ Is the rose orange or red?

☐ Is the pie hot or cold?

☐ Is the watch ticking or not?

☐ Is the soap scented or not?

b) Why do you think it is this one?

Because . . . .
. . . .
. . . .
. . . .

Question page

In a question dealing with the transfer of energy children again encountered problems in explaining their response. To give a satisfactory answer to the example pupils had to use the idea that a wound spring is a source of energy.

Results

(a) 50% ticked B correctly.

(b) Less than 10% gave a correct reason, such as 'winding gives the car energy but when it is moving it is losing energy.'

Partially correct responses were:
'you have to wind it up to make it go'
'when he wound it up and let go of the key it would go faster'
'had a lot of energy when wound up'
'the wheels would be wearing down'.

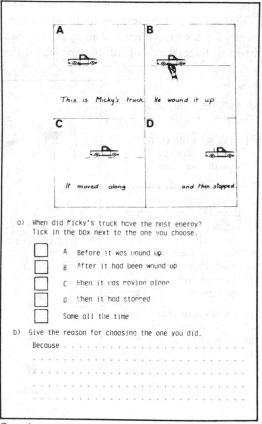

Question page

Hypothesizing. One of the questions which asked pupils to create hypotheses about possible reasons for given events is reproduced on the next page. In some everyday events more than one plausible explanation is possible. Such events were the basis of questions used to test the children's ability to suggest more than one explanation.

The children were able to offer alternative hypotheses. However, their responses suggest that many children do not try to explain events which may be observed in daily life in terms of scientific concepts. In the example below, the two hypotheses most frequently given suggested similar causes but one mentioned only the grass and the other only the ploughed field. The former was that the snow rests on the blades of grass which hold it up where it can be seen and the latter that the ploughed field has ridges or furrows into which the snow falls and cannot be seen.

Results

Most reasons, or hypotheses, were based on the different surface characteristics of the field.

A small proportion mentioned the soil might soak up the snow more than grass or that snow soaks into the earth without mentioning what happens on grass.

Similar small proportions of children mentioned that soil might be warmer than grass and so melt the snow, or that the snow might melt without suggesting how this might happen.

Some suggested that someone or something, often the wind, had moved the snow from the field.

Others said that Jane was mistaken. 13% of responses gave reasons in terms of the existence of the circumstances which were presented – that it was 'because of the grass' or 'because of the ploughing' or were irrelevant in suggesting that the areas were different.

The drawing shows two fields next to each other, one freshly ploughed and one covered with grass. After a snow storm Jane could see more snow on the grass than on the ploughed field.

Before snow   After snow

Grass   Ploughed   Grass   Ploughed

Think of two different reasons why Jane could see more snow on the grass. Write the first at a) and the second at b).

a) It could be because . . . .
   . . . .
   . . . .
   . . . .

b) Or it could be because . . . .
   . . . .
   . . . .
   . . . .

Question page

Using graphs, tables and charts. The example on the next page illustrates one of the types of questions which describes an investigation and tabulates some of the results. The children were asked to add the given data to the table.

Pupils were assessed in reading information from graphs, tables and charts and also in putting information into these forms. Between half and two-thirds of the children succeeded in reading information from flow charts, tables and from symbols, and they could use information in the form of pie charts and bar charts to make qualitative comparisons. Reading quantitative information from line graphs or bar charts proved to be more difficult, and performance was very much lower in putting into words the trends or patterns shown in graphs. As might be expected, the children found it much easier to add information to a partially completed bar chart or line graph than to draw one from scratch.

Results

61% Answered all parts correctly. Very few were partially correct.

Some children cut the bottom off a washing-up bottle and turned it upside down.   They put water in it to 15 cm above the neck and timed how long the water took to run out.   They did this again with water up to 12 cm, then 9 cm and 6 cm.   They put their results in this table:

Height of liquid in cm	Time to empty in seconds		
	Tap water	Soapy water	Washing up liquid
15	55		
12	40		
9	28		
6	20		
3			

Put these other results in the table:

a) With soapy water in up to 9 cm it took 25 seconds.

b) With washing up liquid in up to 12 cm it took 68 seconds.

c) With tap water in up to 3 cm it took 15 seconds.

Question page

6. Summary of implications

[. . .]

The main implications which have emerged [from the surveys] are summarized below. Those who agree with the view of primary science reflected in the surveys may wish to review their own practice in the light of these points.

The survey results suggest that schools are providing suitable opportunities for the children to develop general skills such as observing, measuring and keeping written records which are widely applicable across the curriculum. Given this sound base, there is now a need to consider how to help children to acquire those more specific science skills such as defining patterns in observations, giving explanations, predicting, hypothesizing, controlling variables and planning investigations, in which children are much less competent.

As a first step, schools might review the priorities which they attach to various goals and science-based activities and consider whether, without losing the ground which has been gained, more importance should be given to the more specific science skills. These skills are more likely to be developed if teachers have them firmly in mind when planning their work and in their daily interactions with children.

In planning science activities it is necessary to consider how these process skills will be introduced to the children at various ages and stages of development and to decide what progression can be expected as children gain experience. For example, at any stage of their schooling children can observe objects and phenomena but attention needs to be paid to ways in which the children's skills in observing are developed and how the children can be helped to interpret and use their observations in a scientific way.

Planning must also take account of the teaching approaches which will be used to develop science process skills, since these can only be acquired if the children are given opportunities to use them.

References

DES (1978) *Primary Education in England*, A survey by HM Inspectors of Schools. London, HMSO.

DES (1981) *Science in Schools. Age 11: report no.1*, Report to the DES, DENI and WOED on the 1980 survey of 11 year olds. London, HMSO.

DES (1982) *Science in Schools: Age 13: report no.1*, Report to the DES on the 1980 survey of 13 year olds. London, HMSO.

DES (1982) *Science in Schools. Age 15: report no.1*, Report to the DES, DENI and WOED on the 1980 survey of 15 year olds. London, HMSO.
DES (1983) *Science in Schools: Age 11: report no.2*, Report to the DES, DENI and WOED on the 1981 survey of 11 year olds, DES Research Report.

4.2

LIFE WORLD AND SCIENCE WORLD: PUPILS' IDEAS ABOUT ENERGY

Paul Black and Joan Solomon

1. Introduction

This paper describes investigations into pupils' thinking about energy. Almost all of the results were obtained by one of the authors – Joan Solomon – in her own school in connection with her own physics teaching. Some of the test results have also been repeated in another school. Individual and class discussions have been recorded and analysed. In addition, written tests have been set both before, and at different intervals of time after, teaching on energy. The researcher's detailed knowledge of and control over the teaching itself is a particular feature of the work.

The work is described in four main sections. Section 2 below describes investigations of ideas that pupils had before they had been taught about energy in physics lessons. Section 3 describes a model of pupils thinking about energy which distinguishes between the 'Symbolic World' of the science lessons and the 'Life World' of most of the pupil's daily experience. Section 4 discusses pupils' ideas about conversation and about dissipation after receiving teaching about energy, whilst Section 5 discusses results of a change in the teaching adopted as a result of the outcomes of the first stages of the research. Finally, some of the implications of the work are considered briefly in Section 6.

Source: Marx, G. (ed.) (1983) *Entropy in the School: proceedings of the 6th Danube Seminar on Physics Education: Volume I*, Budapest, Roland Eötvös Physical Society, pp. 43–55

2.   Pupils' ideas about energy

Pupils in two schools were asked to give written answers to the following two questions:

'What does the word *energy* mean?'
'Write three or four sentences to show how you would use the word.'

The pupils tested were at ages 11, 12 and 13. All were following similar courses in science, which included no specific teaching about energy for these age groups.

The responses were first classified into three main groups according to the types of meaning that pupils associated with energy in their sentences.

The first group related energy to *living – usually human – creatures.* The common associations can be summarized in the following list:

Living/people/life/growing
Fitness/health/illness/medicine/vitamins
Exercise/movement/activities/sports/work
Animals
In the body/blood/breathing
Food/carbohydrates/fat/sugar/glucose
Tired/out of breath/sweating/rest/sleep.

The second group related energy to *non-living systems* in the following ways:

Electricity/batteries/power stations
Fuels/petrol/coal/gas/oil/nuclear power
Machines/cars/tractors/industry/moving objects
Lighting/heating/home appliances
Sun/fire/wind/waves/hydroelectric power.

The third group included *universal statements* about energy, common associations being –

Things/all things/everything/all.

Classification in this third category was made only if a sentence expressed an intention to generalize and was applicable across both of the first two categories. Examples of such sentences are:

'A source of power which makes things grow or makes electric.'
'Energy is something we use to move most things.'

The results of this analysis are summarized in Table 1.

Table 1.   Associations with the word energy contained in all of the responses of pupils at ages 11, 12 and 13 in two schools

Sample	Number of pupils	Living	Non-living	Universal	Total number of responses
		Percentages of total number of responses			
Age 11 Boys	45	70%	25%	5%	149
Age 11 Girls	53	93%	6%	1%	174
Age 12 Boys	40	52%	38%	9%	143
Age 12 Girls	60	70%	24%	6%	194
Age 13 Boys	41	35%	52%	13%	119
Age 13 Girls	39	50%	42%	8%	135

Girls' responses had predominantly human associations. For boys, human associations were limited to fitness and sporting activities, and were in the minority by age 13; this may be part of a tendency of many adolescent boys to avoid human and social implications (Head, 1980).

The second- and third-year pupils were also divided on the basis of ability, the top ability group including about half of the total in each case. Table 2 concentrates on the percentage of pupils giving statements in the 'Universal' Category.

Table 2.   Percentages of pupils giving universal statements

Age group	Ability group	Number	Percentage giving at least one Universal Statement
11	All	99	8%
12	Top	53	42%
	Middle	47	4%
	All	100	25%
13	Top	43	51%
	Middle	37	11%
	All	80	33%

The changes with age could not be a direct influence of science teaching: they could be due to influence of other school teaching, or informal learning, or of a more general trend to move from concrete to formal thought about energy.

The large numbers of responses mentioning health, fitness, age and death recalled the old theory of Vitalism. Within the 'Living-Human' responses, the responses could be further divided into strictly 'Vitalist' responses concerned with health, growth, medicines, vitamins and life, and 'Human kinetic energy' responses concerned with sport, activity movement, feeling tired, and food. At age 11, 'Vitalist' responses predominated, at age 13 it was the 'Human kinetic energy' type which predominated. 'Exercise' presented a difficulty, which was explored in class discussion in the two schools. Pupils were asked which of the following two statements could be correct–

'Exercise Uses Up Your Energy'
'Exercise Builds Up Your Energy'.

In both cases the voting was 20 to 2 in favour of the first statement, but a subsequent proposal that 'Either could be right, it depends . . .' attracted support from 10 or more pupils in each school.

The age 13 pupils were also asked 'Can you measure energy?'. Table 3 summarizes the responses according to two categorizations of the pupils concerned. In both cases the results show statistically significant association between positive response to the question and progression from human associations to non-living or more general associations.

Table 3.   Associations of yes/no response to 'Can you measure energy?'

3A Association with 'Living' responses and 'other types'

	Pupils giving only Living ideas	Other ideas
Yes – can measure	7	40
No – can't measure	15	17

3B Association with 'Universal' responses and other types

	Pupils giving only Living, or Non-Living or no ideas	Pupils giving Universal ideas
Yes – can measure	32	18
No – can't measure	26	8

Further details of this particular study are given in a paper by Solomon (1983a). The broad picture is that children widen the range of associations of the term energy in this age range and that by age 13 a notion which is universal and quantifiable seems to be held by about one-third of them. One aspect not discussed here is that the results must be related to the other uses in the language of the word used by science. So these results might not be replicated where English is not the native language (Duit, 1981).

3. Symbolic world and life world

The idea here arises from the writings of Berger and Luckmann (1967) and Schutz and Luckmann (1973). In ordinary living, experiences have to be categorized and absorbed by us into our own 'structures of meaning'. These structures are developed and reinforced by communication and by the language which is our means of communication with others, and so acquire social value which makes them very important to us. Such socially reinforced structures constitute the 'Life World' domain. This domain tends to be composed of many theories, each of application to a limited range of contexts. The theories are not necessarily consistent with one another and are not usually abstract in character.

By contrast, schooling in science will try to create new structures to replace these. These constitute a 'Symbolic World' domain, characterized by few theories, mutually consistent and highly abstract in character.

Pupils will usually use 'Life World' theories for all purposes except the work of school science lessons, and these theories will be those used by most parents and other adults. 'Symbolic World' theories are peculiar to science lessons. To enter this world is to leave reality. To escape from it and return to the 'Life World', is like waking up from a dream. The 'Symbolic World' does not replace the 'Life World', they co-exist, and a study of pupils' responses to teaching may be regarded as a study of these two worlds and of the conditions in which they move from one to the other.

Tests taken by pupils after teaching of energy in their fourth year at secondary school (age 14) can be analysed in terms of this model. One example, discussed in detail by Solomon (1983b), illustrates the approach. Pupils were asked the following question –

> 'An electric drill, working at a rate of 500 watts is used to drill a hole in a piece of wood. How much work could it do in 20 minutes? What energy changes are taking place?'

A diagram illustrated the situation. The analysis was concerned only with the final part of the question. The teaching would have equipped pupils to answer in terms of a chain as follows:

$$\text{electrical energy} \longrightarrow \text{kinetic energy} \longrightarrow \text{heat energy.}$$

Some pupils gave answers in these terms, but amongst them were a set who added to the formal terms some extra terms relating them to the electric drill, to friction in the hole drilled, to drill vibrations producing noise, and so on. These extra terms would be classified as part of the 'Life World' and pupils linking these to the 'Symbolic World' terms would be showing ability to transfer between the two. This gives two categories of response, *'Life plus Symbolic'* and *'Symbolic'* only. A third category was also needed, to classify those whose answers were in the 'Life World' only, talking of the switch, the cable, the plug, the cutting of the bit, the shavings, the friction and heating at the hole, but not relating these to energy terms or to any chain of energy changes. Table 4 shows how responses of 42 pupils were categorized in these three groups. These same pupils were asked a question in a similar form ('Name all the energy changes taking place in . . .') but about a different situation ('. . . in a coal-fired steam engine or turbine' – again with a diagram), as part of an examination held $2\frac{1}{2}$ months after the energy teaching. The responses are also in Table 4 only here the *'Symbolic'* and *'Life plus Symbolic'* have been collapsed to include all those who used energy concepts in their answers.

Table 4.   Classification of pupils by response to the drill problem, and responses of these sub-groups $2\frac{1}{2}$ months later

Nature of ⟶ response / Test occasion	Life plus Symbolic	Symbolic only	Life only or wrong response
Drill problem – at end of teaching	11	25	6
Steam engine problem $2\frac{1}{2}$ months later	↓	↓	↓
Using energy ideas	10	14	0
Life world terms only	1	11	6

These figures give statistically significant confirmation of two hypotheses, that with lapse of time, life-world meanings will tend to replace symbolic ones, and that the ability to cross over between the two domains will be a good prediction of future success and perhaps an indicator of a deeper level of understanding.

In another test, pupils were asked one question calling for 'examples of energy' and another about 'energy changes' taking place when a ball bounces. The numbers giving *only* 'Life World' responses were: 30 (out of 128) on 'Examples of Energy' but only 1 on 'Energy Changes'.

The results are consistent with those reported by Viennot (1979). The response given to a question may depend on which of the pupils' two worlds is evoked by it in those cases where pupils cannot readily move between or relate the two worlds. Thus Viennot found that a general and abstract question – 'If the same force acts on two identical masses, are the notions necessarily identical' was correctly answered by 80 percent of her sample, whereas a question showing three identical balls at the same height but moving along different trajectories with different velocities, led to only a 57 percent correct response rate to the question 'Are the forces the same?'

4.   Conservation and dissipation

The recording and analysis of class discussions give a rich variety of evidence about the ways in which pupils think about energy. These discussions were held both before and during teaching about energy in the fourth year (age 14).

For example, pupils often believe that the energy associated with food (learnt in biology lessons?) is not stored in it but is created by our bodies when we eat it. For fuels which we burn, the energy is created by the burning processes. More generally, stored energy is a confused notion because energy is thought of as a substance stored *with* food, or *with* coal, or *with* my body.

Conservation of energy is also a confused notion. One meaning is concerned with storage only – to conserve is to save up, to keep, to hold back. Another meaning is to save, to prevent waste – public campaigns to improve house insulation talk about 'energy conservation' in this sense.

Neither of these meanings is the same as that applied by the Principle of Conservation of Energy. But a statement of that principle, in the form 'Energy cannot be created or destroyed but can be changed from one form to another' also raises difficulties with pupils. The negative 'not created' is easy to understand and accept, but the other negative 'not destroyed' is not. As one pupil put it to his teacher.

'That Principle of Conservation of Energy, Miss, I don't believe it. You know, when you have a battery and a lamp, and the battery has electrical energy, right? And it goes to heat and light in the lamp. Well, I mean, the heat evaporates and the light goes dim. So the energy has gone. It isn't there, is it?'

The following extract, from a class discussion, illustrates the point in another way.

Teacher	'Can we actually run out of energy?'
Pupil A	'No you can't, can't destroy it.'
Teacher	'Can you run out of fuel?'
Several pupils	'Yes, yes'
Pupil B	'Then you change the energy back.'
Teacher	'Can you change energy back into fuel?'
Several pupils	'No, no'
Pupil B	'Yes you can'
Pupil A	'If you could, you'd be a millionaire!'

The above example arose in a discussion provoked by a problem about a car running out of fuel, where pupils were asked to say what had happened to the energy. A systematic analysis of the discussions suggested that the conservation principle could be applied – whether correctly or not – in the following five ways:

First   Using 'Life World' ideas only: 'I mustn't use created or destroyed but still I do know that the energy is lost or burnt up'.

Second   Using the idea that energy is stored in the original system: 'If energy is not created or destroyed it must still be there, stored up in some way'.

Third   Using the idea that energy is reversible, using the notion also that this relates to its being a substance: 'If energy is conserved, it must turn up again in the same form as it was in the beginning'.

Fourth   Using a model of Simple Transformation, often blindly from rote learning: 'Like the Conservation Principle says, it can be changed, so it must have been'.

Fifth   Using both ideas of Transformation and of Dissipation: 'The energy must have been turned into some form which then leaks away, so that is why the object eventually stops'.

The overall picture given by this part of the study was that pupils' natural tendency to revert to 'Life World' explanations was enhanced here because teaching which concentrated on conservation was under a double difficulty. First that it seemed to fly in the face of all common experience, second that it depended on a term that had at least three related but distinct meanings.

5. Teaching dissipation

The conventional sequence in energy teaching has been to discuss work, then energy changes, leading to quantitative measures and calculations for energy in its various forms. This could culminate in statements about conservation. Energy dissipation or degradation *might* then be mentioned as an afterthought.

For teaching classes in 1982, a different sequence was adopted in an attempt to meet some of the problems exposed by the work described above, particularly in Section 4. After initial work on the ideas of work and on various forms of energy transformation, the teaching concentrated on the idea of energy dissipation. A variety of demonstration experiments, including a steam engine, a water siphon, a pendulum in which the damping of the swings was evident, and the expansion of CO_2 from a high pressure cylinder, was used to provoke discussion. This lead to an overall principle, stated in the following general form –

> 'In all energy changes, there is a running down towards sameness in which some of the energy becomes useless'.

After this, work on heat loss and on world energy problems was developed. Finally, the idea of energy conservation was discussed, but in the light of the preceding work on dissipation.

One piece of evidence about the outcome can be quoted. A question set at the end of the energy teaching showed a golfer striking a ball, which bounced repeatedly as it travelled forward, with the heights of the bounces becoming successively smaller. The question was an open one 'Describe all the energy changes that have taken place as completely as you can'.

The same question was set in 1980, after the old teaching scheme, with no instruction on energy dissipation, and in 1982 after the new one. Table 5 shows the percentages of pupils whose response fell into each of five main categories, one for those omitting to answer and four derived from the five described for the class discussion data in Section 4 above.

Table 5. Classification of answers to describe energy changes for a bouncing golf ball at end of energy teaching in old (1980) and new (1982) sequences

				% in each category		
Year	Number of pupils	Omit	Life World	Storage or reversible	Transform- ation	Transform- ation & Dissipation
1980	46	17%	9%	30%	30%	15%
1982	56	14%	12%	6%	29%	40%

The results show a well-marked improvement. The more able pupils particularly had shifted from the 'Storage or Reversible Group' to the 'Transformation and Dissipation Group'. Of the 22 in this group in 1982, 19 also gave a correct statement of the Principle of Conservation of Energy in the same test, compared with 9 out of the 16 in the 'Transformation Group' and 6 out of the 18 in the first three groups. Thus, teaching about dissipation had not cause obvious confusion about the Conservation principle. There was also strong association between ability to state the 'Running Down' principle and ability to use it, as characterized by the categorization of responses to the question described above.

6. Conclusions

The discussion of the significance and interpretation of the above results have been kept brief and are left largely to the reader. However, certain general conclusions are strongly supported by the work.

First, if we want pupils to learn any physics principles effectively, we must find ways to help them to link the 'Symbolic World' of our physics to the 'Life World' of their everyday experience. In order to do this, we need to study and understand this 'Life World' for the areas of experience which relate to the principles being taught.

Secondly, for teaching about energy, the above principle must lead to the conclusion that dissipation and transformation of energy should be taught first, and that the Conservation Principle comes later. It should also be mentioned that there are good general arguments within engineering thermodynamics for teaching a Running Down principle in its own right (Solomon, 1982). So the Second Law comes first, and we should teach it, not only because we want it to be understood for its own sake, but also because appreciation of it is a necessary condition for pupils to make sense of the concept of energy and of its conservation.

References

Berger, P. L. and Luckmann, T. (1967) *The Social Construction of Reality*. London, Penguin.

Duit, R. (1981) An instrument to investigate the learning of the energy concept. Paper presented at the International Conference on Energy Education, Providence, U.S.A.

Head, J. (1980) A model to link personality characteristics to a preference for science, *European Journal of Science Education*, 2, 295–300.

Schutz, A. and Luckmann, T. (1973) *The Structures of the Life World*. London, Heinemann.

Solomon, J. (1982) How children learn about energy or does the first law come first? *School Science Review*, 63, 415–422.

Solomon, J. (1983a) Socially acquired knowledge: an inquiry into British children's notions about energy prior to teaching. Submitted to *Science Education*.

Solomon, J. (1983b) Learning about energy – how pupils think in two domains, *European Journal of Science Education* 5, 49–59.

Viennot, L. (1979) Spontaneous reasoning in elementary dynamics, *European Journal of Science Education*, 1, 203–221.

4.3

PUPILS' ALTERNATIVE FRAMEWORKS IN SCIENCE

Rosalind Driver

Attention has been given recently in Britain and elsewhere to studies of children's thinking in science. The main focus of this research work has tended to be on the development of logical thought by children, based on Piagetian stage theory.

In this paper I shall be considering a complementary aspect of children's thinking and learning: that is the sets of beliefs or expectations they hold about the way natural phenomena occur, and how they affect the sense pupils make of experiences we give them in science classes. I shall indicate that in some areas pupils hold beliefs which differ from the currently accepted view and from the intended outcome of learning experiences. Such beliefs I shall call 'alternate frameworks'.

In the first part of this paper the status of alternate frameworks will be explored from a philosophical point of view. The second part gives further examples of pupils' frameworks and briefly comments on literature in this area. The last part of the paper addresses itself to the question of implications for classroom practice.

Alternate frameworks: a philosophical perspective

We all have sets of beliefs about how things happen, and have expectations which enable us to predict future events. A piece of chalk rolls along the table and I know where to grasp for it to stop it falling. The fact that so many of us

Source: Driver, R (1981), Pupils' alternative Frameworks in Science, *European Journal of Science Education*, *3* (1), pp. 94–101.

can drive around on our roads without more accidents occurring is possible because of the sets of expectations we have developed which enable us to predict the speed and movement of other vehicles on the road. Such sets of expectations enable us to operate our daily lives without being constantly in a state of disorientation and shock. The children we teach also have built up sets of expectations and their own beliefs about a range of natural phenomena and these may differ from those the teacher wishes to develop.

Here is an example of the kind of situation to which I am referring. Two 11-year-old boys, Tim and Ricky, are doing simple experiments on the extension of springs when loaded. They have made their own springs by winding wire round a length of dowel and are now studying the way one of their springs extends as they add ball-bearings to a polystyrene cup hanging from it (Figure 1). Ricky is intent on adding ball-bearings one at a time and

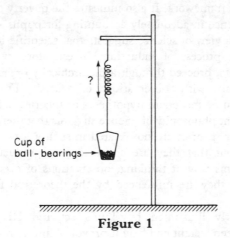

Cup of
ball-bearings→

Figure 1

measuring the new length of the spring after each addition. Tim is watching him, then interrupts: 'Wait. What happens if we lift it up?' He unclamps the spring, raises it higher up the stand, and measures its length again. Apparently satisfied that the length is the same he continues with the experiment.

Later, when he was asked the reason for doing this, Tim picks up two marbles, holds one up higher than the other and explains:

'this is farther up and gravity is pulling it down harder – I mean the gravity is still the same but it turns out it is pulling harder the farther away. The higher it gets the more effect gravity will have on it because if you just stood over there and someone dropped a pebble on him, it would just sting him, it wouldn't hurt him. But if I dropped it from an aeroplane it would be accelerating faster and faster and when it hit someone on the head it would kill him.'

Of course it should not be a surprise to us that children have developed expectations of common physical phenomena. Their experiences of pushing, pulling, lifting, throwing, feeling and seeing things contribute to these ideas, as does everyday language (as opposed to the specialist use of words in science). But we would be misled if we thought that these frameworks derived only from children's experiences, that they are arrived at through a process of induction. There is also a creative and imaginative element involved on the part of each child in constructing the meanings he imposes on events.

The example of Tim's idea about weight serves not only as an illustration of a pupil's alternate framework. It also indicates the poverty of an inductionist philosophy of science in adequately accounting for pupils' learning.

The empiricist's view of science suggests that scientific ideas and theories are reached by a process of induction. Investigators, whether pupils or practising scientists, proceed through a hierarchically organized sequence of processes, starting with observation of 'facts'. From such 'facts' generalizations can be made and hypotheses or theories induced.

However, current philosophy of science suggests that there is a fallacy here; that hypotheses or theories are not related in such a way with the so-called 'objective' data but that they are constructions, products of the human imagination. In this way of thinking, observations of events are not being objective because they are influenced by the theoretical framework of the observer.

This was clearly illustrated by Tim's activity. His idea about the relationship between weight and height provoked him to raise the spring and make the observation of its length under this new condition. His observation in this sense was 'theory laden'.

Because any theory is not related in a deductive and hence unique way to observations, there can be multiple explanations of events. Pupils can and do bring alternate frameworks to explain observations which are in keeping with their experience and in this respect are not 'wrong'. However, we may recognize them as partial and limited in their scope.

Recently I visited a school in which the science for 11- to 13-year-old pupils was organized on an individualized basis. Pupils were programmed through a series of activities on work cards. The teacher let me audio-record some of the groups at work.

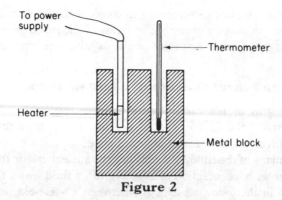

Figure 2

One group of girls was doing an experiment in which an immersion heater was placed in blocks of equal weight but made of different metals (Figure 2). The pupils had been instructed to draw a temperature-time graph as each block is heated. (The function of the experiment was to demonstrate variation in heat capacity.)

Towards the end of the lesson the girls were instructed to look at the graphs they had produced and compare them, suggesting an explanation. Here are their comments.

Pupil 1   'We've got to do a graph for the aluminium.'
Pupil 2   'Good. Aluminium isn't so – um – it.'
Pupil 1   'Don't forget it has to go through doesn't it?'
           'Through the thickness to reach there – the thermometer.'
Pupil 2   'That was only thin to get to that.'
Pupil 1   'Come on we've got to put it away now.'

The teacher enters the discussion.

Teacher   'What has your experiment shown you?'
Pupil 2   'That different – um – that different materials and that see how heat could travel through them.'
Teacher   'What did you find out?'
Pupil 1   'Well – er – that heat went through the – the iron more easier than it did through the er . . .'.
Pupil 2   'Aluminium.'

The pupils had had first-hand experiences – they had collected their data, but these had not been assimilated into the way of thinking that the teacher had expected. Later, we shall be returning to consider the implications of such a 'constructivist' philosophy of science in terms of classroom practice. First we will return to give further examples of pupils' alternate frameworks.

Examples and characteristics of alternate frameworks

A common feature of new curriculum projects in science is the introduction of ideas of molecular kinetic theory to children to help them interpret phenomena involving heat and changes of state.

However, many of the children seem, like the ancient caloric theorists, to be much happier with a conception of heat as stuff, a fluid which flows. We see this reflected in the following dialogue between 12-year-old pupils who are explaining how a balloon on a tin-can gets bigger when the tin is heated.

Pupil 1	'What do you think will happen, Kevin?'
Pupil 2	'I think it will – er – blow up and – er – bop [smiles] with the force of the heat.'
Pupil 1	'But where's the force coming from?'
Pupil 2	'From bottom going through that [points to can] then – er . . .'.
Pupil 1	'What do you think, Susan?'
Pupil 3	'The heat's coming and its collecting in that can and its blowing the bubble up.'
Pupil 1	'Well, there is air in there at first. And the heat gets into it and it's rising up and it's making the balloon bigger.'
Teacher	'So, what's pushing the balloon out?'
Pupils 1, 2 and 3	'The air inside that can.'
Teacher	'How does the air do that?'
Pupil 1	'The heats pushing the air so it blows the balloon up.'
Teacher	'What's the heat making the air do?'
Pupil 3	'Rise.'
Pupil 1	'Force up – it's forcing it up.'

Despite having been introduced to ideas of moving molecules these are not being used in the pupils' explanations. Instead we see evidence of ideas such as 'the force of the heat', 'the heat forcing the air to rise'.

The following example shows even more clearly the struggle that children have in using the kinetic-molecular model when it is presented to them. In this example, 13- and 14-year-old pupils have been presented with the elementary ideas of the molecular-kinetic theory of matter. They have then been asked to use those ideas to explain some simple observations. In this case, two pupils have observed a metal rod expand when it is heated (Figure 3).

Here they are attempting to explain their observations.

Pupil 1   'Yes, well that the – er – the heat molecules are pushing the . . .'.
Pupil 2   'No, they're not.'
Pupil 1   'Well, anyway, that thing is going down.'
Pupil 2   'They're expanding. The – er – heat molecules are giving more energy, so they need more room to move about and so the bar needs to get longer, so it goes down, the needle.'

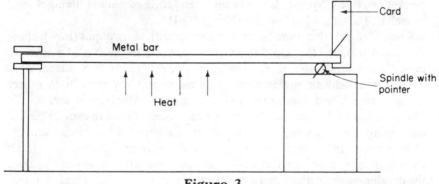

Figure 3

Pupil 1   'If that's the heat, and molecules have to expand, right? [Yes] and you've got that thing like that, so when the molecules turn it round like that, and when that bar pushes it, it pushes the things round and that goes down.'
(Transcript provided by M. Torbe.)

In this excerpt we see indications of how the notion of molecules is being assimilated by these pupils. For example, we see reference made to 'molecules of heat' and 'molecules expanding' on heating. The examples of alternate frameworks given here are only indications of the different ways pupils may interpret events. Little attention has been given to systematic studies on such alternate frameworks.

194   Research approaches

In general, of course, Piaget's work is a major source for studying children's ideas. But here I suggest his work should be read with more attention given to children's causal thinking than to the logical structures which Piaget postulates to explain them.

The way that younger children explain and interpret natural events was explored by Piaget in his well-known early works (Piaget, 1929, 1930), in which he used verbal methods to explore pupils' explanations of questions such as 'What causes night?' and 'How do clouds move?' These studies have been extensively replicated (see, for example, Laurendeau and Pinard, 1962). The results of such studies are still worth scrutiny not in terms of the logical structures they reveal but in terms of the content of the responses of pupils of different ages. One might ask, for example, what implications it might have for introductory biology courses if you take seriously the finding that over 10 percent of 11- to 12-year-olds in Britain extend their concept of 'living things' to include the sun, wind and fire (King, 1961).

Studies indicate that a similar problem exists with older pupils (Boyd, 1966; Za'rour, 1976), and that some alternate frameworks in the area of mechanics persist among university physics students (Viennot, 1974). In Scotland, work by Johnstone and his students has illuminated problem areas in chemistry topics (Duncan and Johnstone, 1973; Johnstone, MacDonald and Webb, 1977). At Leeds, Lovell and his students have done studies to explore pupils' developing understanding of ideas of gravitational and potential energy. (Archenhold, 1975) and certain biological concepts (Okeke, 1976). Of particular interest are the few studies which systematically attempt to trace the developmental path in understanding important scientific ideas. A recent study with American children, for example, traces the development of children's understanding of the 'earth concept' from that of a flat platform to a sphere in unlimited space (Nussbaum and Novak, 1976).

Such studies indicate that although individual children will bring unique perspectives to learning there are enough common trends in their thinking to make a study of more common alternate frameworks worthwhile.

In the next section we will consider how such information may be used in curriculum design and in teaching.

Implications for classroom practice

One may well ask why attention should be paid to children's alternative frameworks. If such ideas are wrong, perhaps like the misdemeanours of a naughty child they are best extinguished by being ignored.

Over a decade ago, Ausubel commented on the importance of considering what he called children's preconceptions, suggesting that they are 'amazingly tenacious and resistant to extinction' and that 'unlearning of preconceptions might well prove to be the most determinative single factor in the acquisition and retention of subject matter knowledge' (Ausubel, 1968). We have seen an indication of this problem in the case of pupils' understanding of the molecular-kinetic theory. Studies referred to in the previous section indicated the strength of Aristotelian ideas in pupils' understanding of mechanics.

If there is a problem in terms of the persistence of alternate frameworks, is it not important to be aware of these ideas in order to help pupils see their limitations and to develop their thinking? Let us now turn to look at how such information might be used and what implications it may have for classroom practice. Here I will suggest four points:

1. Curriculum development in science needs to pay as much attention to the structure of thought of the child as it has recently paid to the structure of the disciplines in organizing learning experiences.

Currently our concern for the structure of thought of the child has been focused on Piagetian logical operations. I would argue that the content as much as the process of thought requires our attention.

2. Teaching programmes may need to be structured so as to be more in keeping with the developmental path in understanding important scientific ideas. The logical order of teaching a topic may not correspond with the psychological order in learning.

This is a word of caution for those who are enthusiastic about structured learning programmes involving such hierarchies.

3. Activities in science may need to include those which enable pupils to disprove alternate interpretations as well as affirm the accepted ones. (This of course also has bearing on the shortcomings of learning hierarchies.) If we think back to the example discussed earlier of Tim's idea of weight related to height above the ground, we see an example of this kind of activity. Tim needed to explore that idea to disprove it to himself. Studies which indicate the possible importance of this are reported by Cole and Raven (1969), and Rowell and Dawson (1977).

4. Lastly, if we are to take seriously the philosophical issues discussed earlier we need to include opportunities for pupils to think through the implications of observations and measurements made in science lessons. We must realize that our explanations do not spring clearly from the data.

As teachers we know how to expect an experiment to be interpreted. We have been along that route before. Our pupils perhaps have not – nor is it always an easy route to follow. Theory is not related in a unique deductive way to data; activities with apparatus in the laboratory and outside it are not enough to develop children's thinking.

Modern philosophers of science have indicated the limitations of rational empiricism, and yet I would hold that rational empiricism is still the view of science which predominates in our classrooms.

In England, the Nuffield O-level physics materials were launched on the slogan 'I do and I understand'. We now have classrooms in which activities play a central part. Pupils can spend a major portion of their time pushing trolleys up runways; gathering, cutting and sticking tangling metres of ticker-tape; marbles are rattled around in trays simulating solids, liquids and gases; batteries and bulbs are clicked in and out of specially designed circuit boards. To what end? Sometimes I suspect 'I do and I am even more confused'. Activity by itself is not enough. It is the sense we make of it that matters.

I am not here arguing for less practical work. What I am suggesting is that practical work by itself is not enough. Pupils need time both individually, in groups and with their teacher to think and talk through the implications and possible explanations of what they are observing – *and this takes time* – more time than often we see being given in classrooms. In the jargon of the philosophers of science, pupils' thinking may need to undergo a paradigm shift in learning science. A study of the history of science shows how difficult this can be for many scientists. In fact, Max Planck commented that 'New theories do not convert people; it is just that old men die.' If scientists have this difficulty in reformulating their conceptions of the world, is it a wonder that children sometimes have a struggle to do so?

Some tentative suggestions have been made as to the role of talk and writing in helping pupils make these changes in their thinking, for example by Barnes (1976).

The writers of the Bullock Report (1975), which reported on language development of pupils in British Schools, also saw language as a tool in learning:

> What the teacher has in mind may well be the desirable destination of a thinking process; but a learner needs to trace the steps from the familiar to the new, from the fact or idea he possesses to that which he is to acquire. In other words, the learner has to make a journey in thought for himself.

References

Archenhold, W. F. (1975) *A study of the understanding by sixth form students of the concept of potential in physics*, M.Phil. Thesis, University of Leeds.
Ausubel, D. (1968) *Educational Psychology: a Cognitive View*. Holt, Rinehart and Winston Inc.
Barnes, D. (1976) *From Communication to Curriculum*. Harmondsworth, Penguin.
Boyd, C. A. (1966) A study of unfounded beliefs, *Science Education*, Vol. 50, pp. 396–398.
The Bullock Report (1975) *A Language for Life*. London, H.M.S.O., pp. 141–142.
Cole, H. and Raven, R. (1969) Principle learning as a function of instruction on excluding irrelevant variables, *Journal of Research in Science Teaching*, Vol. 6, pp. 234–241.
Duncan, I. M. and Johnstone, A. H. (1973) The mole concept, *Education in Chemistry*, Vol. 10, No. 6, pp. 213–214.
Johnstone, A. H., MacDonald, J. J. and Webb, G. (1977) A thermodynamic approach to chemical equilibrium, *Physics Education*, Vol. 12, No. 4, pp. 248–251.
King, W. H. (1961) Studies of children's scientific concepts and interests, *British Journal of Educational Psychology*, Vol. 31, pp. 1–20.
Laurendeau, M. and Pinard, A. (1962) *Causal Thinking in the Child*. New York, International University Press.
Nussbaum, J. and Novak, J. D. (1976) An assessment of children's concepts of the earth utilizing structured interviews, *Science Education*, Vol. 60, No. 4, pp. 535–550.
Okeke, E. A. C. (1976) *A study of the understanding in Nigerian School Certificate Biology candidates of the concepts of reproduction, transportation and growth*, Ph.D. Thesis, University of Leeds.
Piaget, J. (1929) *The Child's Conception of the World*. New York, Harcourt, Brace.
Piaget, J. (1930) *The Child's Conception of Physical Causality*. London, Kegan Paul.
Rowell, J. A. and Dawson, C. J. (1977) Teaching about floating and sinking: an attempt to link cognitive psychology with classroom practice. *Science Education*, Vol. 61, No. 2, pp. 245–253.
Viennot, L. (1974) Sens physique et raisonnement formel en dynamique elementaire. *Encart Pedagogique*, Vol. II, pp. 34–46.
Za'rour, G. (1976) Interpretation of natural phenomena by Lebanese school children. *Science Education*, Vol. 60, pp. 277–287.

Further reading

Driver, R. (1983) *The Pupil as Scientist*. Open University Press.
Driver, R., Guesne, E. and Tiberghien, A. (1985) *Children's Ideas in Science*. Open University Press.

4.4

A STUDY OF SCHOOLCHILDREN'S ALTERNATIVE FRAMEWORKS OF THE CONCEPT OF FORCE

D. Michael Watts

Introduction

A number of recent reports have highlighted the substantive aspects of children's thinking concerning concepts in science. This welcome change of emphasis, away from the exclusive concern for pupils' logical reasoning, towards the substance of their conceptual frameworks, has prompted new lines of enquiry. Clement (1977), Viennot (1979), Osborne and Gilbert (1980), Jung (1981), Watts and Zylbersztajn (1981) have all discussed some concepts of *force*; Saltiel and Malgrange (1980), Trowbridge and McDermott (1980) about *velocity*; Nussbaum and Novak (1976), Gunstone and White (1980) about *gravity*; Duit (1981) about *energy*; Erickson (1979) about *heat* and *temperature*; Pfundt (1981) about *chemicals*, and so on.

These studies have typically focused their attention on pupils' perceptions of some common phenomena and have referred to childrens' perceptions variously as 'conceptual inventories', 'spontaneous ways of reasoning', 'intuitive physics', 'notions', and 'alternative frameworks'. This last term, taken from the work of Driver and Easley (1978), is the one to be used here. An alternative framework can be thought of as a person's imaginative efforts to describe and explain their physical world. The systematic and rigorous exploration of schoolchildren's alternative frameworks has major implications for science education. It has been persuasively argued that the more teachers know about and appreciate these alternative conceptions, the better they will

Source: Watts, D. M. (1983) A study of schoolchildren's alternative frameworks of the concept of force, *European Journal of Science Education*, 5 (2), pp. 217–230

be able to provide effective learning experiences for their pupils to modify the conceptions (Sutton, 1980; Gilbert, Osborne and Fensham, 1981).

One of the main aims of the study is to provide science teachers with quick and useful insights into children's thinking. By augmenting teachers' diagnostic skills it may be possible to promote more effective teaching based upon what a learner already knows and understands.

The methods employed

This study of force is part of a continuing series of efforts to describe youngsters' conceptions in physics. Pupils of different ages and academic achievement were interviewed individually using a method called the Interview-about-Instances approach (Gilbert and Osborne, 1980; Gilbert, Watts and Osborne, 1981). The interviews centred on a collection of simple line drawings which the pupils were required to interpret as examples or non-examples of their concept of force. They were asked for their reasons for each choice and, wherever possible, their own language was used to probe their understandings. The pictures did not follow a rigid sequence, and an informal conversation was allowed to develop around the instances presented. Some examples of the drawings are shown in Figure 1.

The interviews were audiotaped and then fully transcribed to a detailed notation (Watts, 1980a). The participants in this study were the author together with twelve schoolchildren ranging in age from 11 to 18 years, from schools in the Greater London urban area. They were drawn from both junior science classes and advanced level physics groups. Some more biographical details are given in Table 1.

Methods of presenting the alternative frameworks

The alternative frameworks are presented here in three ways, using the following methods:

(a) A simplified description – a pithy summary statement of each framework. These short descriptions are called 'vignettes'.

(b) Illustrations of the framework, by means of extracts taken from the transcripts of the pupils' responses. Included within these quotes are [in squared brackets] immediate interview questions and, often, some indication of what was referred to in the discussion. The numbers at the end of each quote refer to the number of the interview and the age of the interviewee.

Thus, (14:13) would denote the fourteenth interview which took place with a 13-year-old. These extracts are taken directly from the transcripts and are unpunctuated and often ungrammatical. A series of dots indicates a pause between phrases; the letter I means 'Interviewer'.

(c)   Comments about the ways in which frameworks differ from the orthodox physics view.

The frameworks described here come from no *one* pupil. They have been pieced together from the implicit and explicit conceptions used by the children during the course of the interview. Each framework was used by at least two pupils and used at least twice during the interviews. The frameworks form a composite picture based on ideas shared by a number of pupils, an approach termed, the 'mosaic' method (Bloor, 1973). The need is to develop models of student understanding that are powerful enough to capture important individual differences, yet not so specific that the end product is the same number of models as there are pupils. Many of the frameworks are consistent with the findings of other research workers, and where this is the case, the similarities have been commented upon. The task of exploring the generality of the frameworks with large samples is now in progress (Watts and Zylbersztajn, 1981).

Table 1.   The participants in the interviews

Tape number	Name	M/F	Age	Group
01	Zeba	F	17	Physics extension group (CEE)
02	Sarah	F	15	Examination physics group (O Level)
03	Susan	F	15	Examination physics group (O Level)
04	Stephanie	F	15	Examination physics group (O Level)
05	Julie	F	16	Standard physics group (CSE)
06	Steve	M	17	Advanced physics group (A Level)
07	Carol	F	14	General Science class
08	Richard	M	14	General Science class
09	Ted	M	12	Junior Science class
10	Sally	F	11	Junior Science class
11	Jonathon	M	15	Examination physics group (O Level)
12	Giany	M	15	Examination physics group (O Level)

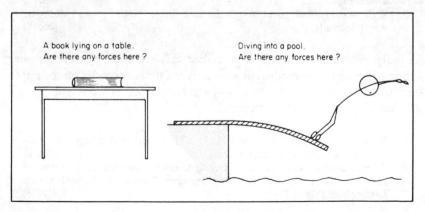

Figure 1.   Some examples of the cards

Descriptions of the frameworks

A: Affective forces

The word 'affect' can be defined as 'desire, especially as leading to action: disposed or inclined to action'. It seems an appropriate description of this framework for force where objects are seen as inclined, or attempting, to produce action. Pupils of all ages frequently use this kind of framework, as was also noted by Osborne (1980) with children in New Zealand. He calls it children's 'everyday views', views that are characterized by very anthropomorphic language. For example, a golfball in flight 'wants' to fall down, a bicycle 'wants' to slow down when the cyclist stops pedalling. Osborne puts 'everyday views' at one end of a continuum between 'children's science' and 'scientists' science'. The frameworks described here are neither a continuum, nor a hierarchy, but conceptions common to a broad group of students, both novice and advanced students.

This framework comes in three parts, and can be paraphrased as:

Forces are obligations to complete an action against some resistance.

Firstly, force is seen as compulsion, very much the 'everyday' meaning, to force someone or something to act.

> Z.   That [ball] *has* to do it . . . if you hit the ball there it *has* to go up. [Golfball]
> (01:17)
> S.   Well, gravity is a kind of power isn't it . . . forcing something to *do* something.
> (04:15)
> S.   Well, as the golfball goes through the air it forces the air . . . to get out of its way. [Golfball]
> (06:17)

Secondly, the framework is best described as visceral. It conveys an *inner* feeling of trying to accomplish some activity an inner drive. When the pupils described some occurrences (like a spacecraft lifting off) one got the impression of a gut-wrenching effort.

> S.   Well the tree is forcing itself to stay up . . . it's being pulled by gravity but– the tree's sort of *working* against the two. [Tree and wind]
> (04:15)
> G.   There's quite a lot of force there *driving* the man down the slope because of gravity and weight and the force is going against the wind . . . the friction is *fighting* back [Sledge]
> (12:15)

The third sense of the word suggests that forces are also international. It contrasts with 'accidental' or 'naturally' occurring incidents:

T. No I don't think he's forcing himself to trip over . . . uhh it's just an accident. [Astronaut on the moon]   (09:12)

J. If you *do* something . . . actually physically sort of dig something up . . . *then* you would be causing forces . . . like playing the piano. (11:15)

Clearly these views are very different from the orthodox physics way of describing force. By 'orthodox' is meant the normal school programme of Newtonian physics, crystallized in Newton's law of universal gravitation and his three laws of motion. The 'neutral' language of physics uses force as a noun (not a verb) and as a description of interactions in nature.

C: Configuration forces

The framework can be expressed as:

Objects restrained in a position have force.

It has a notion of force as a 'bonding' between objects that hold them stable in relation to each other. Without that bonding, objects would not be expected to stay in position, but would move apart. It is a framework that tries to account for the *absence* of movement. Immobility seems to need a cause and forces, both singly and in combination, are described to account for it: youngsters describe forces in situations where nothing is happening, when they might otherwise expect something to occur.

Z. I think it [a force] is holding him up in space . . . Yes, he needs a force to stay there [Astronaut in space]   (01:17)

S. And that [a force] is what keeps it down instead of flying off when you know there's nothing else pulling it   (02:15)

I. What is force?

S. Something being held . . . yes, held together by forces.   (04:15)

The second part is an idea of force due to an object's position, usually its height. For instance, a ball rolling down a slope would have more force at the top of the slope than at the bottom. Other positions are important too: the stability of an object; the flexing of a diving springboard from its 'natural' horizontal position. When something is unstable and likely to fall, then it has force.

> J. Well . . . you've got more force the higher up you are . . . it's obvious isn't
> it . . .   (05:16)
> S. The force is actually . . . in how the torch is positioned [Torches]   (04:15)

The third part has a suggestion of constraint about it – a pent-up, ready-to-burst configuration. For example, within this sense, a bomb which is stationary on the floor but about to explode, would be considered a very large force.

> C. It'll try to get above all the air . . . and *force* its way above all the air . . . or
> try to . . . but it won't be able to 'cos he's holding it. [Balloon]   (07:14)

All three parts to the framework have a sense similar to the physicist's idea of potential energy, particularly gravitational potential energy. It is interesting to speculate on the educational implications for an 11-year-old having an intuitive feel for elastic potential energy, which she calls force. For example, Sally (10:11) says

> S. Well, it's like a spring and when you get onto it . . . I don't know . . . it's
> got a force . . . to push you out . . . the spring. [Diving board]   (10:11)

At points of no apparent motion forces are sometimes seen as 'equal' and 'opposite'. This contrasted with those pupils who thought there are *no* forces at these points.

> S. Oh yes, they're equal because . . . there the force downwards equals the
> force upwards. [I. Why?] Well, it's not moving, is it. [Golfball at maximum
> height]   (02:15)
> S. Something that's not moving must be stable . . . the force is downwards . . .
> which is gravitational force . . . it has to be equal to the force going
> upwards which is the force or thrust. [Golfball at maximum height] (03:15)

Pupils frequently cited an 'upward force' or 'thrust' on a golfball that cause it to move through the air long after leaving the golfclub. This is discussed more fully under *Motive forces*.

Viennot (1979) notes a similar framework for students in their last year of secondary school and first year of university both in Britain and Belgium. She points to 'local' and 'global' types of structures of spontaneous thought and describes 'local' as 'a "local" or "static" type which considers the *positions* of the objects in the system, or its *state*, and which makes a *local* analysis of the motion, and thus uses force of interaction only'.

She concludes, too, that these students also have difficulty in differentiating between the concepts of force and energy. Gunstone and White (1980) also comment on the role that 'equilibrium' plays in student thinking. Using a pulley-system demonstration with first year university students at Monash University, Australia, they say: 'Equilibrium was seen in an odd way by many students. It was, during this demonstration, "shattered", "lost", "upset", "destroyed", "sought", "immediately re-established", "obtained", systems "wanted to go back to it" '. It was apparently seen as some sort of real entity contained in objects rather than as a description of a particular physical state.

D: Designated forces

The children in these interviews seem to decide that certain objects are endowed with force, and others, in the same picture, are not. Force seems to reside within the objects; force is immanent. Immanence means 'indwelling' or 'inherent', and suggests some sort of power residing within an object or body. Immanence is designated by the pupils not arbitrarily, but on the basis of 'activity'. Force is seen to 'activate' a body, and those objects that *have* force are those that seem most likely to create an occurrence. The occurrence may actually be happening within the picture (sledging down a hill, for example) or be about to happen. In either case, the objects most likely to be the seat of activity are the objects designated to have force. This can be paraphrased as:

Forces are designated to those objects that are causing or will cause events to occur.

The term 'object' includes both animate and inanimate bodies. This framework can be separated into three main parts as follows: firstly, humans are centres of force: which is a very anthropocentric notion. Where there are people shown in a situation, they are commonly the focus of attention, and are seen as the focus of forces. Sometimes they are the *only* forces mentioned, at other times other forces are mentioned but not emphasized. For example:

Z. The force is coming from the man who whacks it. [The golfball] (01:17)
S. The force is coming originally from his arm and he's giving it to the ball. [Golfer] (04:15)
S. There's some force there from the teacher . . . his power to tell the boy off . . . (56) [Being told off] (10:11)
J. *He* is energy . . . moving energy . . . he swings it . . . which is the force . . . so he creates the force. [Golfer] (11:15)

Not only are people the centre of forces, the causes of events or the agents of force, but the forces are *inside* their bodies. Some pupils list these innervative forces to the exclusion of all others. They are commonly found in the body's large muscles, though the hands and feet are often mentioned too.

> Z. Let me think . . . no . . . they're pulling it with their backs, aren't they . . . it's more in their legs . . . backs . . . in their muscles. [Pulling a stone]
> (01:17)
> [I. Where are the forces?] S. Umh . . . his knee . . . maybe in his feet you know . . . pushing up . . . Oh, his arms I forgot those. [Diver] (10:11)
> S. The force is *in him* . . . striking the ball . . . the movement of his arms. [Golfer] (04:15)

Thirdly some objects were seen as 'having' force, others were not. The pupils' language often sounds anthropomorphic as they describe objects in this way. Not all the pictures had human actors in them. Some of the objects depicted as 'having' force might have been expected (a tree, a diving board, a golfball), whereas others were less obvious (a book, a balloon, an astronaut's boots).

> C. Well, there *will* be forces if he was wearing those boots . . . those big ones . . . . [I. Why would they make a difference?] Well maybe they're made so that they go down on the moon . . . aren't they? . . . They stay there . . . so they're exerting a force . . . 'cos if there was no force there he'd just float away so they must be exerting *some* force. [Astronaut on moon] (07:14)
> S. Yes, there is force in *the ball* . . . in the movement . . . the whack of the thing. [Golfer] (10:11)
> R. Well, he's suffering a force from the *crater* . . . when he's got onto the crater. [Astronaut on moon] (08:14)

The example of the astronaut's boots being special was very popular. Weight and force are treated as two separate, only vaguely related concepts. Weight often means the 'heaviness' of an object or person, that is, the amount of muscular effort required to lift it. Force could take any one of the meanings suggested in these frameworks. The boots were seen to hold the astronaut onto the moon: if the fastenings were to accidentally come undone he would no longer be held down and would float away from the moon's surface. In space the boots held the astronaut 'upright' (earthwards?) and were able to 'right' him should he go upside down.

The first two parts of the framework are particularly anthropocentric (people centred) and anthropomorphic. Clement (1977) notes similar tendencies amongst physics undergraduates at the University of

Massachussetts. Discussing a 'conceptual system' which he calls 'source of force', he says, 'Elastic bands, people and motors are sources of force. This belief would appear to be related to an anthropomorphic, root metaphor that underlies one's conception of force, namely one's own very basic experience of pushing and pulling an object. In order to be compatible with this basic conceptual model of "force", an object perceived as a source of force must be an active agent against something at least remotely like the way humans are active agents'.

Osborne (1980), too, notes the prevalence of anthropocentrism. Both authors seem to ignore the all-pervasiveness of language and the scientist's willingness to enslave words for his own particular purposes. As Helm (1981) points out, the apparent objectivity of physics still imagines forces to 'be exerting', or 'to act'. Exertion has strong overtones of strenuous muscular activity, and if a force is exerted is it not natural to look for an agent producing that exertion?

E: Encounter forces

Throughout the interviews it was common for the pupils to treat force as a single entity, rather than as an interaction between bodies or forces. As described in other frameworks ('impetus' and 'motive' forces) *the* force was usually seen as the element in the situation that produces an effect. This *encounter framework* deals with a number of forces. When forces come together they don't *always* seem to produce movement. If they are in objects already moving they might combine to co-operate in the movement: otherwise they tend to balance and become 'equal and opposite'. This particular adage is used to explain a range of phenomena in a similar way to framework C. A paraphrase for the framework would be:

When two or more forces come together they can be combined to change the movement of an object.

S. The force would be in that direction [along line of motion] and eventually it would stop going upwards . . . and start being pulled downwards and so you get a curve . . . [Golfball]   (06:17)

J. If he was travelling with speed around the earth . . . orbiting round it . . . he would have a force . . . acting outwards . . . as his velocity would want to pull him . . . his velocity would want to go straight on at a tangent out into space . . . though gravitational forces would want to pull him down so he'd get circular motion. [Astronaut in space]   (05:16)

Pupils, as in these examples, were willing to treat velocity and speed as forces and to combine them with other forces (like gravity or air resistance) in order to describe changes in direction or magnitude. Trowbridge and McDermott (1980) report how college students in an introductory physics course were unsuccessful in using the concept of velocity in real physics situations, although they were able to give an acceptable definition of it. Saltiel and Malgrange (1980) also make the point that for French 11-year-old pupils and fourth-year university students: 'Forces and velocities are often intermixed even when all motion is uniform. Our results, together with our co-workers, point to the fact that velocities as well as forces exist *per se* independently of reference frames, and are endowed with causal properties, so that they are invoked to explain motion on a quite similar basis'.

I: Impact forces

This is a model of forces very similar to the concepts of 'momentum' in physics. Objects that are moving have force by virtue of their movement. When moving objects collide, then the collision itself is seen as a force, and the greater the speed of the object, the greater is the force it has. The larger the bulk of the body, then again, the more force it has. This can be paraphrased as:

> *Moving objects are a force, which is made manifest when the object collides with some other body*

I.   Where does the wind get its force from?
S.   I think it's movement . . . the wind moves and it gets its force from that . . . [I. Oh?] . . . it's movement pushing . . . probably that's what it is . . . moving force . . . a force caused by movement. [Wind and tree]   (02:15)
S.   Well, basically it [force] is a push or a pull or a movement of some kind.   (04:15)
J.   Moving things have got forces.   (05:16)

Secondly, force depends on speed and size of object.

R.   Yes . . . the faster you go . . . you've got more force . . . you have to lean further over. [Motorbike taking a corner]   (08:14)
I.   Where do golfballs get their force from?
T.   Umh . . . from their height and their speed. [Golfball]   (09:12)

Force is also seen as a property of collisions – force happens when things collide. This is said of objects that continue to move after the collision, *or* that remain unmoved. It has strong similarity with the physicist's notion of momentum in elastic and inelastic collisions.

S.   By hitting the ground it's able to move off again . . . it's the force it lands with you know . . . [I. Oh?] Yes, the front is hitting something so it's moving . . . It's hitting the ground . . . I suppose getting extra energy from this . . . from the force of the hit. [Golfball]   (04:15)

R.   There's a force of the wind actually hitting . . . when it hits against the tree. [Tree and wind]   (08:14)

M: Motive forces

This was a common framework in the interviews. It is different from the *impact framework* in that forces are not seen as being the motion itself, but are required to cause and maintain the motion. In the impact model, the force *is* the motion. A paraphrasing has been used here that is borrowed from another study (Watts and Zylbersztajn, 1981). Here, the term force has replaced the words 'net force' in the original.

If a body is moving there is a force acting upon it in the direction of the movement. If a body is not moving there is no force acting upon it.

It is evident that some of the pupils *do* consider the force causing motion to be a net force. Others make no distinction between force and net force. These two groups are described in different aspects of the framework as follows. The more general of the two descriptions suggests that the pupils see motion as a necessary consequence of any force. If it is moving it *has* force.

I.   Oh, what's the difference then between force and weight?

G.   . . . Force is *driving* something and weight is just weight . . . force as I see it . . . I think force is something that should *drive* something . . .   (12:15)

S.   If you push something you're pushing energy from *you* into the thing and it'll start going . . . moving.   (02:15)

The second part of the framework gives the impression of a number of forces acting, and that notion occurs when there is an imbalance of force. It suggests a conflict of forces and motion occurring because one force is larger, or in some cases, weakening in the face of opposition.

S.   When a net force is applied to something there . . . is going to be given
     movement or something.   (06:17)
Z.   It's got a lot of force and so it goes up . . . and the force that hits it up is
     greater than the force that brings it down . . . when it gets up there it'll
     even out and then the other will win. [Golfball]   (01:17)

The final aspect of the framework comes from the latter part of the paraphrasing. If motion is caused by a force and that force acts along the line of motion, then when the force stops, so will the motion.

Z.   Unless you're pushed you don't keep going on the flat [Sledge]   (01:17)
J.   Well, if you carry on going straight you'd slow down and eventually stop
     . . . there's nothing helping him along . . . you know, unless he pushed his
     hands along or something he wouldn't move [Sledge]   (05:16)

Both the *motive forces* and the *impact forces* frameworks have been widely reported by other researchers. Osborne (1980), Clement (1977) and Viennot (1979) have each commented on the prevalence of these ideas. As Clement says, 'What has surprised us is the pervasiveness of this belief and the incredible diversity of situations in which it shows up, once one begins to listen to students' commonsense theories'.

Both frameworks are conceptions that are at odds with the Newtonian perspective that a net force acts to change the velocity of an object. Warren (1979) points to textbooks as a major cause of difficulty for students, because of the imprecision of their statements: 'Some elementary books "define" force by saying that "a force will cause a body to move, or tend to move". It is hard to say which is worse, the bad physics (*move* instead of *accelerate*) or the absurd logic. Since "tending to move" a body is contrasted with moving it, the statement above can only mean that a force is something that either moves a body or does not!'

O: Operative forces

To operate is to be in action, to produce an effect or to exercise some influence. This framework of force is very similar to the physicist's notion of *energy*. Children who describe forces this way seem to suggest some form of action that will accomplish an effect. The activity is seen as the property of some objects (see *designed forces*) whilst here the *activity* is described as a force. The activity is consumable, in that it wears off after, or during, the event. It also transforms from one to another during the occurrence.

Force is an action. The amount of force is proportional to the amount of activity taking place.

Physicists describe *energy* as 'the capacity to do work' a definition that seems remarkably similar to some of the pupils' definitions of force.

S.   Something that makes something else happen . . . you can't actually see it.
                                                                          (02:15)

Forces are seen to be 'used up' at a rate that is commensurate with the level of activity. A force can only operate for so long and then it has to be replenished.

R.   The force also gets less after it's hit the golfball . . . as the force wears off the ball just falls down.   (08:14)

Moreover, forces are seen to transfer from one kind to another, so that a chain of events can be accounted for. The force for one particular object may not have been used entirely, but partly transformed to some other kind to continue the activity in another object.

S.   When something pushes something it transfers sort of energy . . . the force is an energy.   (02:15)
J.   It's primarily forced by him . . . and the force of him hitting it and transference from his arms to the club . . . Some of the energy stays with the club and some is transferred into the ball. [Golfball]   (11:15)

In this framework the pupils make both implicit and explicit links between their concept of energy and force, and even go so far as to say that force *is* energy, or *an* energy. Clement (1978), Viennot (1979) and Watts (1980b) have all encountered a similar framework. Clement says, 'Various references to the "stress meaning energy is present", the pillar "resisting compression" and the "force acting through the pillar" being energy, all seem to indicate that the notions of force, force of resistance, elastic force and energy were not clearly distinguished by the students as they are in physics'. Viennot, too, notes that energy is, 'inextricably mixed with the concept of force in a single undifferentiated explanatory complex'.

S: Substantial forces

It seems difficult for pupils to conceive of forces acting-at-a-distance, and they describe forces as *necessarily* having a medium to act through. A force is seen as an actual event, and is presented as a physical presence, a positive, large entity. It is rather similar to a physics notion of *pressure*. It is a property of a substance that is transmitted to all parts of the substance and acts at the surface with other objects. This framework is positive in the sense that events have outcomes, they are clear, overt and obvious. Forces are often substantial, too, in that they are large. A paraphrasing would be:

> *Forces are positive actions that are effective when they come into contact with objects.*

Like the word *power* force has a suggestion of something overwhelming. In this sense of the word, force is contrasted with a gentle action, a light touch or a slight movement.

I.   Is there a force here?
Z.   ... It depends how heavy it is. [Book on a table]   (01:17)
C.   I wouldn't say a tiny drop of water ... I'd say a stone or something has a force on the table ... it'd confuse me if I said something as small as that had. [Water drops]   (07:14)

The 'positive force' framework treats force as out-and-out occurrences: large, intentional and in this sense, overwhelming. This is not a model of a *net* force or the result of a combination of forces, but a view of forces that are only present when some obvious, large scale activity takes place.

Z.   It's only a force if the table breaks ... yes ... they would all come down to the bottom and fall down. [Book on a table]   (01:17)
S.   There's a force in the balloon ... especially if it's a helium one because they rise ... the other ones just sort of rise and then they come down. [Balloon]   (10:11)

Lastly, forces need to have some substance to operate through, and against.

S.   Something to travel through ... a medium to travel through ... forces to travel through ... a solid liquid or gas ... you could say gravity travels through solids ... yes it travels through everything.   (06:17)
G.   Force is a physical reaction to make someone do it but there is not sort of bond between ... not touching ... I'm not *too* sure about it ... I think there *should* be some sort of touching.   (12:15)

Newton himself was reluctant to entertain the idea of action-at-a-distance (See Nuffield Advanced Physics, 1971). Moreover, as can be seen from these extracts, the youngsters do not treat forces as acting along 'a line of application' or acting at a 'point of application'. For them forces are rather more expanded and wholesome. Robertson and Richardson (1975), working with 12- to 15-year-olds in Sydney, Australia, say, 'The tests of conservation of pressure, force, acceleration, work and potential energy, provide dramatic evidence on the lack of understanding of these concepts'. They note that some groups of pupils interpret force as pressure, whilst others distinguish between force and pressure. Some could define and calculate pressure without *conserving* it (being aware of the invariant aspects of the concept in the face of transformations).

Summary

The study in this paper has contented itself with describing eight distinctive frameworks that pupils use when describing common phenomena in terms of their concept of force. It is the work of future studies to:

(a)   describe quantitatively the prevalence of these frameworks in various student populations, possibly along the lines of the study by Watts and Zylbersztajn (1981); and
(b)   explore the classroom implications for school children (and teachers) who may subscribe to these frameworks.

Within each of the eight frameworks some extracts have been provided from interviews conducted by the author with pupils of mixed age and academic achievement. Views have been compiled to construct a composite picture of the ideas.

Some impression of the commonality of the frameworks has been provided by reference to the work of others who have noted similar tendencies in interviewing and testing physics students.

Throughout the study children's alternative frameworks have been given a respected status that reflects their widespread use, their internal coherence and their tenacity in the face of classroom teaching. In analysing individual interview transcripts, an attempt was made to construct frameworks that can account for statements by a pupil in such a way that statements are compatible with each other. The assumption that all of a person's statements are logically consistent to a listener (or reader), is difficult to maintain. However, it is one that has to be made as a working hypothesis, otherwise it is too easy to discount sections of a student's discourse that seem inconsistent with understandable sections.

The aim of the study has been to provide science educators with a repertoire of common frameworks, and some ways in which they differ from the orthodox physics view. By better understanding the beliefs and commitments of pupils about the concept of force, the teacher has a firmer basis from which to choose particular teaching approaches.

Apart from making possible the types of future studies mentioned above, this kind of work might serve the important task of raising teachers' awareness of the difficulties in communicating with children and the need to probe their understanding.

References

Bloor, D. C. (1973) Are philosophers averse to science? In D. O. Edge and J. N. Wolpe (eds.), *Meaning and Control: Essays in Social Aspects of Science and Technology*. London, Tavistock Publications Ltd.

Clement, J. (1977) Catalogue of Students' Conceptual Models in Physics. Section 1: Movement and Force. Mimeograph Department of Physics and Astronomy, University of Massachusetts, USA.

Clement, J. (1978) Student Responses to Questions on the Concept of Energy. Mimeograph, Department of Physics and Astronomy, University of Massachusetts, USA.

Driver, R. and Easley, J. (1978) Pupils and paradigms: a review of the literature related to concept development in adolescent science students, *Studies in Science Education*, Vol. 5, pp. 61–84.

Duit, R. (1981) Students' notions about the energy concept – before and after physics instructions. Paper presented at the International Workshop on problems concerning students' representation of Physics and Chemistry Knowledge, Pädagogische Hochschule Ludwisberg, September 1981.

Erickson, G. L. (1979) Children's conceptions of heat and temperature, *Science Education*, Vol. 63, No. 2, pp. 221–230.

Gilbert, J. K. and Osborne, R. J. (1980) 'I understand, but I don't get it': Some problems of learning science, *School Science Review*, Vol. 61, No. 217, pp. 664–678.

Gilbert, J. K., Osborne, R. J. and Fensham, P. (1982) Children's science and its consequences for teaching, *Science Education*, Vol. 66, No. 4, pp. 623–633.

Gilbert, J. K., Watts, D. M. and Osborne, R. J. (1982) Eliciting student views using an Interview-about-Instances technique, *Physics Education*, Vol. 17, No. 2, pp. 62–65.

Gunstone, R. F. and White, R. T. (1980) A Matter of Gravity. Paper given at the Australian Science Education Association, Melbourne, May 1980.

Helm, H. (1981) Conceptual Misunderstandings in Physics. In *Perspectives 3*, School of Education, University of Exeter, UK.

Jung, W. (1981) Conceptual frameworks in Elementary Optics. Paper presented at the International Workshop on problems concerning students' representation of Physics and Chemistry Knowledge, Pädagogishche Hochschule Ludwisberg, September, 1981.

Nuffield Advanced Physics (1971) *Teachers' Guide Unit 3, Field and Potential*, London, Longmans.

Nussbaum, J. and Novak, J. D. (1976) An assessment of children's concept of the earth using structural interviews, *Science Education*, Vol. 60, pp. 535–550.

Osborne, R. J. (1980) Force, Learning in Science Project, Working Paper No. 13, University of Waikato, Hamilton, NZ.

Osborne, R. J. and Gilbert, J. K. (1980) A technique for exploring students' views of the world, *Physics Education*, Vol. 15, pp. 376–379.

Pfundt, H. (1981) Pre-instructional conceptions about substances and transformations of substances. Paper presented at the International Workshop on problems concerning students' representation of Physics and Chemistry Knowledge, Pädagogische Hochschule Ludwisberg, September 1981.

Robertson, W. W. and Richardson, E. (1975) The development of some physical science concepts in secondary school students, *Journal of Research in Science Teaching*, Vol. 12, No. 4, pp. 319–329.

Saltiel, E. and Malgrange, J. L. (1980) Spontaneous ways of reasoning in elementary kinematics, *European Journal of Physics*, pp. 73–80.

Sutton, C. (1980) The Learner's prior knowledge – a critical review of techniques for probing its organization, *European Journal of Science Education*, Vol. 2, No. 2, pp. 107–120.

Trowbridge, D. and McDermott, L. C. (1980) Investigation of student understanding of the concept of velocity in one dimension, *American Journal of Physics*, Vol. 48, No. 12, pp. 1020–28.

Viennot, L. (1981) The Implication of Mathematical Structure versus Physical Content. Report on a research done by S. Fauconnet. Paper presented at the International Workshop on problems concerning students' representation of Physics and Chemistry Knowledge, Pädagogische Hochschule Ludwisberg, September 1981.

Viennot, L. (1979) Spontaneous reasoning in elementary dynamics. *European Journal of Science Education*, Vol. 1, No. 2, pp. 205–21.

Warren, J. (1979) *Understanding Force*. London, J. Murray.

Watts, D. M. (1980a) A transcription notation. Mimeograph. Institute for Educational Technology, University of Surrey, UK.

Watts, D. M. (1980b) An Exploration of Students' Understanding of the Concepts of Force and Energy. Paper presented for discussion to the International Conference on Education for Physics Teaching, Trieste, Italy, September.

Watts, D. M. and Zylbersztajn, A. (1981) A Survey of Some Ideas about Force. *Physics Education*, Vol. 15, pp. 360–365.

PART FIVE

Classroom Practice

Introduction

In this part we focus on classroom practice.

The Jelly article provides a thought-provoking analysis of how to carry out one of the most important roles a teacher in the classroom can play – questioning.

The remaining articles consist of practical case studies – teachers describing their own approach to the introduction of a science topic in their classroom. Ross describes a project carried out by 10-year-olds whose aim was to find 'the strongest conker in the world'; a micro-computer was used in data collection. Chadwick, a peripatetic teacher of technology, describes a project on the road-holding of cars carried out by 8-year-olds. The Purnell paper contains a description of the use of a scheme on a mechanics topic carried out with top infants using work cards produced by Purnell's primary science project.

These three case studies, all on physical science topics, illustrate the variety of approaches available to the primary science teacher.

5.1

HELPING CHILDREN RAISE QUESTIONS – AND ANSWERING THEM

Sheila Jelly

In my experience, many of the questions children ask spontaneously are not profitable starting points for science. The commonest questions I get asked in infant classrooms are along the lines, 'Is Mr Jelly your husband/father/brother?' I quote this not as a facetious example, but to make the point that questions from young children reflect an urge to make associations with their previous experience. Even when this associative process is triggered by interesting materials with great potential for scientific investigation, a child's curiosity often does not show itself as spontaneous questioning but rather as a statement of interests. 'Look it (snail) has little eyes on stalks.' In situations like this, teachers have to intervene in order to frame problems that children can investigate in a scientific way: 'Are they really eyes?' 'Can snails see?' 'How might we find out?' So in practice it is very often a *teacher's* questioning, not a child's that initiates scientific activity. For this reason any consideration of handling children's questions in science must be closely related to the way in which a teacher handles her own questioning.

[. . .] Productive questions, which stimulate productive activity, are distinguished from unproductive questions, which do not lead to scientific activity but the recall of factual knowledge. Unproductive questions are those to which a child either knows the answer ('Where did you find it?') or, if he does not ('What's it called?'), he obtains it from secondary sources – the teacher or books. Such questions may be very useful for encouraging conversation, or with the development of reading skills in mind, for sending children to books to acquire information, but as starting points for scientific

Source: Harlen, W. (ed) (1985) *Primary Science: Taking the Plunge.* London, Heinemann, pp.47–57

activity they are very limited and unproductive. The features of these two types of question are summarized in the Table below.

Unproductive	Productive
Promote science as information	Promote science as a way of working
Answers derived from secondary sources by talking/reading	Answers derived from first hand experience involving practical action with materials
Tend to emphasize answering as the achievement of a correct end product (the right answer)	Encourage awareness that varied answers may each be 'correct' on their own terms and view achievement as what is learnt in the process of arriving at an answer
Successful answering is most readily achieved by verbally fluent children who have confidence and facility with words	Successful answering is achievable by all children

Productive questions are the type we need to encourage in the classroom if we wish to promote science as a way of working, but experience shows that teachers ask far more unproductive questions than productive ones and frequently find the framing of productive questions a difficult task. This is not at all surprising because most of us have acquired our formal education in bookish environments and have accordingly established questioning styles that tend to require factual answers. But it is important to make the effort to change the pattern of questioning, since productive questions are a very powerful tool for the teacher. They have considerable value when planning science work; they are extremely useful in those 'thinking on the feet' situations where we make an instantaneous response to something a child says or does, and importantly, they are the kind of question that children can profitably 'catch' if we wish them to find their own problems for investigation.

If we are to improve the range and quality of questioning in a classroom three things are required:

1. Improve our own ability to ask questions.
2. Establish a climate of curiosity and questioning that is conducive to question-asking by the children.
3. Develop strategies for handling children's spontaneous questions.

Improving teachers' own questioning skills

From the various types of productive question [. . .] it is possible to see that there are general frameworks which can be applied in a variety of situations:

'Which _____ is best for _____?'

'Who has the _____?' (strongest hair, best sight, keenest hearing)

'Will it _____ if we _____?' (swing more quickly if we make it longer)

'Do _____ prefer _____?' (any animal/any food or condition)

The key to generating specific questions for particular situations is *practice*. With this in mind here are three activities for teachers to help improve questioning skills.

1. Try taping conversation when there is science work going on in the classroom. Later analyse the quesions the teacher asks. Are they unproductive or productive? What is the proportion of each type? Of the productive questions what kind of child activity did each promote? This is a salutory experience for us all! The first analysis may well prove a little disheartening but, over time, it becomes very encouraging to note how questioning styles can alter.

2. Scrutinize the questions posed in primary science books. Are they unproductive or productive? If productive, what scientific experiences are they encouraging? Many teachers who have carried out this activity report an increased awareness of question types and an increased facility in generating their own productive questions.

3. Use odd moments to practise question-finding. Suppose, for example, you are waiting in a car park (a useful situation, since all schools will have one). What is its potential for science? What productive questions could you ask about it to stimulate children's scientific activity? Make a list of attention-focusing questions. [. . .] Try to go beyond the obvious properties such as colour/shape/kind/age and include questions involving patterns and relationships. For example:

Which of the cars are rusting?
Which parts of a car rust?

Which parts have no rust?
Do all cars rust in the same place?
Is there any connection between the amount of rust and the age of a car?
What attention-focusing questions might you ask about car tyres, windows or lights?

Try also to identify problem-posing questions, such as which colour is the best safety colour for a car? Can you think of others? What productive questions are appropriate for a study of the buildings around the car park?

It's also useful to apply question-finding practice to normal classroom events. Think, for example, of the water play area of an infant classroom. The children will have observational experience of things that float and things that sink. How might their work be extended to involve fair-testing experience? What questions could they be asked? 'Who can make the best boat?' is one that can promote interesting discussion and activity. Can you think of another?

Establishing a classroom climate conducive to children's question-asking

If questioning styles are not taught, a teacher's verbal questioning will probably be the most important factor in establishing a climate conducive to question-asking by children. But it is not the only factor and so it is useful to consider ways by which curiosity might be aroused and how such curiosity can be linked to particularly questioning frameworks. As a first step we need to get children's interest stimulated and this means giving them direct contact with materials. It also means that we need to think carefully about the nature of the materials that make children curious. Materials brought in spontaneously by the children have a built-in curiosity factor and need no further discussion; but what of materials selected by teachers? These can usefully be considered in two categories: those with immediate appeal and those that are commonplace when seen through a child's eyes, but which can evoke curiosity if teacher tactics present them in a new and challenging light. The first kind present fewest problems because we know that certain properties such as colour, shape and movement can, in themselves, trigger curiosity. Indeed we constantly capitalize on these facts when we introduce materials into the classroom. But if we remember that children's response is shaped largely by what they guess to be the expectations their teacher has for them, then in many classes materials will promote activities of the kind summarized in Figure 1.

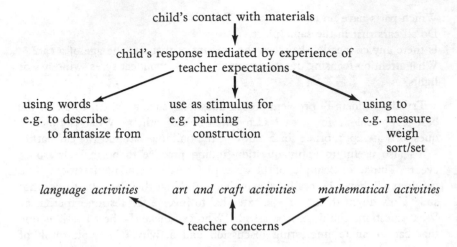

Figure 1

Not surprisingly, therefore, a child's response tends to show itself as an application of the known (procedures and techniques), rather than in a concern for the unknown and an associated generation of questions. For this reason it is helpful to concentrate consciously on building up what we might call the questioning dimension in children's expectations of how teacher would like them to respond. This dimension can be developed when they associate with a teacher's productive questioning style. It can also be strengthened by teacher-promoted activities which reinforce the style; activities that bring children into contact with materials linked to appropriate questions, and activities that provide opportunities for children to frame their own productive questions. Increased contact with appropriate questions can be achieved in a variety of ways. For example:

1. By making sure that displays and collections have associated enquiry questions for the children to read, ponder and perhaps explore incidentally to the main work of the class.
2. By introducing a problem corner or a 'question of the week' activity where materials and associated questions are on offer to the children as a stimulus to thought and action which might be incorporated into classwork.
3. By making 'questions to investigate' lists that can be linked to popular information books.

4. By ensuring that in any teacher-made science work cards there is a question framed to encourage children to see their work as enquiry-based and which also provides a useful heading for any resultant work displayed in the classroom.

Opportunities for children to frame productive questions include activities such as:

1. Using regular class time (such as news time or equivalent) to encourage children to talk about something interesting they have observed, and to tell others of the questions it prompts.
2. Encouraging children to supply 'questions of the week' (as in the activity described above).
3. Establishing procedures by which children, having completed a piece of work, are encouraged to list further questions about it. For example, individually when completing a work card or collectively when discussing work on display.

With techniques such as these it is often surprising how much the quality of children's questioning improves over a period of time. However, it should be stated that, initially, most children find it a very difficult task and tend to ask only unproductive questions. They will need lots of encouragement and quite clearly too much emphasis on question-asking too soon can be counter-productive and may result in a 'not another question' dismissal rather than the excitement and enthusiasm we wish to develop.

Curiously, materials that are very 'ordinary' in children's eyes often generate more sustained question-asking than materials with obvious child appeal. Perhaps this is because a child's particular involvement with things with immediate appeal is sufficient satisfaction in itself and further scrutiny becomes an intrusive and unwanted distraction. Whatever the reason, it is worth considering how commonplace things can be used to promote question-generating situations. For example:

1. By using collections of everyday things as a focus for linking materials with teacher-framed questions. A collection of kitchen utensils, say, has little immediate appeal but associated with appropriate questions it can provide challenging involvement. If for example the tools are sorted by function many enquiry questions can follow. In time, children can be encouraged to organize their own collections of 'ordinary' things and supply questions for others to investigate.

2. By selecting materials for practical investigation that do unexpected things. As for example, the effect of dropping a plasticine ball on polystyrene when investigating bouncing balls. Anomalous happenings are very good question stimulators.

3. By using magnifiers and microscopes to extend children's observation so that they will see exciting detail in familiar things.

4. By considering the extent to which the conventional aesthetic approach to display can be broadened to include materials which may not be visually pleasing but which justify inclusion in display themes because of their potential for enquiry work. For example, a display centred on the theme of the sea is made richer educationally by the inclusion of some tatty, ugly shoreline debris if the material is linked to challenging questions.

Teacher tactics of the kind described do, undoubtedly, improve the climate of enquiry in a classroom and, as a consequence, lead to more spontaneous questioning by children.

Handling children's spontaneous questions

Spontaneous questions from children come in various forms and carry a variety of meanings. Consider for example the following questions. How would you respond to each?

1. What is a baby tiger called?
2. What makes it rain?
3. Why can you see yourself in a window?
4. Why is the hamster ill?
5. If I mix these (paints), what colour will I get?
6. If God made the world, who made God?
7. How long do cows live?
8. How does a computer work?
9. When will the tadpoles be frogs?
10. Are there people in outer space?

Clearly the nature of each question shapes our response to it. Even assuming we wanted to give children the correct answers, we could not do so in all cases. Question 6 has no answer, but we can of course respond to it. Question 10 is similar; it has no certain answer but we could provide a conjectural one based on some relevant evidence. All the other questions do have answers, but this does not mean that each answer is similar in kind, nor does it mean that all answers are known to the teacher, nor are all answers equally accessible to children.

When we analyse what we do everyday as part of our stock-in-trade, namely respond to children's questions, we encounter a highly complex situation. Not only do questions vary in kind, requiring answers that differ in kind, but children also have different reasons for asking a question. The question may mean 'I want a direct answer', it might mean 'I've asked the question to show you I'm interested but I'm not after a literal answer.' Or, it could mean, 'I've asked the question because I want your attention – the answer is not important.' Given all these variables how then should we handle the questions raised spontaneously in science work? The comment of one teacher is pertinent here:

> 'The children's questions worry me. I can deal with the child who just wants attention, but because I've no science background I take other questions at face value and get bothered when I don't know the answer. I don't mind saying I don't know, though I don't want to do it too often. I've tried the "let's find out together" approach, but it's not easy and can be very frustrating.'

Many teachers will identify with these remarks and what follows is a suggested strategy for those in a similar position. It's not the only strategy possible, nor is it completely fail-safe, but it has helped a large number of teachers deal with difficult questions. By difficult questions I mean those that require complex information and/or explanation for a full answer. The approach does not apply to simple informational questions such as 1, 7 and 9 on the list above because these are easy to handle, either by telling or by reference to books, or expertise, in ways familiar to the children in other subject areas. Nor is it relevant to spontaneous questions of the productive kind discussed earlier, because these can be answered by doing. Essentially it is a strategy for handling complex questions and in particular those of the 'why' kind that are the most frequent of all spontaneous questions. They are difficult questions because they carry an apparent request for a full explanation which may not be known to the teacher and, in any case, is likely to be conceptually beyond a child's understanding.

The strategy recommended is one that turns the question to practical action with a 'let's see what we can do to understand more' approach. The teaching skill involved is the ability to 'turn' the question. Consider, for example, a situation in which children are exploring the properties of fabrics. They have dropped water on different fabrics and become fascinated by the fact that water stays, 'like a little ball' on felt. They tilt the felt, rolling the ball around, and someone asks, 'Why is it like a ball?' How might the question be turned by applying the 'doing more to understand' approach? We need to analyse the situation quickly and use what I call a 'variables scan'. The explanation must relate to something 'going on' between the water and the felt surface so causing the ball. That being so, ideas for children's activities will come if we consider ways in which the situation could be varied to better understand the making of the ball. We could explore surfaces keeping the drop the same, and explore drops keeping the surface the same. These thoughts can prompt others that bring ideas nearer to what children might do. For example:

1. Focusing on the surface, keeping the drop the same:
    What is special about the felt that helps make the ball?
    Which fabrics are good 'ball-makers'?
    Which are poor?
    What have the good ball-making fabrics in common?
    What surfaces are good ball-makers?
    What properties do these share with the good ball-making fabrics?
    Can we turn the felt into a poor ball-maker?
2. Focusing on the water drop, keeping the surface the same:
    Are all fluids good ball-makers?
    Can we turn the water into a poor ball-maker?

Notice how the 'variables scan' results in the development of productive questions than can be explored by the children. The original question has been turned to practical activity and children exploring along these lines will certainly enlarge their understanding of what is involved in the phenomenon. They will not arrive at a detailed explanation but may be led towards simple generalization of their experience, such as 'A ball will form when . . . ' or 'It will not form when . . . '

Some teachers see the strategy as one of diversion (which it is) and are uneasy that the original question remains unanswered, but does this matter? The question has promoted worthwhile scientific enquiry and we must remember that its meaning for the child may well have been 'I'm asking it to communicate my interest'. For such children interest has certainly been developed and children who may have initiated the question as a request for explanation in practice, are normally satisfied by the work their question generates.

The strategy can be summarized as follows:

Analyse the question
↓
Consider if it can be 'turned'
to practical activity (with its
'real' materials or by simulating them)
↓
Carry out a 'variables scan' and identify
productive questions
↓
Use questions to promote activity
↓
Consider simple generalizations children
might make *from experience*

It is not a blue print for handling *all* difficult questions, but it does provide a framework that helps us to cope with many of them. Its use becomes easier with practice. Try using it to respond to the question 'Why can you see yourself in a window?' (a comparatively simple application) and to the question 'Why do aeroplanes stay up?' which is a more complex application. The task may be difficult initially, indeed several aspects of the analysis and use of questions put forward in this chapter may prove likewise. But the effective handling of questions is vital in any science programme.

Summary of main points

Children learn their question-asking habits from teachers. If children are to be encouraged to raise questions that lead to investigation, this is one more reason for teachers making the effort to ask more productive questions and fewer unproductive ones. Some specific ways in which teachers can practise and improve question skills have been suggested.

The atmosphere in the classroom must also be conducive to encouraging children to ask questions. Some ways of showing that questions are welcome are by adding questions to displays and collections, introducing a problem corner in the classroom, creating lists of 'questions to investigate', making sure any work cards or sheets are framed in terms of investigable questions. Regular discussion of questions is also important. Children, like teachers, do not find it easy at first to change the emphasis in their questioning from unproductive to productive. Novel materials are not necessarily the best stimulus; often more familiar ones help children raise questions, especially with a lead from the teacher to the kind of productive questions that can be asked.

Once children begin to ask questions they will ask ones of all kinds; some will be difficult for teachers to handle, but it is important to find a way of doing this which does not make the child wish (s)he had not asked. A strategy has been described for analysing children's questions so that unproductive ones can be used productively.

Guidelines for encouraging children's questioning

1. Provide a wide range of materials for children to respond to.
2. Practise and improve your questioning style so that it provides an example for the children.
3. Provide a climate of enquiry for children to work in.
4. Encourage children to form and to discuss their own questions.
5. Respond positively to children's spontaneous questions.
6. Turn children's unproductive questions into productive ones that promote investigation of real materials.

5.2

THE STRONGEST CONKER IN THE WORLD

Alistair Ross

It had been a particulary good conker season. London parks and playgrounds were awash with them. Before school one morning I came upon a group of my third-year junior class (9–10 year olds) engaged in a heated discussion about what exactly constituted a strong conker. Most of the proposals were for semi-secret recipes – some favoured long slow baking in the oven, others soaking in vinegar.

When the class started, I opened the discussion up to the whole class. After we had discussed what we were told about the secret recipes, I moved the discussion on to the 'normal' attributes of a conker. Lots of suggestions were made: 'Very big ones are best, and very little ones, but not the in-between ones'; 'Heavy ones are best'; 'Float them in water – the ones that float are not good'; 'The older the better. Save them up for a year, or even two or three years'. It was noticeable that lots of children were joining in with ideas, and not just the regular conker players made suggestions.

I asked them all to write down, very briefly, what they thought were the important things to look for in a conker. I suggested that we might go on to make some tests on conkers, to see if we could find the strongest conker. Some of the suggestions were pithy and concise:

'Big, thick-skinned, hard-middled, heavy, and about a week-old conker'
'When the shell is 2 mm thick, it is 2 years old, quite small or big'
'The inside should be hard; the older the better'

Source: The Open University (1984) P542 *Micros in Schools: Micros in Action in the Classroom: case studies*, Milton Keynes, The Open University Press, pp.20–23

Others were more expansive:

'What I think makes a good conker:
1. The age of the conker – the older the better.
2. The size – the big ones and small ones are better than the medium-sized ones.
3. The thickness of the shell also matters.
4. As well as being hard outside, it should be inside too.
I think that in the game conkers the more you use it the weaker it will get.'

Some were technical, using conker-users' jargon: 'An old conker will crack by itself, because it is a death crack', or used their experience to write suggestions: 'I don't think that age makes any difference, because some year-old ones were just as good as new ones. I think it depends on how you treat the conker, because if you bump it around it will probably get cracked. I think that heavy conkers are good conkers, because they travel at such a speed they smash the other conker'; 'If a little conker doesn't break, it is normally because it is bouncey. That's why little conkers are good. Big ones are also good'.

We then discussed how we could test conkers for strength. I managed to steer the conversation away from the suggestion that we have a long series of in-classroom conker fights, and towards the idea that we try to measure the strength in some way. Dropping them out of the window on to the playground seemed a good idea at first, but then somebody pointed out that there were only a limited number of heights from which we could drop conkers. More interestingly, several of them knew that although each conker, whatever its weight, would hit the ground at the same speed if it was dropped from the same height, different weight conkers would hit the playground with a force dependent on their weight. This, they argued, would make the test unfair to heavier conkers – they would hit the playground harder and therefore break at lower weights. ('Unless', suggested one boy, 'we worked out a sort of scale of heights and weights, so we knew how much less we had to drop heavy ones to be fair'. Nobody else seemed able to follow this.)

Then someone had a brainwave. If we couldn't drop the conkers, why not drop something on the conker? A regular weight would mean that we only need measure the height from which it was dropped. All we had to do was to gradually increase the height until the conker cracked, and use this height as a measure of its strength. We tried the idea with a 1 kilogram weight, but it wasn't quite as simple as it sounded. Just dropping the weight wasn't good enough. Sometimes the edge of the weight caught the conker and cut into it, and this seemed unfair. One child suggested making a cardboard tube, positioning this over the conker, and dropping the weight in at the top. Of course, to get a range of heights, we would have to have a range of different length tubes. And so the 'destructor' shown in Figure 1 was born. However, after trying it out for a couple of dozen conkers, we began to have second thoughts. Children noticed that the weights seemed to be going down the longer tubes more slowly. We discovered that they were gradually buckling, and thus slowing down the passage of the weight. The tubes were relegated to 'Destructor Mark 1', and the search was on for Mark 2.

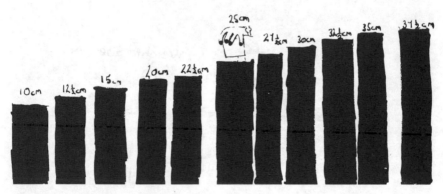

Figure 1   Destructor Mark 1

We finally fixed a cardboard aiming box on to the upright rule used for measuring children's heights, and placed a target underneath it. We found that if we carefully placed the conkers on the target, we could accurately drop the weight through the aiming box on the centre of the conker as shown in Figure 2. With the 'Destructor Mark 2' operational, we began serious testing.

Conkers had been gathered for several days. We assumed that they were 'fresh' on the day that they were picked up in the parks, and we amassed trays of conkers of various dates over a 2-week span. Each conker was then numbered with a waterproof felt-tip pen, and a catalogue begun, showing each conker's record number and the date it was collected. Each conker was then weighed (to the nearest gram) and its volume measured, by displacement of water in a measuring cylinder. The volumes were not measured terribly accurately, due to the generally poor level of accurate measuring devices found in primary schools, but I felt that measurements were sufficiently close to be worthwhile including.

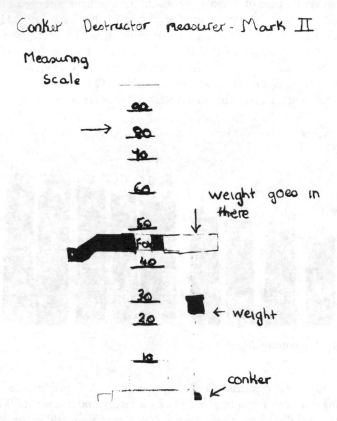

Figure 2   Destructor Mark 2

'We measured the volume of conkers by measuring 20 cc of water in a plastic measuring tube, and then put the conker in and saw how much the water had risen. The highest a conker made the water rise was 20 cc, and these conkers had that volume.' (See Figure 3.)

Some conkers floated:

'If the conker floated we would push it under the water with the tip of our pencil, and measure how much the water went up. We wrote this down and put an F next to it, but if it sank we just recorded how much the water had gone up.'

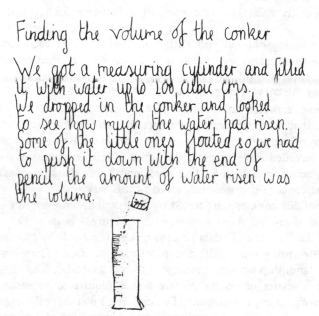

Finding the volume of the conker

We got a measuring cylinder and filled it with water up to 100 cubic cms. We dropped in the conker and looked to see how much the water had risen. Some of the little ones floated so we had to push it down with the end of pencil, the amount of water risen was the volume.

Figure 3   Finding the volume of the conkers

Several conkers also had hair-line cracks in the skin before they were tested. This was also noted on the catalogue: these conkers were tested until a 'real' crack appeared. The other conkers were tested until the first crack appeared. The children usually started to drop the weight from a height of 10 centimetres, and worked up from these in 2.5-centimetre stages. However, I did notice that certain groups acquired a knack of better estimating the strength of conkers, and would sometimes start with a higher initial drop.

Figure 4   Some conker data

Ref. no.	Found	Weight (grms)	Volume (cc)	Conkered	Strength (cms)	Age when tested	Skin thickness (mm)
1	16 Sept.	17	16	N	22.5	6	0.6
2	18 Sept.	12	14F	N	27.5	4	0.35
3	14 Sept.	15	12	Y	17.5	8	0.65

Our efforts to obtain a range of old and new conkers were helped when one collector brought in a batch of 40 one-year-old conkers for testing. Not knowing exactly when they were collected, we gave them a notional age of 365 days!

The measuring did not end with the destruction of each conker. One hypothesis to be tested was that skin thickness had an effect on strength, so they peeled the skin off each conker and used a micrometer screw gauge to measure its thickness. However, they quickly discovered that there was some considerable variation in the thickness of each shell. At first one child suggested that they consistently measure the whiter skin area, but this was rejected by others as unfair. In the end they made three measurements of each skin and recorded the average of the three. The instruments available were not really sensitive enough for this work, and it was also time-consuming, so not all the conker skins were measured in this way.

A total of 209 conkers were tested by destruction, however. We now had a large table of results, about 4 metres long! Figure 4 is an extract from this. This was ideal material for data-processing on the school's microcomputer, an RML 380Z, using the LEEP data-processing package. There was no self-evident relationship between the various factors we had measured – there was obviously a scatter of results and we would require to do some statistical analysis to detect any correlations. The children's own hypotheses, when they talked about them now, slipped into more generalised statements, such as 'Most large conkers will be stronger than most small conkers'.

The class and I devised a data file, with nine fields (or vertical columns), and entered the data of 209 conkers, each conker constituting one record. The file structure included the length of each field (the number of characters wide it needed to be to accommodate the data), and the type of field – whether it included only numerical data (N), or a mixture of numerical and alphabetical data (A).

Fieldname	Length	Type	Notes
No two	3	N	serial number*
FOUND	7	A	date of finding conker*
WEIGHT	2	N	grms
VOLUME	2	N	cc
STRENGTH	4	N	cms (with a decimal point)
AGE	3	N	days
SKIN	3	N	mm (with a decimal point)
BUST	1	A	Y or N (yes or no)
FLOAT	1	A	F or N (float or not)

*These fields are in fact redundant.

The information was then typed into the computer and stored on disk. Each child typed in between six and a dozen records in all. This was a fairly quick task, and had started during the testing.

When the datafile was complete, we were almost ready to start testing the various hypotheses. But, as the children themselves observed, we would first need to decide what we meant by categories such as 'large' and 'small' conkers. I divided the class into five groups, and asked each to make a computer enquiry that would help them decide what should be the exact categories for different weights, volumes, ages, strengths and skin thicknesses. To do this, each group made a simple enquiry: they used the LEEP program to search for all records, and to output one field in order. For example, VOLUME in order produced a list of 209 weights, starting at 2 cc (of which there were three conkers) and increasing up to 22 cc (of which there were seven). With a pen they marked off the various volumes of conker in 2 cc intervals, added up the number in each group, and made a bar-graph. There was a bell-shaped distribution of volumes. This work is shown in Figure 5.

The children decided that 'small' was going to mean 'with volume < 10 cc', large would be 'with volume > 15 cc' and all those in between would be 'medium'. Thus about 30 percent of the conkers were 'large', and 30 percent 'small'. Similar categories were arrived at by other groups. For example, 'strong' conkers were the 73 with a cracking point of over 32 centimetres, the 'weak' conkers were the 67 of 20 centimetres or less, and the average strength were the 67 in between 20 and 32 centimetres.

Hypotheses were now tested. This was done in a variety of ways. For a start, scatter graphs were drawn showing the range of results. This was rather difficult to do, but had the advantage of demonstrating that we could only arrive at a possible rule, not an absolute one – some conkers did not obey the rules! They attempted to draw a line of correlation though the scatter of points, but this was extremely difficult.

Better, they found, was to sort out and block graph three sets of conkers: for example, one group made three enquiries, to produce lists of the strengths of large, small and medium-sized conkers. Their enquiries were respectively for VOLUME > 15, VOLUME < 10, AND VOLUME > 9, AND VOLUME < 16. Each list was then examined to discover the number of strong, weak and average-strengthened conkers in it. Three bar-charts were drawn. This work is shown in Figure 6.

(Conkers that had cracks already were eliminated in this table.)

'Most of the big conkers are the strong ones . . . The medium-sized conkers aren't as good as the big-sized conkers, but the small-sized conkers are

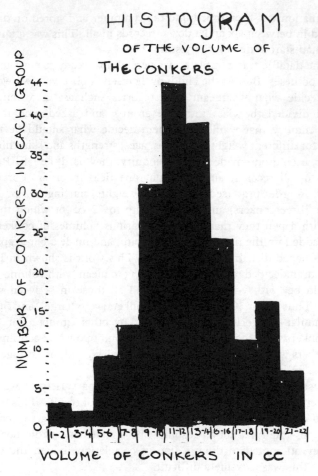

Figure 5   Some children's work on conker volumes

definitely the worst.' A third method of showing results was to make smaller groups of one variable – say all 1–2 day-old conkers, all 3–4 day-old conkers, and so on – and to find the average strength of each group. The micro-computer could do both the sorting and the averaging, and some striking graphs were made. In particular, they were all astounded to discover that there was a negative correlation between age and strength: fresh conkers, less than 3 days old, were on average twice as strong as conkers 13–14 days old.

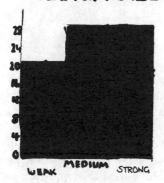

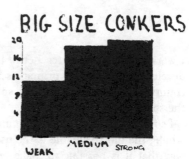

Figure 6   Categorizing the conkers

This did not hold completely true, because the year-old conkers proved to have somehow regained some (but not all) of their strength.

There was much discussion about this discovery, and also that skin thickness doesn't make a great deal of difference to strength. Finally a composite formula was arrived at to help decide which conkers were likely to be strong. This formula eliminated references to skin thickness, partly because no one was very happy about the accuracy of our measurements, but also (more pertinently) there wasn't much point in destroying a conker by peeling its skin off to see how strong it was!

The conclusion:

'The strongest conker in the world is . . .
   with a weight of over 17 grams
   with a volume of over 14 cc
   it should be 1–4 days old (or over 365 days old)
Big conkers are better than small conkers, and new conkers are better than old ones'.

5.3

ROAD HOLDING

Eileen Chadwick

I work as a peripatetic teacher of technology, my task being to introduce and develop the subject in primary schools in Berkshire in accordance with the county's concern that children should develop a technological awareness of the society in which we live.

I could accomplish my task in many ways. However, a strategy I have found among the most valuable is the use of science for solving problems in such a way that it is possible to make end products. I have used this approach to produce articles in concrete, small wooden bridges, food items, Christmas cards and packaging. I believe it is an extremely effective way to teach science to primary school children. They recognize science as a problem-solving activity and look more keenly for its application in society after their experience in the classroom. Children learn best by doing and no amount of telling can replace this. If we want them to be aware of technology it is therefore essential that they practise it for themselves and see its merits.

It is my experience that teachers often feel at a loss when it comes to using science to solve problems and wonder how on earth to organize 30 children while following an open-ended approach to teaching. Open-ended teaching seems to ask much of its practitioners in that they start out not only not knowing what the end result of any lesson will be but also not knowing where the search for the result is likely to start! The aim of this paper is to show not only how open-ended teaching may occur in a framework of organization rather than chaos but also to demonstrate how children might discover physics concepts for themselves.

Source: specially commissioned for this volume

The project described here concerns the design and making of a small wooden car which has good road-holding qualities but which uses as little energy as possible. (There are several good projects which have similar design briefs).

I have used this project in four different schools over 3 years, and no two sets of experiments were the same.

Ask the children to organize themselves into threes or fours. Each group should then choose a name, such as Clever Cars Ltd. Children who are often difficult are frequently not so in this situation, as working with friends is a great motivator. Children are highly social beings if we give them opportunities to develop as such. It is amazing how group membership motivates at this age. Remember children have an intrinsic need to learn.

To avoid classroom chaos when the children are all engaged in practical work, it is useful to have a method of restoring order. I use the signal 'Waxworks'. It means be as still as figures at the waxworks, stop talking and listen. This works even when the children are all absorbed in their own activities. Children should be reminded of the acceptable working level of noise. They should also be reminded that if a class member or yourself is talking, everyone listens to that person; it is rude not to do so.

Each group should appoint a new manager each week. The manager's task is to ensure (without being bossy) that everyone has something to do, to collect additional materials needed during the course of experiments and to seek the teacher's advice if necessary. This prevents too many people wandering around the class at the same time and too many demands on the teacher's time.

I have found the following compartments to a 75-minute science lesson to be useful:

0 – 20 minutes	Lesson introduction by teacher. A dramatic beginning, using a toy or something gimmicky which appeals to them, sets a project off to a flying start. Once their enthusiasm is aroused they can't wait to begin.
20 – 60 minutes	Experimenting themselves.
60 – 75 minutes	Class discussion. Groups present findings. One member (often manager for that week) communicates results to the rest. This is an ideal opportunity to develop communication skills – a necessity in modern society.

The case study

The school in which this case study was carried out was Churchend Primary School, Tilehurst, near Reading. It was chosen as representative of many schools on the outskirts of a large town or city and one in which there was a large number of 'average' children. The catchment area consists of children from council estate and privately owned houses. There are some children whose academic performance is above average and there are some whose performance is below, as well as a large number in the middle. The language development of the below-average attainers is poor and probably a major cause of their low attainment. However, most of the children have average or higher than averge reading scores for their age, and this is something the school prides itself upon. Standards of written work and spelling are also high.

All parts of the school, including the nursery unit, were taking part in a co-operative topic on transport, and the science work was developed to fit into this. The school also uses the West Sussex scheme Science Horizons, from which the teachers extract workcards for their relevance to their current topic.

Lesson 1

I introduced the design brief to the children: to design, make and test a small car which had good road holding but used as little energy as possible. We looked at two home-made wooden cars I had brought and toys they had brought and predicted which would have the desired qualities. Not many seemed to understand the words 'energy' or 'road-holding' and had difficulty in finding one car which would fit both aspects of the problem. I felt the children would benefit more from group rather than class discussion on this so I deferred the question and asked them how we would know how to make the finished article. Someone suggested making a test car, another suggested testing the cars brought in, and another suggested going outside to look at cars. Any of these would have been acceptable beginnings but I decided to put them in groups and to ask each group to make a test car.

The children were reminded of the rules and were allowed to group themselves into threes or fours, to choose a group manager and to select a company name. This seemed to appeal to them as much as the idea of making a test car.

At any one time, one third of the class were making simple test cars. They sawed up some scrap wood about 18cm × 9cm, used panel pins for axles and fastened small aeroplane wheels (purchased at a model shop) to their cars. The

Design

Invent and make a small car which has good road holding ability and uses as little energy as possible

We made this test bed for some experiments I'm in a company called "Tracks" LTD

Desk floor Worktop Newspaper

rest were copying down the design brief and drawing plans for cars which might answer the problem. The children, on completing their cars, naturally began running them on different surfaces. I saw this as a golden opportunity to introduce the children to the scientific method.

I gathered the class together (Waxworks works well!) and asked if they had noticed anything about how the cars ran on different surfaces. They had lots to say on this. I asked them how we could do a fair test to find out. As they were unsure about what I meant, I phrased if differently – would it be fair if we ran the test car along the floor, a table or a work-surface but put different passengers on each time? We did this. Most *seemed* to know what I meant. As time ran out, the experiments were left until next time.

Lesson 2

I introduced the lesson to the class by showing them working models of vehicles which used different sources of energy. One was driven by a propeller and electric motor, another by an elastic band, and the third was a steam engine. I asked them where the 'go' came from in each case, and then where the 'go' in cars came from. We related 'go' to energy. The reason for this was that I was not sure most of this class understood energy as an abstract concept.

We discussed why the test cars moved more easily over one surface than another. The children rubbed their hands together and felt friction effects. I told them we were going to attach an elastic band to the test car and were going to pull it along different surfaces. I demonstrated with a child's help the effect of small pulls and large pulls on the elastic band. The children were then asked to divide themselves into their groups and I asked them to think about how we could carry out a fair test for each surface.

Each group manager told the rest of the class what sort of test that group thought would work. We decided on a single fair test for all the groups: pulling the test cars over a distance of $\frac{1}{2}$ metre and measuring the difference in the stretch of the band. Each group recorded its results as follows:

Surface	Amount of stretch
Desk	
Floor	
Worktop	
Newspaper	

Does the elastic band stretch differently on different surfaces?

CW

Surface	stretch
Desk	11 cm
Floor	8 cm
Work top	5 cm
Newspaper	1 cm

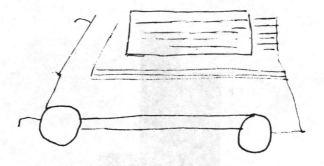

Our table shows that the desk uses most energy and the newspaper uses least.

Does the elastic band stretch
differently on different surfaces?

Surfaces . . . . Stretch

floor 9cm   2nd

desk 11cm   1st

worktop 5cm   3rd

Newspaper . . . . -2cm   4th

The desk used most energy because
it was rough and it had most friction

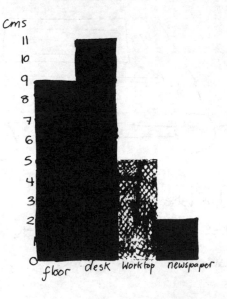

The groups presented their findings to others. They equated friction with roughness and we discussed which roads near to the school would use most petrol.

I found children varied in their ability to calculate the difference in stretch. Most had no trouble with this, but a poorer group did not understand. I think the experience was still very useful for them as a means of developing mathematical concepts.

Lesson 3

I decided that the children were still not ready to work on their own hypotheses (each group on a different experiment) and that the whole class should work on a single idea suggested by a class member. So, at the start of the lesson, I drew the children's attention to the design problem and asked what sort of experiment we could do to solve the problem.

The ideas were sorted into two classes:

Seeing if different cars use different amounts of energy	*Seeing if different cars have different road holding*
1. Change the mass of the car and pull it up a slope.	1. Change the mass of cars and see which turn over as they run down a slope.
2. Change the mass of the car and let it run down a slope	2. See if heavier cars are better at road holding if they are catapulted.
3. Change the mass of the car, make a force-giver and see how far the car goes.	3. Change the mass and see how they hold the road after a series of bends.

I ended up deciding that they should work on two ideas – the first and third ideas in the first column. The rest of the ideas were written down and saved for a later date.

We changed the mass of the car by adding weights. In the first test the car was pulled up a slope and the stretch of the elastic band attached to it was measured. In the second test, catapult elastic (available from model shops) was tied around chair legs and was used as a force-giver to move the car forward.

(The children can fix a piece of wood or coat-hanger wire to their test cars so that the catapult elastic has something to push against.) The groups were asked to discuss how to make the tests fair and how to make them accurate. Each group chose one of the two tests to work on and recorded the results as follows:

Mass	Band stretch

Mass added	Distance travelled

During this experiment it became obvious that this was the last time the children could work together on the same theme as they were at different conceptual levels. We discussed the results at the end of the lesson, and the following interesting questions arose:

- Why does a car need more energy going up a hill?
- What is gravity?
- Do buses with more passengers go further if they freewheel down a hill?
- What other forces apart from gravity are at work when cars go up and down hill?

Lessons 4, 5 and 6

I made a display of the conclusions arrived at during the two previous lessons and then asked the children for ideas for experiments. The groups were then allowed to choose their own experiment. They also discussed experimental design, including how to make the test fair.

The chosen experiments were:

1. Freewheeling the cars down a slope kept at constant angle and measuring the distance travelled.
2. Making and fixing different cardboard shapes to a car and measuring the distance travelled down a slope.
3. Making a series of bends, adding different masses to the cars and seeing which hold the road best.

4. Seeing if cars of different masses are more likely to go off course when they freewheel down a slope.
5. Catapulting the cars and seeing if they turn over as different masses are added.

One group went on to look at changing the angle of the slope and seeing how much energy was used up as the car was pulled uphill. (PE planks can be used for slopes and blackboard protractors may be used for measuring angles.) They later tried the same experiment downhill. This was an excellent opportunity not only for mathematics concepts to be transferred but also to talk about pushes and pulls.

Another group suggested changing the wheels to see if this caused a difference. One group clearly could not manage to control the variables for their experiments. I found that this group needed to be given very precise instructions on what and how to measure. Not all the groups completed their experiments.

Lessons 7 and 8

Results from all experiments were displayed under two headings:

Energy experiments   *Road-holding experiments*

The groups were then asked to design a car which held the road well but used as little energy as possible. Some children incorporated into their designs free-running axles which could be propelled by an elastic band.

The children were then given the task of making their cars. Jelutong is an ideal softwood for the children to use as it is easily cut and shaped. Axles can be made from wooden dowelling, coat-hanger wire or piano wire. Some groups tried to solve both the road-holding and energy problems in their final design, but one group in particular could not do this. This group all along had been at a more concrete conceptual level. They did, however, gain a lot from the language experiences the project provided as well as from using mathematical skills for real reasons.

WORKING WITH WORKCARDS

Roy Purnell

, There seems to be a diversity of opinion concerning workcards. On the one hand they are said to be restricting and to stifle freedom of discovery, and on the other hand cards can be seen as a useful tool, guiding children through the steps of a subject at their own pace and their own level of intellectual development. With any mode or technique of teaching style there are, thank goodness, supporters and detractors. There is no one perfect approach; the ingredients of child, teacher, classroom, home environment, head and yes even the school caretaker form a complex amalgam. What is educationally successful one year fails abysmally the next. Teaching is also extremely fashion-conscious – bandwagons move past and disappear into the mists of time, but while around can cause panic and create havoc among the profession, making some teachers feel guilty, some aggressively indifferent and some, who have climbed on the wagon, smug in their endeavours.

A lot of the work that poses as science in today's schools removes the children from involvement, making them at best second-hand long-term observers and at worst passive receivers. Copying from science books, watching tadpoles die, looking at pictures of leaves, etc. remove children from first-hand experience. They must be their own scientist in their world, making their tests, making their observations and communicating their results and thoughts. What a particular child sees and thinks is most important, so that initial responses rather than 'what is supposed to happen' are vital.

Recognizing the paucity of suitable experimental science available to primary schools, there was an attempt in Gwent to rectify the deficit at the local level. So much published material is too difficult, too diffuse, too ambitious, too dangerous and mostly biased towards the biological sciences. Such books also seem to think that the teacher has at the very least a degree in a biological   science and expertise in physics and chemistry. Under the sponsorship of the Manpower Services Commission (MSC) and the direction

Source: specially commissioned for this volume

of Dr Roy Purnell and Dr Peter Johnston, it was decided to try to produce science material containing all the elements that seem to be missing in contemporary publications.

How was the material to be produced? Should it be written by a scientist whose experience is limited in the primary school, or should it be written by a trained teacher without a science background, somebody who could see the problems in the science rather than in the teaching? The latter is more likely to see the difficulties with the subject in the same way as would the prospective teacher and pupil. Herein lies the problem with much so-called curriculum reform. Teachers sometimes feel that ideas and schemes are foisted onto the profession by gangs of academics whose appreciation and knowledge of what is needed is light years away.

A team of researchers, who were trained but relatively inexperienced teachers and whose qualifications in science in the main were non-existent, initiated and tested science experiments with children in the age range 5 to 11 years. The product was put into workcard form. The brief for the cards was:

1. The cards should give children 'hands-on' experience with experiments using apparatus which is cheap and readily available.
2. Each card should be aimed at the level of ability and the age of the child.
3. The content of each card should introduce a new scientific concept and show development.
4. The cards should be attractive without being distractive, and instructions should be unambiguous and crystal clear to the teacher and the child.

A tall order, but it is apparent that much of present-day published material does not obey these obvious rules.

Using the sponsorship money from the MSC, copies of the cards were printed in Gwent College of Higher Education by extremely helpful and co-operative technicians and some one hundred free sets were distributed to the schools of Gwent. The cards were printed in black type on coloured card. This style has three main advantages: firstly, it was cheap and its production was within the capabilities of the college printing facilities; secondly, different colours would be instantly recognized as belonging to a particular topic or ability range; thirdly, many teachers have said that too much colour distracts the customer, i.e. the pupil.

A card designed for upper junior average ability is shown in Figure A. The apparatus suggested is easily obtainable and familiar to a child. The experiment for the child involves mechanical manipulation and planning

Air 3

As light as air.   You need: two balloons, a ball of string,
                                  scissors, a thin stick 50 cms
                                  long, plasticine, two drawing pins

Here is a good way to find out if
air weighs anything.

1. Tie a long piece of string to
    the middle of the stick.
    Suspend the stick by pinning
    the other end of the string
    to a door frame or ceiling
    with a drawing pin.
    Look at your balance, is it
    level?
    If not, stick a very small piece
    of plasticine on the lighter
    end in order to level the balance.

2. Blow up two balloons to the same
    size.
    Tie the necks with string.
    Tie a balloon onto each end of
    the stick.
    Slide the strings along the stick
    until the stick hangs exactly
    level again.

3. Now prick one of the balloons
    with a pin and watch what
    happens.
    Which end is heavier?
    Why has the other end become
    lighter?
    Write down what happened and
    what this experiment shows.

Figure A

Variety can be introduced, and within this simple operation a vast amount of discussion can arise. Does it make any difference if the stick is longer or shorter than 50 cm? Why not try? What happens when the balloon is pricked and pieces of rubber drop off? Is it a fair test? The concept of fairness burns strongly and deeply in children. What could the child do to make it a fair test? Once the air has been expelled and the comparison shows that air has weight, how can the amount of air in the unpricked balloon be quantified? The teacher could suggest using tacks or paper clips to restore the balance. The child could then find the amount of air in terms of tacks or clips. Thus measure or quantity in terms of number has been introduced, and the child has found the amount of air in one balloon in terms of repeatable quantity – a quantity that has meaning for other people.

Any child who has worked through this particular card has been taken through the scientific process of being posed a problem, devising an apparatus and using the apparatus to solve the problem. The work could then be extended by the teacher – or hopefully by the child – to quantify or measure, a refinement which will give the child a sense of achievement and which will stop the feeling that when the card is finished the job is done. Children have fertile imaginations and once started will run to a multitude of variations.

The talk this far has been of a general nature. How were the cards used in the front line, that is with children? Some teachers used them as an aid to topic work, some in a group situation with different groups tackling different cards, some as a class demonstration. The uses were wide and varied. Their success can be gauged by the fact that they were recommended by teachers to their colleagues and demand has exceeded supply. Thomas Nelson are to publish the cards nationally under the title 'Links'.

The following account, by Beryl James, tells of her experience in the use of the science workcards:

West End School has approximately 160 infant children (who are in six classes arranged by age only), 9 full-time nursery children and 60 part-time nursery children. The children come from very varied family backgrounds and a mixture of private and council accommodation. The staff consists of eight teachers, two nursery nurses, one peripatetic nursery nurse attending 2 days per week for a profoundly deaf child, one student nursery nurse, plus myself, the headteacher. I am timetabled to work with groups of children from all classes.

In the curriculum at West End School, science is not set apart but comes under the umbrella heading of 'Interest Studies', so named because, when planning a topic of interest, various aspects of the curriculum will link together in developing the children's skills, attitudes, concepts and language.

Teachers of infant children must be adaptable, as the following example of how work on mechanics arose shows. It began with the 'Opposites: Fast/Slow' workcards, as shown in the following chart:

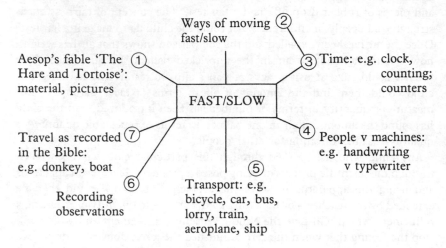

From the transport area, the children became interested in the way things moved, and in particular the use of wheels. Thus mechanics work developed out of this area of work as shown in the following chart:

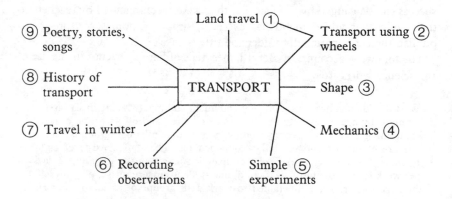

The group of top infant children who worked on this project were of mixed ability but they could all read, write, and had basic computational skills. I selected the workcards to be used either as a basis for group discussion or for the children to use individually, in pairs, or as groups for practical work.

The 'Mechanics' set of workcards are planned in this way:

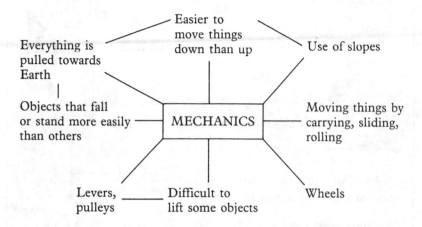

Lesson using the 'Everything is pulled towards Earth' workcards (see Figure B)
Apparatus needed: jug of water, paper cup, cotton reels, buttons, plasticine, blocks of wood, pieces of paper, workcards, paper, pencils, felt-tipped pens.

1. As a group the children read, discussed, and interpreted practically the small workcards with the teacher in the following way.
   (a) Water falls downwards – one child poured water from jug to cup – observed water poured downwards.
   (b) Things fall if you drop them – children chose what to hold, e.g. pencil, ruler, book – released the objects from their hold – all fell downwards.

Everything is pulled towards Earth 2.

You need:

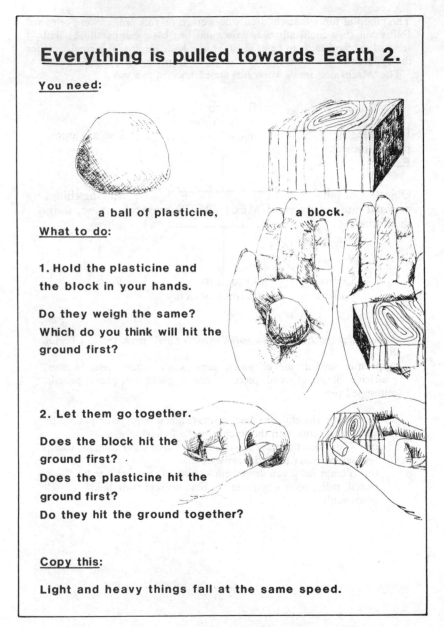

a ball of plasticine,   a block.

What to do:

1. Hold the plasticine and
the block in your hands.

Do they weigh the same?
Which do you think will hit the
ground first?

2. Let them go together.

Does the block hit the
ground first?
Does the plasticine hit the
ground first?
Do they hit the ground together?

Copy this:

Light and heavy things fall at the same speed.

Figure B.

2. Then the children were divided into small groups for practical experiment work using the large workcards. The children read the cards themselves, helping each other with the instructions, and making sure they used the correct objects. In each group much good discussion, observation and interpretation took place, and great interest and enjoyment was shown.

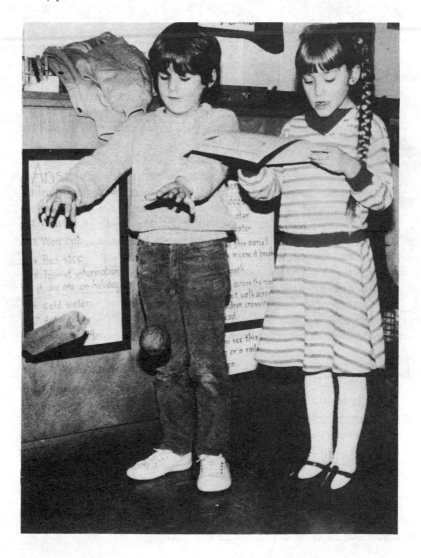

3. As each group of children finished their experiments they recorded, individually, their observations and findings by writing and drawing.
4. While the children were experimenting and interpreting the information from the workcards, the teacher was able to discuss the work of each group in turn and assist with the individual recording.

The block hit the ground first
because the paper floated down to
the floor. When the paper was
crumpled it hit the ground at the
same time as the block.

Lessons were given in a similar manner, using the relevant workcards for:

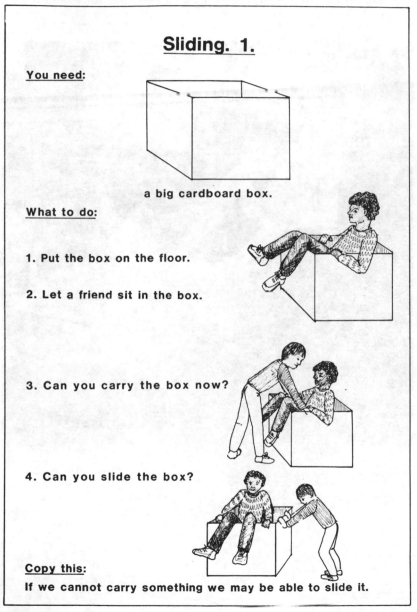

Sliding. 1.

You need:

a big cardboard box.

What to do:

1. Put the box on the floor.

2. Let a friend sit in the box.

3. Can you carry the box now?

4. Can you slide the box?

Copy this:
If we cannot carry something we may be able to slide it.

Figure C

1.   Moving things by sliding (see Figure C). There was great hilarity when the children took it in turns to try and move the cardboard box with another child sitting in it.

To move the box. The easier way is the front way to push

when Irene was in the box. I had to lift Irene

up and I could not lift her up she

was to heavy in the box.

2. Moving things by rolling.

3. Moving things by use of wheels (see below). Using the workcards as a base, this section on wheels was expanded by discussion, practical/experimental work and recording observations in separate lessons on:

(a) Wheel shapes.

(b) Making cardboard cars, vans, wheels and axles using thick plastic wiring.

(c) Observing and recording the many things that have wheels apart from transport.

These science workcards are most informative and helpful. They are designed in a logical, instructive manner and are written so that infant children can use them on their own after discussion with the teacher and other children. The workcards are also adaptable so that the teacher may choose the relevant cards from any section, or use them as a base to enlarge upon as required, for any topic undertaken with the children.

The editors wish to thank M. B. Hughes for photographs reproduced in this case study.

INDEX OF NAMES

Main references, and page-numbers of articles contributed to this reader, are in **bold**. *The suffix n denotes a bibliographical reference or footnote.*

Conran, R.J.,   148, 149n
Cooper, K. and Whitfield,   148, 149n
Copernicus, Nicolas,   12
Crick, Francis,   9

Dawson, C.J., Rowell and,   112, 115n,
   195, 197n
Deadman, J.A. and Kelly,   29, 33n
Delacôte, G.,   112
   Tiberghien and,   112, 116n
Department of Education and Science
   (DES),   84n, 85n, 175n–6n
Desforges, C.
   Brown and   107, 113n
   McNamara and   32, 33n
Dewey, John,   27, 101
Dihoff, R.E., Hooper and,   127, 132n
Donaldson, M.,   108, 114n, 142, 149,
   149n
Driver, Rosalind,   **98–113, 188–96**, 188n
   (1973)   111, 114n
   (1979)   104, 114n
   (1983)   197n
   and Easley   29, 33n, 104, 114n, 198,
   214n
   and Guesne and Tiberghien,   197n
Duckworth, E.,   122–3, 132n
Duit, R.,   181, 187n, 198, 214n
Duncan, I.M. and Johnstone,   194, 197n

Easley, J., Driver and,   29, 33n, 104,
   114n, 198, 214n
Einstein, Albert,   11, 13, 144
Elkind, E.,   106, 114n
Engel, Elizabeth,   **25–33**, 25n
Ennever, L. and Harlen,   65, 71n, 73,
   85n, 114n
Ennis, B.,   107, 114n
Erickson, G.L.,   112, 114n, 198, 214n
Evans, P.,   148, 149n

Fensham, P. see Gilbert
Ferriero, E.,   123, 132n
Finch, Irene,   29
Floyd, A.,   117n
Freeman, N. and Lloyd and Sinha,   142,
   149n
Froebel, Friedrich,   101

Gagné, Robert,   97
Galileo Galilei,   12–13, 105
Gelman,   125

Gilbert, J.K.
   and Osborne   199, 214n
   and Osborne and Fensham   199, 214n
   and Watts and Osborne   199, 214n
   Osborne and   198, 215n
Goldsmith, M.,   11, 23n
Gruber, H. and Vorèche,   142, 149n
Guesne, E.,   112, 114n
   see also Driver
Gunstone, R.F. and White,   198, 205,
   214n

Halford, G.S.,   129, 132n
Harlen, Wynne,   **72–84, 152–75**, 152n
   (1978)   25, 28, 33n, 63, 67
   (1981)   71n
   (1985)   218n
   et al   65, 69, 71n
   Ennever and   65, 71n, 73, 85n, 114n
Haysom, J.T. and Sutton,   32, 33n
Head, J.,   179, 187n
Helm, H.,   207, 214n
Helmont, Jean Baptiste van,   13
Her Majesty's Inspectorate of Schools
   (HMIs),
   (1961)   73
   (1978)   **3–8**, 3n, 27, 33, 33n, 61
   (1983)   **35–41**, 35n
   see also Dept of Education and Science
Hirst, P.H.,   15, 16, 23n
Hooper, F,
   and Dihoff   127, 132n
   and Sipple   127, 132n
Howe, A.C., Johnson and,   102, 114n

Inhelder, B.
   and Piaget   107, 114n, 122, 127, 128,
   132n
   and Sinclair and Bovet   122, 125, 127,
   132n
   Karmiloff-Smith and   111, 114n
   Piaget and   118, 133n
Isaacs, Nathan,   84n
Isaacs, Susan,   27

Jelly, Sheila,   **218–28**
Johnson, J.K. and Howe,   102, 114n
Johnson, Dr Peter,   249
Johnson-Laird, P.N., Wason and,   108,
   116n, 128, 134n
Johnstone, A.H.
   and MacDonald and Webb   194, 187n

INDEX OF SUBJECTS

Main references are in **bold**. *All names of persons, whether or not cited as references in the text, will be found in the Index of Names.*